KU-485-296

USES AND ABUSES OF PSYCHOLOGY

BY

H. J. EYSENCK

*

PENGUIN BOOKS

Penguin Books Ltd, Harmondsworth, Middlesex
U.S.A. : Penguin Books Inc., 3300 Clipper Mill Road, Baltimore 11, Md
AUSTRALIA: Penguin Books Pty Ltd, 762 Whitehorse Road,
Mitcham, Victoria
—

First published 1953
Reprinted 1954, 1955, 1958, 1959, 1960

Made and printed in Great Britain
by T. and A. Constable Ltd
Edinburgh

PELICAN BOOKS

A 281

USES AND ABUSES OF PSYCHOLOGY

H. J. EYSENCK

CONTENTS

It cannot be that axioms established by argumentation can suffice for the discovery of new works, since the subtlety of nature is greater many times over than the subtlety of argument.

*

FRANCIS BACON

INTRODUCTION

CLEMENCEAU, in one of his more insightful moments, said that war was too serious a business to be left to the generals. In recent years the feeling has been growing that science is too serious a business to be left entirely to the scientists. From birth to death the life of modern man is conditioned and determined by forces and discoveries which he so little understands that he customarily applies the term 'miracles' to them. Statements such as these are platitudes when applied to physical forces and physical discoveries; few people realize to what extent their lives are being shaped by the application of discoveries in the social sciences, more particularly by the recent advances in psychology.

Yet in one way or another almost everyone has come up against the mixed blessings which applied psychology bestows on humanity. Decisions regarding the child's future education are being made on the basis of intelligence tests applied at the tender age of eleven or twelve; indeed, the whole modern system of education is based on psychological discoveries and theories which are relatively recent. The soldier's allocation to a particular arm or trade inside the service, as well as his advancement to officer status, are determined in part by psychological tests; our new rulers, the upper ranks of the Civil Service, are being selected by 'new type' selection methods; vocational guidance and occupational selection are affecting the every-day working lives of many thousands. The extremely numerous nervous breakdowns which appear to characterize modern society are being diagnosed and treated by what purport to be psychological methods. Attitudes are being measured by Gallup and other polls, and the results of such surveys, some of them carried out by Government agencies on a fact-finding basis, help to lay the foundations for legislation and policy-making. Radio programmes and many commercial products take into account survey figures regarding 'audience reactions'. Psychologists investigate optimum working conditions, spacing of rest pauses, systems of incentives, the spreading of rumours, causes of industrial unrest, and large numbers of other friction points in the political and social organism. Even old age is not safe from their scrutiny; the intellectual and emotional development of old people is being studied more and more intensely, and action based on the results.

This brief and incomplete survey shows to what an extent psychology is already taking a part in transforming our lives; almost unnoticed, and certainly within the memory of most people now in their forties and fifties, there has taken place the beginning of a revolution which may influence the pattern of our lives as much as, or even more than, the Industrial Revolution did in its time.

The beginnings of this new revolution can be traced with considerable accuracy. The new scientific discoveries of Binet, Spearman, and Stern in the field of intelligence testing were put to the crucial test of practical application by the American Army during the first World War; their triumphant success there established psychology once and for all as an indispensable adjunct to all selection procedures. It may be of interest to quote the directive setting out the tasks which the Army authorities expected the intelligence test to perform. The test was to 'designate and select men whose superior intelligence indicated the desirability of advancement or special assignment; to select and recommend for "development battalions" such men as were so inferior intellectually as to be unsuited for regular military training; to enable officers to build up organizations of uniform mental strength, or in accordance with definite specifications concerning intellectual requirements; to select men for various types of military duty or for special assignments; to eliminate men whose intelligence was so inferior as to make it impossible to use them at all.'

The very success of the intelligence test in this difficult assignment became the reason for subsequent disappointment. Thousands of enthusiasts, ignorant of the scientific principles of intelligence testing, but eager to cash in on the new fad, invaded the field and tried to apply the Army testing procedures in industrial and commercial institutions. Impossible claims were made, and the inevitable reaction was severe and lasting. Many intelligent people, unable to separate the chaff from the wheat, or the get-rich-quick charlatan from the genuine scientist, became sceptical and finally hostile to 'psychology', and carried this attitude over to other, newer developments and claims.

It took another war, and the gigantic selection problems associated with it, to overcome this hostility, and to enable psychologists to prove once and for all the superiority of their methods to all others. The proof was so clear and devastating that in the end psychological selection procedures were used by almost all belligerents. To anyone familiar with the conservatism of Army authorities in every country, this acceptance, reluctant and hesitant though it was, will speak louder than any testimonial. Even in peacetime, selection along psychological lines has remained, and has indeed been extended to other equally conservative fields, such as the Civil Service.

Unfortunately, there is no guarantee that what happened before may not happen again. Uncritical enthusiasts, fired with the conviction of righteousness given them by some 'system' or other, are again trying to extend these methods to fields where they may not be appropriate; claims which are at present impossible of fulfilment are again being made. There is every possibility that once more the intelligent layman may in his disappointment reject the good with the bad, and visit the sins of the interlopers on those who have laboriously built up the beginnings of a genuine science.

This danger is particularly acute because in this field at least 'the devil has the best hymns'. Citizens of a democratic society need to be told in clear, unambiguous language just what is the present position in a scientific field; what can and cannot be done at the present time; what developments are taking place; what is likely to happen in the near future. Without such knowledge, there arises a dangerous gap between scientist and citizen, a gap which

prevents the one from making the best use of the contribution the other has to offer, and which encourages the misunderstandings which have bedevilled their relations for so
long. Yet unfortunately psychologists, for various reasons,
have usually fought shy of writing for anyone but other
psychologists; they have preferred to leave the popular ex-
position of their achievements to people without the scientific
background necessary in order to stay on firm ground, and
without the ability to say 'We don't know' instead of 'It is
certain'. Thus popularization of psychology has usually been
of a kind to encourage over-optimistic attitudes in some, and
exaggerated scepticism in others.

It is in the hope of redressing this balance to some extent
that I have written this book. The title will indicate the
thread which runs through the various chapters. They all
deal with the application of psychological discoveries to
social problems. In some cases the evidence is strong enough
to make it possible to say that here is an area of usefulness
which society would be ill advised to neglect. In some cases
the evidence is strong enough to make it possible to say that
here is a method, or a technique, which in its present form is
useless, and should either be discarded or improved beyond
recognition. In some cases the only possible answer is that
not enough is known to say whether or not a given procedure is useful, and that research is urgently required. I
have chosen fields where there is little doubt about the
answer; few psychologists who have studied the evidence
carefully would probably disagree on more than a few minor
points. In so far as they are likely to disagree, it would probably be in the direction of considering my account unduly
critical and conservative.

This point will bear amplification. The majority of psychologists are working in the applied field – educational,
clinical, industrial, military, or counselling. They have to
make decisions on the basis of the available evidence; if
probabilities favour one solution over another, even though
the margin be relatively narrow, they will decide according
to the available evidence. This is perfectly correct, because

a decision must be made, and usually cannot wait until new facts are discovered. But it is not the way of science. The 'pure' scientist is concerned with getting the correct answer; it is not only his right, but also his duty, to say that on the basis of the present evidence it is not possible to come to any definite conclusion. This may be infuriating to the applied worker, who is convinced that a given technique is working perfectly well, but it is an essential safeguard against the 'premature crystallization of spurious orthodoxies'.

An experiment may illustrate this dichotomy. An American investigator gave a test to a group of 'pure' and a group of 'applied' psychologists. Essentially, the test was the old 'pea under the thimble' trick, in which the subject has to say under which of three thimbles the pea is hidden. After demonstrating the test, the experimenter abstracted the pea, so that the subject could not possibly succeed in guessing right, and waited to see how many repetitions of the trick would be necessary before the subject came to the conclusion that there was no pea. The expected result was found in actual fact. The 'applied' group declared after some six repetitions that there was probably no pea; the 'pure' group plodded on for over twice as many trials before coming to the same conclusion.

Now obviously neither group could be sure; in either case it was a question of probability. The 'applied' group were content to base their decision on probabilities which to most people would probably appear adequate (about 1 chance in 10 of being wrong). The 'pure' group required repetitions to a point where there could be no reasonable doubt whatever about their conclusion (about 1 chance in 200 of being wrong). Both types of reaction are intelligible and appropriate in relation to the problems and tasks which face 'pure' and 'applied' scientists respectively. The 'applied' scientist may experience considerable annoyance at his colleague's refusal to accept his cherished beliefs and methods without asking for detailed documentation and proof; the 'pure' scientist may wring his hands at the easy acceptance by his colleague of procedures and hypotheses for which the evidence is insufficient and sometimes contradictory. Probably personality factors play some part in the creation of this dichotomy, as well as the demands of the groups for which these two types of scientists work – employers and clients on the one hand, fellow scientists on the other.

This distinction between 'pure' and 'applied' can of course be taken too far. It certainly does not correspond in any way with 'usefulness'. The 'ivory tower' scientist may make discoveries whose usefulness far outweighs the contribution of his colleague who spends all his time in the rough-and-tumble of industry. As an example may be quoted the researches conducted during the first decade of this century by Seashore into 'auditory illusions' – a subject which he thought would be as pure and undefiled by considerations of practical usefulness as could possibly be imagined. These illusions are similar in some ways to the better-known visual ones, in which strokes affixed arrow-fashion to the ends of a line make it appear longer or shorter, or in which an unusual use of the rules of perspective make things appear other than they are.

Came the war, and with it the U-boat menace. In the absence of mechanical detection devices, warships had to rely on reports of special 'look-outs' sitting in the hull listening for the engine noise of the U-boat, and indicating the direction from which the noise was coming. It was soon found that there were systematic errors involved in these reports due to 'auditory illusions', and Seashore was called in to advise on methods of correction. For a few crucial months, his 'ivory tower' research findings succeeded in keeping the U-boat menace at bay, until mechanical devices were perfected which dispensed with the faulty human element.

Pure and applied psychology, then, should not be pictured as in any sense opposed to each other, but as marching hand in hand towards the combined goals of greater scientific understanding and greater social usefulness. Unfortunately there has been a tendency for them to get out of step recently. The reason for this has been a rather simple one. The problems which are crying out for a solution in the social field – problems of maladjustment, of guidance, of selection, of education, even of war and peace – are so pressing that application has outrun knowledge. Many psychologists feel such an urge to give help that they forget that it is only scientific knowledge which enables them to do so effectively. Unwilling to subject their intuitive certainties and their admirable intentions to the unimpassioned appraisal of scientific verification, they have for all intents and purposes left the field of science, while still claiming the prestige which attaches to that term.

Before turning to the main part of this book, there are one or two further points which may require discussion. Many people are finding great difficulties in keeping apart psychologists, psychiatrists, and psycho-analysts, and it may be worth while to indicate briefly the main differences between these three groups. A psychologist is concerned with the scientific study of human behaviour; he has a degree from a University, taken in the faculty of either Arts or Science, which certifies that he has studied the foundations of his subject. This does not qualify him to do applied work, for which post-graduate courses are required, nor does it qualify him for research work in the absence of two years' further academic work for the Doctorate. A psychiatrist is a medically qualified person who has followed certain post-graduate courses which make him a specialist in mental disorders arising from various causes; courses in psychology form an important part of such training. The main function of the psychiatrist is in the treatment of mental and nervous troubles. The psycho-analyst is usually a psychiatrist who has specialized in one particular form of treatment, namely psychotherapy, and who accepts essentially the teachings of S. Freud. A few psycho-analysts lack medical qualifications, but this is becoming something of an anomaly in this country. The relation between psychology and psychiatry may be pictured as something like that between physiologist and physician, with the psychoanalyst corresponding to a physician who has specialized in one type of disease and treatment.

Sometimes there is conflict between these different groups.

In the United States, clinical psychologists often carry out treatment – sometimes under the direction of a psychiatrist, sometimes without; this is rightly frowned upon by many psychiatrists who point out that man is not a 'ghost in a corpse', where the illness of the 'ghost' could be treated in isolation from the 'corpse', but rather an integrated unity where mental and physical functions constantly interact in such a way as to make treatment in non-medical hands a danger. On the other side, psycho-analysts often make oracular pronouncements on the fate of the world, the origins of war and peace, the causes of industrial unrest, or the nature of national differences, which are very tenuously based on the sick-room fantasies of neurotic patients; psychologists rightly resent this light-hearted invasion of their territory by those not versed in the rigours of scientific methodology. On the whole, however, there is harmonious co-operation between these various groups on the basis of divided responsibility.

Psychologists, psychiatrists, and psycho-analysts would certainly all agree on one point which the man in the street is likely to dispute, namely the predictability of human behaviour. To most people, prediction in the physical sciences has become a commonplace; we take its miraculous accuracy almost for granted. But we tend to boggle at the application of scientific methods to the prediction of human behaviour; we like to feel that in some way we are 'masters of our fate', and not subject to general rules and laws which alone make prediction possible. Yet it has rightly been pointed out that many of our everyday decisions depend on the assumption of human predictability, and that frequently our predictions of human actions are more accurate than our predictions in the physical field. Many people have been delayed because of some mechanical defect of the train or bus, but very few because the driver suddenly decided to stop and pick daisies. There is sufficient regularity in human behaviour to make it subject to scientific study; whether human conduct is *completely* determined is a question outside the scope of a factual account.

the place of detailed discussion. Little wonder that most people don't know just where they stand with respect to psychology, and that they regard it as a mixture of black magic and quackery. It is the aim of this book to show that it is neither, but merely a science in its early, formative period, not sufficiently advanced to answer all the vital questions which are often asked of it, but already in a position to offer solutions to some of our problems. Greater public understanding of what psychology is doing is one important prerequisite for further advance along this road.

There is one great difficulty in presenting an account of psychological experiments and conclusions in popular terms, a difficulty equally great with that which besets the physicist trying to give a clear picture of what he is doing. The results of the physicist are expressed in mathematical terms, and even with the greatest ingenuity it is often impossible to translate them with any exactitude into ordinary language. Similarly, the results of the psychologist are so closely tied up with mathematics and statistics that an adequate understanding is impossible without at least a smattering of knowledge in these fields. To many laymen, a statistician may be merely a man who draws a mathematically straight line from an unwarranted assumption to a foregone conclusion; to the psychologist the statistician appears as one who provides him with certain indispensable tools which alone enable him to sort out the very complex interaction of facts which confront him at every turn. If there are lies, big lies, and statistics, then only a thorough mastery of the latter will prevent the psychologist from drawing false conclusions from his data. It would be an error to imagine that by denigrating statistics we can manage to avoid it; opposition to statistics too frequently merely means the use of bad and inefficient statistics.

Given that physics and psychology share this handicap to easy communication, how can they overcome it? The physicist is in a rather favourable position. Few people imagine themselves to be experts in his field, or to know more about it than he does. In addition, the great prestige of his science makes most people accept his statements without apparent proof. How different is the position of the psychologist! There are few people who in their heart of hearts do not resent his assumption of superior knowledge about human behaviour, who do not feel that they know far more about 'people' than any scientific textbook can tell, and who would be willing to accept his statements without explicit proof. And woe to the psychologist if his proof consists, as it inevitably must, in complex experimentation and mathematical formulae! These are dismissed after cursory inspection as 'unintelligible', and he is urged to furnish his proof without any mention even of the very methods of which it consists.

I have tried to leave out complex and difficult material as far as possible in this book, and have eschewed almost completely the mention of mathematics or statistics. This inevitably means that many statements are much less precise than they would otherwise have been, and the reader who feels critical of any particular statement, before voicing his criticism, should remember the handicap under which the writer has been labouring. If the reader still feels dissatisfied, then his only course is to look at the technical literature and familiarize himself with the facts as given there. In doing so he may find it necessary to spend a few years on courses in mathematics and statistics, followed by work in physics, chemistry, genetics, sociology, economics, physiology, neurology, anatomy, biology, and a whole host of other sciences which have a very close and direct bearing on modern psychology. The right to criticize scientific results and theories has to be bought in terms of knowledge, and should not be too easily assumed.

As an illustration of the kind of criticism which is often directed at psychology I may perhaps quote an occasion which made a considerable impression on me. A representative of H.M. Government had been asked a question in Parliament about the use of certain tests in connexion with selection procedures, and in his answer managed to epitomize all the shallow thinking, profound ignorance, and biassed method of argument which are so characteristic of politicians in their dealings with scientific subjects. Brandishing the test in question in his hand, he proceeded to read out one question from it, a question which apparently had little to do with the objective the test was supposed to serve. Basing his argument on this apparent inappropriateness, the Minister then went on to say that such tests were obviously useless, and that he refused to have them introduced.

The following points should be noted. The test referred to consisted of certain questions which were relevant, i.e. on

the answer to which action would be taken, and a number of 'camouflage' questions, which served merely to make the purpose of the test less obvious. It was one of the latter questions which was quoted, so that its apparent relevance or irrelevance to the purpose of the test could hardly be made an excuse for dropping the test as a whole. Even if the question cited had been one of the 'relevant' ones, however, it is difficult to see how one could judge its value by simple inspection. A test item which distinguishes between good and poor risks at a high level of significance is *eo ipso* a good item; an item which fails to discriminate is a bad item. It would be very nice, of course, if we could distinguish between good and poor items by simple inspection, but unfortunately that has been found to be quite impossible. Many years of detailed research are required before the validity of a given test or test item is known, and it is often found that superficially attractive items and tests are quite worthless, while apparently less attractive items are successful.

Even if the item in question had been relevant, and shown poor discrimination, it might still deserve its place in the questionnaire as a measure of some important quality known to influence responses to other items. Thus some people try to give a good impression of themselves on questionnaires, rather than answer the items truthfully and to the best of their ability; a special set of questions is often included which measures this tendency and makes it possible to discount its influence on the test proper.

This episode has been quoted because in many ways it is typical of the careless way in which psychological methods are often dismissed in utter disregard of the facts. What is written in the daily newspapers about intelligence tests might serve as another example; facts are either twisted out of all recognition, or else disregarded completely, and the opinion of journalists is given greater weight than that of people with life-long experience in the field of intelligence-testing. The immense complexities of the problem are not taken into account, and slogans and partial statements take

PART ONE

INTELLIGENCE TESTING

1

WHAT DO INTELLIGENCE TESTS REALLY MEASURE?

THE great increase in the use of intelligence tests, particularly in schools, has made more and more people realize the importance of the question: 'What do intelligence tests really measure?' Answers range all the way from that of the faithful believer – 'Why, intelligence of course' – to that of the confirmed sceptic – 'Nothing but monkey tricks!' Even psychologists tend to blanch a little when this question is put to them in brains trusts, by W.E.A. audiences, or in conversation. Their reaction is prompted not so much by ignorance of the right answer as by a realization of the complexity of the problem. The meaning of a scientific concept is bound up so intimately with the whole process of measurement and the theoretical structure into which it fits that to isolate one question and expect an answer, in the absence of knowledge regarding all the other variables which have to be considered, is to make sure that the answer, when it comes, will be unsatisfactory and apparently quite arbitrary. Short of writing a whole text-book, filled with experimental data and incomprehensible mathematical shorthand notation involving Gramian matrices or Kronecker's deltas, it is impossible to give an accurate answer. It may be possible, however, to give a reasonably complete answer within the compass of a brief chapter if the reader is willing to take the mathematics as given.

First of all, then, we must purge our minds of one notion which underlies much popular thinking. It is often thought that scientific concepts refer to things which actually exist, and that the scientist's cleverness lies in isolating these really existing things and measuring them. Thus it might be thought that bodies have length, and that the scientist discovers this fact and then proceeds to measure that length. Similarly, it might be thought that people have intelligence, and that the scientist discovers this fact and then proceeds to measure this intelligence. Thus we would be dealing with scientific laws and concepts which existed in nature independently of man, and which could be discovered by diligent search. This exceedingly popular view of science is quite false. Thurstone has expressed the true position when he says:

'It is the faith of all science that an unlimited number of phenomena can be comprehended in terms of a limited number of concepts or ideal constructs. Without this faith no science could ever have any motivation. To deny this faith is to affirm the primary chaos of nature and the consequent futility of scientific effort. The constructs in terms of which natural phenomena are comprehended are man-made inventions. To discover a scientific law is merely to discover that a man-made scheme serves to unify, and thereby to simplify, comprehension of a certain class of natural phenomena. A scientific law is not to be thought of as having an independent existence which some scientist is fortunate to stumble upon. A scientific law is not a part of nature. It is only a way of comprehending nature.'

If we return to our example of 'height' we will see immediately how necessary this warning is. If we measure the height of a person, or the length of a metal bar, in the summer, it will be found that the person is taller, and the bar is longer, than it would be in the winter. If we measured a given distance in terms of the number of times we had to apply the metal bar, we would find that the distance varied according to the temperature prevailing at the time of measurement. We rationalize all these facts in terms of a scientific law relating the phenomena of length and temperature and saying that 'bodies expand in the heat and contract in the cold'. We formulate this law because it helps us to unify our observations; it makes our description of nature simpler, and aids our comprehension. A person's height, then, is not something absolute; it is a construct derived from scientific theory, and interlocking with many other concepts which superficially appear to have little relation to it.

Intelligence, similarly, is not something directly given in nature, which we may succeed in isolating and measuring. It is a concept which we find useful in describing human conduct. 'A science of psychology will deal with the activities of people as its central theme. A large class of human activity is that which differentiates individuals as regards their overt accomplishments. Just as it is convenient to postulate physical forces in describing the movements of physical objects, so it is also natural to postulate abilities and their absence as primary causes of the successful completion of a task by some individuals and of the failure of other individuals in the same task.'

These remarks may serve as a salutary warning to those who like to argue that, in their opinion, intelligence is the ability to acquire knowledge, or the capacity for abstract thinking, or the equivalent of wisdom, or quickness of thinking, or depth of profundity, or a combination of some of these, or else something quite different. The argument usually continues that because intelligence tests *obviously* do not measure these particular qualities, therefore intelligence tests certainly do not measure intelligence, whatever else they may measure. As Hobbes remarked, 'Words are wise men's counters, but they are the money of fools', and it is to be feared that in the absence of an agreed definition of wisdom, or profundity, or learning ability, and lacking any acceptable measures of these qualities, to equate them with intelligence, and to make any assertions regarding the degree to which they might be measured by current intelligence tests, is mere semantic obscurantism. It complicates the problem unnecessarily, rather than aids in its solution, and substitutes a host of vague and meaningless terms for the objective, clear-cut standard against which we wish to measure the adequacy of our tests.

There is ample proof that laymen do not agree in their definitions of intelligence; there is equally ample proof that psychologists do not agree very much more closely among themselves when asked for a formal, verbal definition. This does not mean that they are not all referring to the same thing. If we take a given substance, X, and ask a politician, a garage proprietor, and a housewife to define it, they might say that it was ‘ the cause of present troubles with several mid-Eastern countries’, that it was ‘the ultimate cause of propulsion of motor cars’, or that it was ‘a stain remover’. These definitions are all quite different, but they refer to one and the same thing, namely what most of us would call ‘petrol’. This diversity of definitions does mean, however, that we cannot use any one of them as a standard to compare our tests with, because such a choice would be purely arbitrary and contrary to the procedure of science. We may therefore try quite a different tack and resort to what are known as practical definitions.

A practical definition, in contradistinction to a verbal one, is one which sets up agreed practical criteria which are universally deemed to contain the definient, though not in pure form. Thus almost everyone would agree that intelligence was required in order to do well at school, or at University, to be an efficient officer, or a successful business executive, or quite generally to do intellectual work of any kind with an outstandingly high degree of success. Similarly, almost everyone would agree that the opposite to high intelligence was shown by mental defectives, educationally subnormal children, and people who in spite of persistent efforts could not master even relatively low-level jobs. Obviously other factors, such as good teaching, right connexions, luck, persistent application, and stability are also involved in success in these various spheres, but intelligence certainly exerts a major influence. Consequently we would expect intelligence tests to show high scores for people successful, and low scores for people unsuccessful in school, university, business, and the various other professions and occupations mentioned. Where people with high scores did badly on the job, we should expect to be able to account for their failure in terms of emotional instability, or some other interfering factor. Where people with low scores did well, we should expect to find them to be exceptionally hard-working, or well-connected, or in some other way outstanding along non-intellectual lines.

The facts bear out these predictions. In later chapters I shall quote detailed evidence of the close relationship between success at school, in college, and in later life on the one hand, and high scores on intelligence tests on the other. Similarly, there is usually a close relationship between intelligence test results and ratings of intelligence made by teachers, professors, supervisors, senior officers, and other people in a position to judge the abilities of the testee. Many hundreds of studies have been made along these lines, and they all give results tending in the same direction. From the practical point of view, this evidence is quite sufficient to justify the use of tests of intelligence in selection and prediction. From the scientific point of view, however, it leaves much to be desired.

The main reason for this lack of satisfaction would appear to be this. Suppose we were to measure two people's heights by using a yardstick. We should find that X was taller than Y, regardless of which of the innumerable yardsticks in the country we used. We should find that if X was taller than Y, and Y taller than Z, X would also be taller than Z. If these relations did not hold, we should rightly be suspicious of the accuracy of our measurement, and should consider very carefully the conditions under which it was made. If we found that simple errors of measurement, such as occur inevitably in all physical and mental measurement, could not account for our discrepancies, we should be forced to consider our measurement lacking in what psychologists call 'unidimensionality'. This is such an important attribute and condition of scientific measurement that it may be worth while to discuss it in some detail.

Suppose that the proverbial camel is trying to get through the proverbial eye of a needle. In trying to predict the success of this hazardous enterprise we should wish to know the height and width of the camel, and the height and width of the needle; given these unidimensional measurements we could predict with reasonable accuracy. But suppose we were told merely the 'bigness' of the camel, i.e. its height multiplied by its width, and the 'bigness' of the eye of the needle, calculated in a similar manner. This 'bigness' is a multidimensional measurement, and gives us very little information. The eye of the needle might be 'bigger' than the camel, and yet the camel might get stuck. It might have ample height to spare, but be too broad in the beam. Thus prediction based on tests and concepts which are not unidimensional are much less accurate and powerful than predictions based on unidimensional tests.

In our example we have assumed that 'bigness' was a concept based on an agreed method of combining height and width. In other words, we assumed that the true dimensions involved, as well as their method of combination, were all known. But suppose that instead we have people estimate the 'bigness' of a series of camels. One person might lay great stress on height, and disregard width almost completely in his estimate. Another might base his judgement almost entirely on width. A third might compromise between these two extremes, and a fourth be swayed sometimes by one, sometimes by the other. If we based our predictions on these judgements, we should probably still be right more frequently than chance would allow, but clearly from the point of view of accurate measurement and successful prediction we should have paid a high price for our neglect to analyse the concept of 'bigness' into its main dimensions.

Up to a point, the original concept of 'intelligence' advocated by the early workers in this field, and the tests constructed by them, were 'bigness' concepts and 'bigness' measures. They did not know, and they did not agree, on the unidimensional components which made up this 'bigness'; they were content with the fact that tests constructed on this principle worked reasonably well, and they disregarded criticisms to the effect that there was no rational basis underlying their process of 'measurement', and that the results were often contradictory. Person A might be superior to B on the Stanford-Binet, B might be superior to C on the Porteus Maze test, and C might be superior to A on the Army Alpha. It is possible to show that results such as these cannot be blamed on random errors of measurement, and the only reasonable explanation appears to be that these different tests are combinations of different fundamental dimensions of abilities in different proportions. In either case, more detailed analysis is called for, in spite of the apparent success of old-fashioned intelligence tests. Such analysis inevitably leads to more accurate measurement and to the elimination of incongruities such as those mentioned. Oddly enough, such further analysis has encountered a certain amount of resistance.

One reason for this resistance is to be found in the conservatism of many 'consumers' of intelligence tests. Teachers, psychiatrists, social workers – they all have become used to the concept of the I.Q. (intelligence quotient) which purports to be a measure of a person's general intelligence.* The

* The I.Q. or intelligence quotient is the ratio: $\dfrac{\text{Mental Age}}{\text{Chronological Age}}$ × 100, where 'Mental Age' is defined in terms of a child's ability to do successfully tests which the average child of a given age can do. Thus a child who solves problems which 50 per cent of nine-year olds can solve would have a mental age of 9, regardless of his chronological age. If he himself happened to be 9 years old at the time, he would be of average ability and have an I.Q. of $\dfrac{9}{9}$ × 100=100, because by definition the average child has an I.Q. of 100. If his chronological age happened to be 6, he would obviously be a bright child, very advanced, with an I.Q. of $\dfrac{9}{6}$ × 100=150. With a chronological age of 12, he would be a retarded, dull child having an I.Q. of $\dfrac{9}{12}$ × 100=75. Only one child in 200 has an I.Q. of over 140, or below 60; about 50 per cent of all children have I.Q.s between 90 and 110. Mental defectives tend to be below the I.Q.=70 level. However, the diagnosis of mental deficiency is usually based only in part on intelligence tests, so that this figure may sometimes be misleading.

I.Q. is a typical 'bigness' measure, but its undoubted practical usefulness has blinded many people to its undoubted drawbacks. Another equally powerful reason is the disinclination of many people (including, be it said with feelings of shame, some psychologists) to master matrix algebra and the other mathematical devices which are required to carry out or follow the analysis of 'intelligence' into its constituent parts. But the main objection has come from those who feel that in the I.Q. they are dealing with a concept that describes the totality of an individual's intellectual powers more adequately than do more analytical measures. It is true, of course, that 'bigness' tells us more about a camel than 'height' does, even though 'bigness' is a vague concept, inaccurately measured, while 'height' is a precise concept, accurately measured. But 'height' and 'width' combined tell us more than 'bigness', without loss of rigour and accuracy – indeed, with a notable gain in both. Similarly, if we were reduced to expressing a person's intellectual powers in terms of one single figure alone, we should presumably use something very like the I.Q., while protesting strongly that what we need is not one figure, but as many as there are dimensions in the intellectual realm. Fortunately there is no reason why we should be restricted to one figure, and our picture of a person's intelligence will be a profile, listing his strong and weak points, rather than a single average.

Even so, our description will not be complete. This fact is often used to discredit attempts to measure intelligence, and must therefore be considered. As Thurstone points out, 'if abilities are to be postulated as primary causes of individual differences in overt accomplishment, then the widely different achievements of individuals must be demonstrable functions of a limited number of reference abilities. This implies that individuals will be described in terms of a limited number of faculties. This is contrary to the erroneous contention that since every person is different from every other person in the world, people must not be classified and labelled. Each generalization in the scientific description of

nature results in a loss to the extent to which the ideal constructs of science match the individual events of experience.
. . . From the viewpoint of immediate experience, scientific
description is necessarily incomplete. The scientist always
finds his constructs immersed in the irrelevancies of experience. It seems appropriate to acknowledge this characteristic of science in view of the fact that it is a rather common
notion that the scientific description of a person is not valid
unless the so-called "total situation" has been engulfed. A
study of people does not become scientific because it
attempts to be complete, nor is it invalid because it is restricted. The scientific description of a person will be as
incomplete from the viewpoint of common sense as the
description of other objects in scientific contexts.'

Examples of the type of objection to which Thurstone
refers are easy to find. Thus it is often said that an anxious
person is handicapped in intelligence by his anxiety, so that
the test does not give a fair picture of his 'true' abilities.
Thus 'intelligence' cannot be measured in isolation; we
must take into account the 'whole personality' of our subject. To analyse out 'intelligence' from the whole background of a person's emotional needs, experiences, and
motivations is said to be 'atomistic' and fallacious. But
surely we do the same, with good success, in the physical
sciences? We might say that in measuring the length of a
bar of metal we are surely 'handicapping' the bar by measuring it during a cold spell; it would be much longer in the
heat of summer. This is perfectly true; 'length' and 'temperature' are not independent variables, and we must know
both, as well as the functional law which obtains between
them, before our description is reasonably accurate. Similarly, it is quite possible that anxiety and intelligence interact.
The solution to the problem presented is not to give some
global 'bigness' estimate based on a combination of the two,
but to measure them separately and state the exact mathematical law according to which they interact. We can
measure 'anxiety' almost as accurately as we can measure
'intelligence' (cf. chapter 10); we can experimentally

increase a person's anxiety and note the effects on his intelligence test scores, and we can study persons suffering from anxiety and see whether their intelligence test scores improve as their anxiety diminishes. The outcome of experiments of this type appears to be that anxiety does handicap the individual slightly in the performance of an intelligence test, but that only in really extreme cases is the effect marked enough to require correction.

There are probably many other hypotheses of a similar nature regarding the interaction of 'intelligence' and aspects of the emotional, non-intellectual parts of personality. The existence of such 'interaction' does not make the accurate measurement of ability impossible; it should rather encourage us to investigate such hypotheses with great care, and try to state as accurately as possible the laws of interaction. The set of concepts with which we are working is only a first approximation; we may have to discard many of them and try out new ones. In principle, however, it is safe to state that only by more rigorous and detailed analysis are we likely to discover the most useful concepts, as well as their mode of interaction.

What sort of analysis is required to break down the 'bigness' concept of intelligence into more unidimensional variables? We could try to do this by what are called 'Schreibtischexperiments' – by sitting at the desk thinking about the problem, introspecting, and then setting out the results of our cogitations in lengthy and impressive tomes. This, roughly, is what philosophers have been doing throughout history, and the main outcome of these deliberations appears to have been the doctrine of 'faculties'. According to this doctrine, man possesses a large number of faculties which enable him to perform his various duties – a faculty of memory, of imagination, of consideration, and so forth. These faculties were often considered to be located in a special part of the brain, and the phrenologists even went so far as to claim that by feeling the bumps on a person's head they could tell which of his faculties were particularly strongly developed, and which were outstandingly weak.

Maps were drawn of the brain, with the faculty-areas clearly marked, and many people made fortunes out of this game of 'character-telling'. Even serious scientists were implicated in these speculations, and indeed the whole history of this movement may serve as an eloquent warning against similar fads in more modern dress.

By and large faculty psychology and phrenology were discredited, partly because of the rather obvious absurdity of explaining a person's remembering something by invoking a 'faculty of memory', the only evidence for which consists in his having remembered something; partly because electrical stimulation of the brain became possible, and it was rather damaging to the claims of phrenologists to find that when the 'area of amorousness' was stimulated the patient did not burst forth with lustful cries in pursuit of the nurses, but merely wiggled his big toe. In any case, faculty psychology has left its mark on our common speech, and even on our educational practices; when we teach Latin to children in order to improve 'their logical sense', or make them memorize history dates to 'improve their memory' we are acting in accordance with the notions of an outdated philosophical psychology which has been fairly decisively disproved in its main contentions by experimental work during the past century.

Perhaps we may fare better if we look closely at the different types of intelligence tests now on the market, and ask ourselves in what ways they differ from each other. Our attention there would be drawn first of all to the *material* which went to make up our tests. Some tests use words, others use numbers, yet others abstract visual material like designs; some tests make use of concrete objects such as coloured blocks, jig-saw puzzles, and the like. It seems likely that some people may be superior in dealing with one kind of material, others in dealing with another. Here then is one possible direction in which to look for our hypothetical abilities.

Next we might look at the *mental operations* required to carry out a given task. In one test we might be asked to *learn* the content of a passage, in another to *remember* something, in yet a third to make *inductive judgements*, while in a fourth our main task might be of a *perceptual* nature. This type of classification is more difficult *a priori* because we have little knowledge about the mental processes involved in any particular mental act, but as a hypothesis we may perhaps let it stand.

Yet a third possible approach seems to lie in the distinction often made between speed and power. Perhaps some tests call more for quick and possibly superficial responses, while others measure the depth of our understanding rather than its quickness. As a possibility at least this must be considered; many critics of intelligence tests have put forward some such idea as this, complaining that intelligence tests tend to put a premium on quickness and speed, rather than on profundity.

We thus have three possible ways in which analysis might proceed; by way of differences in test *material*, by way of difference of mental *processes*, and by way of what we may call difference in *quality*. How can we verify these hypotheses or else show them to be ill-founded? The most usual, and in practice the only effective way, has been through a statistical-experimental procedure called factor analysis. This is based on a very simple principle. If you give a series of tests of so-called intelligence to a large, diversified group of people, then each test will give you an order of 'goodness' of performance, with one person at the top, another at the bottom, and the rest strung out in between. Now if two tests measure the same mental process, in the same material, and holding quality constant for both, then they should give exactly the same order, with the same person top in both, the same person at the bottom, and all the others also arranged in the same way. Chance errors of measurement might slightly alter the order in unpredictable ways, but on the whole our expectation is a reasonable one, and indeed one which is borne out in actual practice. Two tests constructed to fulfil these conditions show very high agreement; in some cases the agreement is almost perfect.

Now if we take two tests differing in certain respects – either using different types of material, or different mental processes, or laying different degrees of stress on speed and power respectively, then the respective rank orders of 'goodness' of performance should be less similar. The more dissimilar we make the tests, the less agreement would be expected in the rank orders, until we reach the point where two tests are so unlike each other that knowing who did well on one test would tell us nothing about that person's performance on the other test. In other words, the more similar two tests are with respect to material, mental process, and quality, the more alike will be the performances of our subjects on the two tests. Conversely, the less alike two tests are in these three respects, the less alike will be the performances of our subjects.

It is possible to transform these rather vague concepts of 'like' and 'unlike' into precise mathematical terms by using what is called a 'coefficient of correlation'. This coefficient ranges from 1 (indicating complete and perfect agreement) to 0 (indicating complete absence of agreement). Occasionally negative coefficients are observed, as when there is a tendency for a person who does well on test A to do badly on test B, and vice versa. Such negative coefficients hardly ever appear in work with intelligence tests. A few examples may make the meaning of this coefficient clearer. We know that there is a tendency for tall people to be heavier than short people; the correlation between height and weight is about ·6, i.e. about equally far removed from perfect correspondence and complete lack of correspondence. Height and intelligence only correlate about ·2, i.e. so little that no reasonable prediction of a person's intelligence can be made from his height, although a slight tendency for tall people to be more intelligent is present. The length of a person's right arm correlates with the length of his left arm about ·98, i.e. very near perfection; the length of his nose, however, shows very low correlations on the average with the size of his feet.

We can now restate our hypothesis – tests which are

similar with respect to material, process, and quality will tend to show high correlations, while tests dissimilar with respect to one or all of these will show low correlations. The greater the degree of similarity, the greater the amount of correlation; the less the degree of similarity, the smaller the amount of correlation. We can invert this statement and say – the greater the amount of correlation, the greater the similarity of the tests, and the smaller the amount of correlation, the smaller the degree of similarity. This latter form is more useful, because what we observe in actual fact is the correlations between the tests; from these we deduce the greater similarity. The process of analysis by means of which this is done is a rather complex one; results to date have shown remarkable agreement between many different investigators regarding the nature of the main abilities or factors involved in the process of doing intelligence tests. These results have dealt almost entirely with differences in ability to deal with different types of material, and with the efficiency of different mental processes; until quite recently there has been a relative dearth of investigations into the speed-power complex of qualities.

The main factors* isolated have been named Verbal Ability (V), Verbal Fluency (W), Numerical Ability (N), Spatial Ability (S), Perceptual Ability (P), Memory (M), and Inductive Reasoning (R). It is difficult to describe these abilities in the absence of the tests on which they are based, and in terms of which they are defined, and consequently I have given examples of test items which characterize each

* Factors such as these may seem superficially to resemble the 'faculties' criticized so severely in an earlier part of this chapter. The main difference between the two concepts lies in their derivation. Faculties were posited on the basis of unsystematic observation and verbalization of certain stereotypes and prejudices current at the time; factors are carefully defined in terms of experimental and statistical procedures which follow the usual dictates of the scientific method. Occasional resemblances should not be allowed to obscure the fundamental differences between 'faculties' and 'factors'. To escape erroneous verbal implications, factors are often designated by letters rather than by words; these letters are given below after the verbal classification of each factor.

factor in Chapter 2. Most of the examples are at a very easy level; it will be obvious to the reader how they could with ease be made more difficult. A proper test would contain items at all levels of difficulty. Full instructions would of course be given, and a few minutes would in each case be devoted to sample problems in order to make quite certain that the subjects understood just what they were expected to do.

These seven factors or abilities are relatively independent, but not quite so. A person who scores highly on tests for one of these factors tends to score highly also on tests of the other factors, although this general tendency is much less strong than that linking tests of one and the same ability with each other. Perhaps we may identify this universal tendency to do well in all these multifarious tasks with our hypothetical concept of 'intelligence'? Let us look at the various factors and consider which of them seem to consist of tests requiring to the greatest extent the qualities which we normally call 'intellectual'. Most people would probably agree that the tests identifying the reasoning factor required most intelligence, those identifying the verbal and numerical factors next most, and the other tests the least amount of intelligence. This purely subjective and *a priori* view is borne out by the correlations between the tests; the property which they have in common is most clearly manifested in the reasoning tests, less in the numerical and verbal tests, and least in the memory or spatial tests. We thus arrive at a general view of intelligence as an ability underlying all intellectual operations, but to varying extent; more necessary and important for some, less necessary and important for others. In addition to this general quality, which we may call 'intelligence' or which we may prefer more cautiously to denote by the simple letter 'g', there are more specialized abilities enabling us to deal with particular efficiency with certain types of material, or making for the particularly efficient use of some type of mental process. It is highly unlikely that the seven abilities discovered so far are the only ones which can be isolated; there are suggestions in recent work of many

B

others. So far, however, these seven are the most clearly established ones, and hence they may here stand for all the rest.

We have not hitherto dealt with the problem of speed and power. Here psychology is on less certain ground, partly because interest in these concepts has been dormant for many years, and research has not been directed towards its solution. Recently, interest has been reawakened, and as some of the experimental findings are of very great interest and importance I shall try to summarize them now. In doing so I shall make use of the findings and concepts of D. Furneaux, who has been primarily responsible for the solution of this hoary problem.

Let us take a particular type of intelligence-test item, say the letter-series illustrated on page 61. Suppose we construct a great variety of these items, and administer them without any kind of time limit to a representative sample of the population. We can then assign a difficulty level to each item in terms of the proportion of the population passing or failing that item. An item which is successfully solved by 90 per cent of our sample is a relatively easy item; an item successfully solved by only 10 per cent is a relatively difficult one. If we now apply a test made up of items at all difficulty levels to a new sample of the population, we may get one of three different responses: the subject may get the answer right, he may get the answer wrong, or he may give up all hope of a solution and omit the item. Most intelligence tests give a total score based on the number of items solved correctly over a given period; they therefore mix up inextricably these three possible ways of solving the problem. If we wish to analyse the contribution of speed, we must try to keep these types of answer separate. This requires that we measure the time taken by each subject to solve each of the problems; we clearly cannot get any kind of reasonable average by dividing the number of problems solved correctly by the total time taken, because some people would have spent a good deal of time on giving wrong answers, or on problems finally given up, while other people would waste very little time that way.

If we do this, we can plot the time taken by any one person for items at a given difficulty level. This has been done in Figure 1 A, and it will be seen that as the difficulty level goes up, time taken to solve the problem increases quite disproportionately. We can get over this difficulty by using the logarithm of our time measurement (log time), and when we do that the relationship between our two variables (log time and difficulty level) becomes a straight line, as shown in Fig. 1 B. Three people's results have

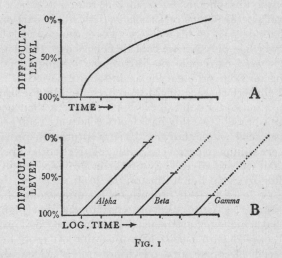

Fig. 1

been plotted there, Messrs Alpha, Beta, and Gamma, and it will be seen that their results can all be represented by straight lines, and that all the lines have equal slopes, i.e. are parallel. This is an experimental finding which could not have been predicted, but which is of the utmost importance; it shows that in our measurement we are here dealing with a universal constant (universal in our culture, at least) such as many people have despaired of being able to find in psychology.

Certain facts will be obvious from the diagram. Alpha is quicker at all levels of difficulty than Beta; Beta is quicker at all levels than Gamma. Gamma solves items only up to a very modest level of difficulty; Beta succeeds up to medium difficult levels; Alpha succeeds even at relatively high levels. It might seem inviting to identify the point at which each person's line intersects with the base line (i.e. the speed with which they solve very simple items such that practically everyone can solve them) with that person's *speed*, and the highest difficulty level at which he succeeds with his *power*. Unfortunately there are two important qualifications to this scheme. There is every reason to expect that a person's performance on problems depends in part on his speed, and in part on his willingess to continue to search for an answer, i.e. on what we call his persistence. If our three subjects were extremely persistent, and willing to go on working on each problem for an indefinite period of time, then their performance might be represented by the broken continuation of the solid lines which represent their actual accomplishment. On this basis even relatively dull people could succeed with relatively difficult problems, provided they were willing to persevere, while relatively bright people might fail with relatively easy problems provided they were unwilling to spend much time on the problem.

The evidence for this proposition is quite strong, and it certainly agrees with common sense to say that high intellectual achievement is the product of high speed of mental work, coupled with persistent application. It must be remembered, of course, that our time scale is a logarithmic scale, so that the required increase in time to solve a difficult problem is quite disproportionate for the dull person; he might require several months of persistent application to solve a problem which the bright person could solve in a few minutes. Nevertheless, the two factors of speed and persistence are relatively independent, and consequently we cannot talk about 'power' as being a useful, unidimensional concept in psychology. Power is usually identified as the highest level of difficulty reached in the correct solutions of problems by a subject; it is clearly a compound concept dependent on the more elementary ones of speed and persistence. It is interesting to note that one of these elementary factors (persistence) is not an intellectual quality at all, but rather a function of personality organization and emotional integration. On the purely cognitive side, speed of mental functioning emerges as the prime determinant of intellectual ability. It may be identified with good reason with 'g' or general mental ability or intelligence.

Even such a combination of speed and persistence, however, does not take into account all the complexities of the problem-solving process. Experimental evidence supports everyday experience in making it clear that failure to solve a problem results just as frequently from writing down a wrong answer, under the impression that it is the right one, as from the failure to persevere for a sufficiently long time. This observation brings a quality rather like 'carelessness' into our analysis, although it may turn out that this is not a very good word to use as a description of what actually happens. The evidence makes it clear that the fast, persistent person may nevertheless achieve relatively little success simply because of the intervention of this further process, which leads to the acceptance of incorrect solutions as right ones, and perhaps also to the rejection of correct answers in favour of wrong ones.

As Furneaux has shown, the facts here summarized, when considered in conjunction with certain relationships between them which can only be given mathematical expression, lead directly to a fairly plausible hypothesis about the nature of the brain processes which underlie problem solving. According to this view, when a problem is first perceived there starts in the brain an orderly sequence of events which results in the production of a chain of 'trial-solutions'. These trial-solutions do not necessarily become conscious, each of them being simply a particular mode of organization of some part of the brain structure. It is the rate at which these 'modes of organization' are set up, broken down, and remodelled which underlies the concept of mental speed. As each trial solution is set up in the brain its adequacy as an answer to the actual problem under consideration is tested, perhaps by the sort of 'feed-back' mechanism which serves the same purpose in electronic computing machines. It is at this stage that 'carelessness' is introduced – perhaps 'error' is a better term – since it may happen that a trial solution which satisfies only some of the requirements of the problem triggers off the testing mechanism and leads to the production of a wrong answer. Provided that no such error interposes, the process of setting up trial-solutions and testing them will continue, either until a valid solution arises, or until lack of persistence results in the transfer of attention to another problem.

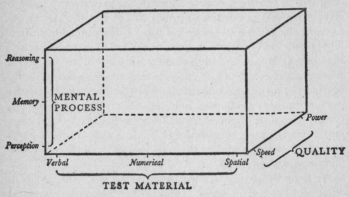

FIG. 2

Shorn of its many complicating features, we thus arrive at the end of our quest for an answer to the question: 'What do tests of intelligence really measure?' If properly constructed along analytic lines, they measure speed of mental functioning, which appears quite basic to intellectual efficiency. They also measure special facility for dealing with different types of material – numbers, words, designs, and so forth – and special excellence of different types of mental processes – perceiving, memorizing, reasoning, and so forth. They also involve non-intellectual components, such as persistence, which are of great importance in determining a person's effective intelligence, i.e. his power to solve problems of higher and higher difficulty and complexity. These various relationships are portrayed diagrammatically in Fig. 2. A poor test will measure a complex of all these different dimensions, thrown together haphazardly, and contributing in unknown proportions to the final I.Q. A well-constructed test (or rather series of tests) will give separate measures of all these qualities, thus making possible much more detailed statements of a person's strong and weak points, and allowing of much more accurate prediction of his future achievements. The conspicuous successes achieved in practical life with poor tests may serve as an indication of what will be achieved in the future when practice catches up with modern theoretical developments; there is evidence already that analytic tests may double and treble the predictive accuracy of older tests.

2

PRIMARY MENTAL ABILITIES

THIS chapter is made up almost completely of examples of tests to illustrate the discussion of the nature of intelligence given in Chapter 1. The main reason for their inclusion is that a purely theoretical argument about such concepts as 'perceptual ability' or 'verbal fluency' cannot mean very much to those not acquainted with the actual instruments used to measure and define these concepts. Professor Thurstone, whose pioneering work in this field has put the study of intelligence on an altogether sounder footing, has kindly agreed to have test-items from his series reproduced here.

It should be noted that these are not complete tests, but merely items illustrating the test-instructions, followed by a few items which the testee has to work through before the test proper begins, in order to show that he has an adequate grasp of the instructions. Consequently most readers will find these pages rather easy going. Even so, however, it will be obvious that very much more difficult items can easily be written, and that tests can be constructed for any desired level of intellectual ability, from the five-year-old level to that of a superior college group.

To those who might feel disposed to dispute the correct grouping of the tests let me emphasize again that this grouping is not an arbitrary one but is dictated by the actual pattern of performance of large groups of people.

(1) VERBAL ABILITY (v)

*

PROVERB TEST

This is a test of your ability to understand what you read. Read Proverb A.

A. *Sail when the wind blows.*

Two and only two of the following sentences have nearly the same meaning as Proverb A. Find these two sentences.

.... √ .... Strike when the iron is hot.

.... One must howl with the wolves.

.... √ .... Make hay while the sun shines.

.... Make not your sail too large for the ship.

The first and third statements have been checked because they have nearly the same meaning as Proverb A.

Now check the two sentences in the group below which have nearly the same meaning as Proverb B.

B. *Tall oaks from little acorns grow.*

.... No grass grows on a beaten road.

.... Large streams from little fountains flow.

.... The exception proves the rule.

.... Great ends from little beginnings.

Verbal Classification

Column 1, below, is a list of *animals*. Column 2 is a list of *furniture*. Column 3 has some words about animals and some words about furniture. *Desk* is furniture, and 2 is written after it. *Sheep* is an animal, and 1 is written after it. The rest of the words under 3 have been marked in the same way.

1	2	3	
cow	table	desk	2
horse	chair	sheep	1
bird	bookcase	rocker	2
dog	lamp	dresser	2
		cat	1
		donkey	1

In the following problems, mark each word under 3.

1	2	3	
lacerate	suffer	wince	____
torture	ache	crucify	____
bite	twinge	crush	____
pinch	writhe	smart	____
		moan	____
		cut	____

VERBAL RELATIONS

Read the following row of words:

1-foot: 2-shoe 3-hand: 4-thumb 5-head 6-glove 7-finger
8-clasp

6

The first two words, *foot* and *shoe*, are united by a certain relation, the shoe is worn on the foot. The next word is *hand*. Which of the five words following can be combined with *hand* in the way given by the *foot-shoe* relation? The answer is *glove* because the glove is worn on the hand. Therefore a 6 is written in the blank at the right.

In the following two exercises find the word at the right which is related to the third word in the same way that the second word is related to the first. Write the corresponding numbers in the blanks at the right.

1-fish: 2-water 3-bird: 4-blue 5-robin 6-ocean
7-sky 8-high

1-mayor: 2-city 3-captain: 4-ship 5-private
6-general 7-store 8-lieutenant

---

(2) VERBAL FLUENCY (w)

*

REARRANGED LETTER

Rearrange the letters on each of the following lines to spell the name of an *animal*. In the first line, the letters (ebar) can be arranged to spell *bear*, which is written in the blank space. In the next line, the letters (odg) spell *dog*, which is written in the blank space. In the same way the letters (atc) spell *cat*.

ANIMALS

ebar   *bear*

odg   *dog*

atc   *cat*

Rearrange the letters on each of the following lines to spell the name of a *bird*.

BIRDS

uckd   ___

cowr   ___

wahk   ___

Word-Finding

In the blanks below, write as many different words as you can that begin with S, and end with L. The words may be long or short. You may write the names of persons, or places, or foreign words. Errors in spelling will not be counted against you.

As examples, the first three lines have already been filled in for you. Write as many other words as you can.

Write words that begin with S and end with L.

1. sell
2. Saul
3. spell
4. _____
5. _____

WORD-MAKING

Make as many different words as you can, using only the letters in the word G-E-N-E-R-A-T-I-O-N-S. You may use long or short words and may include the names of persons, places, or foreign words. In any one word do not use a letter more times than it appears in G-E-N-E-R-A-T-I-O-N-S.

Sample words have been written in the first few lines. Continue writing as many words as you can using only the letters given.

G-E-N-E-R-A-T-I-O-N-S

1. *art*

2. *era*

3. *snore*

4. _____

5. _____

(3) NUMERICAL ABILITY (N)

*

NUMBER CODE

In this test you will be asked to use a number code based on twenty symbols instead of the ten digits to which we are accustomed. There is a symbol for each of the numbers from 0 to 19, as shown below. Notice that a bar means 5 and that a dot means 1. For example, the number 9 is represented by a symbol consisting of a bar and four dots. Zero is represented by a U-shaped symbol as shown.

0 ∪	1 ·	2 ··	3 ···	4 ····	5 —	6 — ·	7 — ··	8 — ···	9 — ····
10 — —	11 — — ·	12 — — ··	13 — — ···	14 — — ····	15 — — —	16 — — — ·	17 — — — ··	18 — — — ···	19 — — — ····

For numbers larger than nineteen, the symbols are combined, one above the other. This is shown in Example 2 below. When there are two symbols, one above the other, the upper one is to be multiplied by 20 and the bottom symbol is to be multiplied by 1. The answer is the sum. Study Example 2.

For numbers larger than 399, three symbols are used, one above the other. The uppermost symbol is multiplied by 400, the next by 20, and the bottom symbol by 1. The answer is the sum. Study Example 3.

Example 1	*Example 2*	*Example 3*
·· × 1 = 7	· × 20 = 120	··· × 400 = 1200
	·· × 1 = 7	··· × 20 = 160
	127	·· × 1 = 12
		1372

Now solve the six practice problems below. The first two have already been solved for you.

	Space for figuring	Answer		Space for figuring	Answer
⋯ ⎯	×1=13	13	⋯ ⋯⋯		
⋅⋅ ∪	×20=140 ×1=0	140	⎯ ⎯ ⋯⋯		
⋅⋅ ⋯⋯ ⎯			⎯ ∪ ⋅		

COMPUTATIONS

In the following table there are blank spaces. Fill in the correct numbers in these spaces. Get the necessary information from the rest of the table. Use the space below each table and on the opposite page for figuring.

Year	MARRIAGES		DIVORCES			
	Number	*Increase over Preceding Year*	*Number*	*Increase over Preceding Year*	*Number Granted to Husband*	*Number Granted to Wife*
1894	566,161	12,512	37,568	100	12,551	25,017
1895	598,855	32,694	40,387	2,819	—	26,931
1896	613,873	15,018	42,937	—	14,448	—
1897	622,350	—	—	1,762	14,765	29,934
Total	2,401,239	No total	165,591	No total	55,220	110,371

ARITHMETICAL PROBLEMS

In this test you are shown some arithmetical problems that have already been worked out. Four answers are given for each problem. One of these is always the right answer. You are asked merely to check the right answer. You may use the space on the page for figuring but do not waste time working out the exact answer.

In the first problem below you can readily see that the first number is nearly 4 and the second number is nearly 7. Since $4 \times 7 = 28$, look for the answer that is nearest 28. This is the third answer and it is checked.

$$4 \cdot 12395 \times 6 \cdot 82187 =$$

$$4 \times 7 = 28$$

7·563327	
14·012468	
28·133051	✓
56·103378	

In the problem below you see that the numerator is nearly 30 and the denominator is nearly 6. Since $30 \div 6 = 5$, we check the second answer which is the one nearest 5.

$$\frac{29 \cdot 6718}{5 \cdot 7261} =$$

$$6\overline{\smash{\big)}30}$$
$$5$$

4·4278	
5·1819	✓
6·9271	
8·4293	

Since you *know* that one answer is *correct*, there are many other tricks for finding out *which* answer that is. For example, in the problem below you see that $30 \times 30 = 900$. Therefore 29×29 must be *less* than 900. You can also see that $9 \times 9 = 81$, so that the right-hand figure of the answer will be 1. Hence 841 is the only possible correct answer.

$$(29)^2 =$$

$$\begin{array}{r} 30 \\ 30 \\ \hline 900 \end{array}$$

755·	
841·	
865·	
901·	

In the problems below use any tricks or short cuts to find out which answer is correct and check that answer. Do not waste time checking exact answers because one of the given answers is the correct one.

	2·621	_____
3·01224×4·86537=	6·782	_____
	14·656	_____
	21·387	_____

	6·5654	_____
	10·6327	_____
$\dfrac{53·29736}{5·01258} =$	91·7136	_____
	134·6973	_____

	7698·	_____
1351+8271+72+3+51+	9875·	_____
2+1+13+9+4+23+	13561·	_____
8+19+22+4+6+16	20679·	_____

	11569·	_____
$(197)^2=$	23417·	_____
	38809·	_____
	62187·	_____

(4) SPATIAL ABILITY (s)

*

HANDS

In this test you will be shown a series of pictures of hands. Some of these pictures represent right hands, others represent left hands. Below each picture you will find two small squares.

If the picture represents a right hand, put a check mark in the right square; if it represents a left hand, put a check mark in the left square, as shown in the following samples, which are correctly marked.

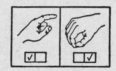

Now mark the samples below in the same way.

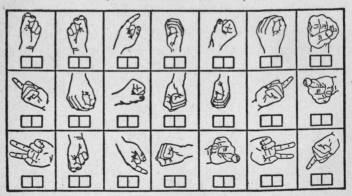

CARDS

Here is a picture of a card. It looks like an *L*, and it has a hole in one end.

Ɬ

The two cards below are alike. You can slide one around on the page to fit the other exactly.

Ɬ ↳

Now look at the next two cards. They are different. You cannot make them fit exactly by sliding them around the page.

Ɬ ⌐

Here are more cards. Some of the cards are marked. The cards which are like the first card in this row are marked.

Ɬ ↳ ⌐ ✓ ⌐ ⌐ ⟨

Below is another row of cards. Mark all the cards which are like the first card in the row.

ᖴ ⅂ ┗ ┛ ᒥ ⟩ ┛

You should have marked the second and third cards. They are like the first card.

Here are some more cards for you to mark. In each row mark every card that is like the first card in the row.

◿ ▽ ◿ ◺ ▽ ▽ ◺

⌓ ⌱ ⌐ ◖ ⌓ ⌐ ⌐

The test contained twenty rows of seven figures.

FLAGS

Here are two pictures of a flag. These two pictures of the flag are the same. You can slide one picture around to fit exactly on the other picture.

S is marked to show that the pictures are the *same*.

The next two pictures of the flag are different. You cannot slide the pictures around to make them fit exactly.

D is marked to show that the pictures are *different*.

Here are some pictures for you to mark. Try to fit the pictures together by sliding them around flat on the paper. If the two pictures of the flag are the same, mark *S*. If the two pictures are different, mark *D*.

You should have marked *S* for the first pair and *D* for the second pair.

The test contained forty-eight items.

(5) PERCEPTUAL ABILITY (P)

*

IDENTICAL NUMBERS

The number at the top of the first column of figures is 634. A mark has been made under each 634 in the column. In the second column a mark has been made under the 876 because 876 is the number at the top of that column. In the third column the two 795's have been marked because 795 is the number at the top of the third column.

The number at the top of each of the other columns is repeated one or more times in that column. Find those numbers as quickly as possible and put a mark under each of them.

634	876	795	423	279	374
693	643	583	837	363	282
850	328	795	115	643	663
634	932	189	423	279	539
513	879	342	528	375	314
398	375	795	969	470	475
696	470	896	274	887	576
634	697	247	423	699	374
574	876	319	627	291	850
628	294	468	423	983	677
634	982	543	962	585	846

Mirror Reading

Look at the two words below.

cat

cat (printed backward)

The first word is *cat*. The second is also *cat*, but it is printed backward.

Below are two lines of words. In the first line the words are printed forward. In the second line the same words are printed backward.

bind	found	dump	skip	aunt
bind *(backward)*	found *(backward)*	dump *(backward)*	skip *(backward)*	aunt *(backward)*

The first word in each column below is printed forward. Below it are four words printed backward. One of the four words printed backward is the same as the word at the top of the column. The word which is the same as the first word is marked.

town	flag
turn *(backward)*	frog *(backward)*
tone *(backward)*	flat *(backward)*
tops *(backward)*	flag *(backward)*
<u>town</u> *(backward)*	farm *(backward)*

In each column of words below, mark the word printed backward which is the same as the first word.

most	horse	purse	book	lamp
more *(backward)*	hunch *(backward)*	purse *(backward)*	bond *(backward)*	look *(backward)*
meat *(backward)*	honey *(backward)*	pedal *(backward)*	bent *(backward)*	lake *(backward)*
most *(backward)*	hedge *(backward)*	phase *(backward)*	bank *(backward)*	lamp *(backward)*
milk *(backward)*	horse *(backward)*	pulley *(backward)*	book *(backward)*	lens *(backward)*

The test contains fifty columns of four words.

FACES

Here is a row of faces. One face is different from the others. The face that is different is marked.

Look closely to be sure that you see why the middle face is marked. The mouth is the part that is different.

Here is another row of faces. Look at them and mark the one that is different.

You should have marked the last face.

Here are more pictures for you to practise on. In each row mark the face which is different from the others.

The test contains sixty rows of faces.

(6) INDUCTIVE REASONING (R)

*

SECRET WRITING

In the first column below, 'Words', are three words: *saw, sat*, and *was*. In the second column, 'Secret Writing', the same words are given in a secret writing or code. Each number stands for a letter. You are to find the letter that corresponds to each number. The words are not in the same order in the first two columns. In the last column, 'Translation', you are to write the words in the same order as in the secret writing.

Words	Secret Writing			Translation		
saw	3	8	6	s	a	t
sat	5	8	3	w	a	s
was	3	8	5	s	a	w

There are several ways to solve this problem. Here is one way:

Look closely at the three words in the first column. Notice that two of the words begin with the same letter. The words *saw* and *sat* begin with *s*. The number which occurs at the beginning of two words is 3. Therefore 3 stands for *s*. Write *s* in each of the three blanks corresponding to the 3's.

The other word begins with *w*, so 5 must stand for *w*. Write *w* in each of the blanks corresponding to the 5's.

The middle letter of each word in the first column is *a*. The middle number of each word in the secret writing is 8. This tells you that 8 stands for *a*. Write *a* in each middle blank in the third column.

The only word which is not complete now is *sat*, so you know that 6 must correspond to *t*. Write *t* in the last blank of the first word.

The words in the last column should be in the order: *sat, was, saw*.

Here is another sample problem. The secret writing is different. Solve the problem to find out which letter each number stands for. Write the words in the correct places in the third column.

Words	Secret	Writing		Translation	
bet	8	o	9	*b* *e* *t*
rat	5	2	8	*c* *a* *b*
cab	4	2	9	*r* *a* *t*

Did you notice that two of the words end in *t*? The number which occurs twice as a last letter is 9. Then 9 must stand for *t*. Write *t* in the last column in the two blanks corresponding to the 9's.

Now notice also that *rat* and *cab* have the same middle letter, *a*. The number which occurs twice in the middle of a word is 2. Write *a* in the blanks corresponding to the 2's.

Now finish the word *rat*. The other word which ends in *t* is *bet*. Write it. Then the second word in the translation must be *cab*, and that checks because 8 is *b* in *bet*. The three words in the last column are *bet*, *cab*, and *rat*.

Here is another problem. Find the letters which correspond to the numbers and write them in the third column. It will help you to get started if you notice that there are three *a*'s in the words. Find the number which occurs three times and write *a*'s in the corresponding blanks in the third column. Finish the solution of the problem.

Words	Secret	Writing		Translation	
are	8	5	1	*s* *a* *w*
oar	2	5	3	*o* *a* *r*
saw	5	3	9	*a* *r* *e*

You should have written the words in the order: *saw, oar, are.*

Here is another problem for you to try. Notice that the letter *g* occurs only once in the three words. Find the number that occurs only once, and you will see the rest of the solution easily.

Words	Secret Writing			Translation		
pig	4	2	7	p	ʟ	t
pit	4	2	9	p	⊥	g
tip	7	2	4	t	⊥	p

You should have written the words in the third column in the order: *pit, pig, tip.*

Here are two more problems for you to practise on. Translate the words in secret writing and write the words in the correct places in the third column.

Words	Secret Writing			Translation		
man	2	4	6	t	a	n
tan	8	3	2	m	e	t
met	8	4	6	m	a	n

Words	Secret Writing			Translation		
run	2	3	9	r	a	n
art	2	4	9	r	u	n
ran	3	2	8	a	r	r

LETTER SERIES

Read the row of letters below.

a b a b a b a b ____

The next letter in this series would be *a*. Write the letter *a* in the blank at the right.

Now read the next row of letters and decide what the next letter should be. Write that letter in the blank.

c a d a e a f a ____

You should have written the letter g.

Now read the series of letters below and fill in each blank with a letter.

c d c d c d <u>c</u>

a a b b c c d d <u>e</u>

a b x c d x e f x g h x <u>i</u>

You should have written *c*, *e*, and *i*.

Now work the following problems for practice. Write the correct letter in each blank.

a a a b b b c c c d d <u>d</u>

a x b y a x b y a x b <u>y</u>

a b m c d m e f m g h m <u>i</u>

r s r t r u r v r w r x r <u>y</u>

a b c d a b c e a b c f a b c <u>g</u>

Letter Differences

Look at the groups of letters below.

AABC   ACAD   ACFH   AACG

Three of the groups have two A's. The group which does not have two A's is marked.

Here is another problem. Three of the groups are alike in some way. Can you find three groups which are alike?

XVRM   ABCD   MNOP   EFGH

In three of the groups the letters are arranged in alphabetical order. The first group is not in alphabetical order. Mark it to show that it is different.

Three of the groups in the next row are alike in some way. Mark the group that is different.

KABC   KEFG   LOPQ   KUVW

Three of the groups start with K. You should have marked the third group, which is different.

Here is another problem. Mark the group that is different.

ACDE   ILMN   LNOP   QSTU

Three of the groups omit only one letter. You should have marked the second group, which is different.

Here are more problems for you to work. In each row three of the groups are alike in some way. Mark the group that is different. Go right ahead.

AAAB   AAAM   AAAR   AATV

DCBA   HGFE   MRVX   PONM

RSTT   LMNL   FGHF   BCDB

ABCE   FGHJ   KLMO   RSTW

(7) MEMORY (M)

*

FIGURE RECOGNITION

Study the figures below so that you can recognize them when you see them again.

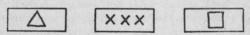

In the list below put a check mark (✓) after each of the figures that were listed above.

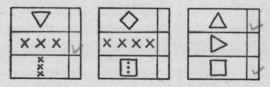

In a similar manner study the list below so that you can check these figures when you see them again on the next page.

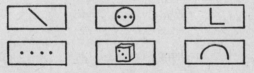

In the test proper twenty figures were shown, and these were to be checked in a longer list of sixty figures presented on a separate sheet.

First and Last Letters

Each object in the list below has a number. The number of *box* is 66, the number of *chair* is 21, and so on. You are to remember the number of each object. On the next page, the names of the objects are listed in a different order. You will be asked to write the number of each object.

If writing helps you to remember, you may copy the pairs of words and numbers on the blanks below. Study silently until you are told to stop. Begin studying now. Do not wait for any signal.

Object	Number	Object	Number	Object	Number
box	66				
chair	21				
fan	92				
lamp	77				

Do not turn back this page.

In the first row the correct number has been written.
Write the number of each of the other objects. Go right ahead.

Object	Number
chair	21
lamp	___
box	___
fan	___

The test proper contains fifteen word-number combinations.

FIRST NAMES

In each row below is written a name. You are to learn the names so well that when the last name is given you can write the first name. On the next page the last names are listed in a different order. You will be asked to write the first names.

If writing helps you to remember, you may copy the first and last names on the blanks below. Study silently until you are told to stop. Begin studying now. Do not wait for any signal.

First Name	Last Name	First Name	Last Name
Mary	Brown	_____	_____
John	Davis	_____	_____
Ruth	Preston	_____	_____
Fred	Smith	_____	_____

In the first row the correct first name has been written. Write the correct first names in the other blanks.

First Name	Last Name
_____	Preston
_____	Brown
_____	Smith
_____	Davis

The test consists in memorizing twenty first names which were to be associated with given surnames.

C

3

THE BRIGHT CHILD GROWS UP

THE lives and future careers of so many children are now in part determined, or at least influenced, by the results of intelligence tests administered at the age of 11 or thereabouts that we may rightly wonder just what is the predictive accuracy of these tests. This is a very important problem which is quite different from another one with which it is usually confused, namely, that of showing to what extent in a given group intelligence is correlated with achievement. Let me exemplify this difference, which has been curiously disregarded by many psychologists, in the following way. Supposing we give an intelligence test to 1000 officer candidates in the Army, all of whom are then sent up to the O.C.T.U.s for training. Some will be rejected as a result of the courses given there, others will be accepted. We can calculate the extent to which intelligence, as measured by our tests, is correlated with success at O.C.T.U., and therefore we can tell to what extent we can use the results of the intelligence test as a predictor of O.C.T.U. success.

Now, let us take a rather different example. Suppose we were to give an intelligence test to the sons of Army officers, all of them around six years of age, and all of them destined by their proud parents for an Army career. Let us also suppose that the very unlikely did happen, and that all these children did decide to make the Army their career and went up to O.C.T.U.s after having been given another intelligence test immediately prior to beginning their training there. Now the intelligence test given at the age of six might be used to predict success at O.C.T.U.; it might also be used to predict the result of the intelligence test given to these boys immediately before going to O.C.T.U. If the I.Q.s of the children remained constant from the time of their first testing at the age of six to the time of their second testing at the age of twenty, say, then obviously the early test would be just as good a predictor of success at O.C.T.U. as would the later test, because the two tests would give essentially the same answer.

But if there are changes in the I.Q. from year to year, then the intelligence test given at the age of six would not predict at all well results of the intelligence test given at the age of twenty: nor would it predict at all well the results of the O.C.T.U. training. If the I.Q. remains constant, then the use of an intelligence test to determine a child's or an adult's position at the moment, relative to others of his own age, would amount to very much the same thing as predicting what his position would be like in the future. If, however, the I.Q. does not remain constant then intelligence tests would still be useful as a measure of the child's or adult's position relative to his peers at the moment, but it could not be used with any great success as an indicator of his future standing. We must therefore enquire into the degree of constancy of the I.Q.

To many people, such an enquiry may seem unnecessary and supererogatory. Repeated assertion has convinced them that I.Q.s remain constant and that we need, therefore, make no distinction between the two uses of the intelligence test, which we may, for the purpose of convenience, call those of *measuring* intelligence and those of *predicting* intelligence respectively. Unfortunately, the evidence appears to point in a different direction. There have been a number of studies, notably a classical one by Dearborn and Rothney, in which large groups of children were followed-up over periods ranging up to ten years or more, and in which the children were tested and retested every year, so that changes in I.Q. could be observed and followed. From a survey of some 30 such studies, the following conclusions seem justified. The correlation between test and retest is a direct function of the length of time intervening. For a highly reliable, well-constructed test, like the Stanford Binet, which is perhaps the most widely used intelligence test of all, we may expect a correlation of about ·95 between test and retest with only a few days or a week intervening. If test and retest are separated by a whole year, the correlation will drop to ·91; if two years intervene it will go down to ·87. For every additional year intervening, the correlation will drop by ·04 points, so that after three years the correlation will be ·83, after four years it will be ·79, after ten years it will be down to ·55. This correlation of ·55, it may be noted, is an extremely low one as far as prediction goes; improvement over a chance prediction, i.e. one based on the tossing of a coin, is only about 10 per cent. This, clearly, is not very good.

It may be noted, incidentally, that these figures only hold within rather a restricted range. Before the age of six, prediction is considerably more inaccurate than might be indicated by these figures. Testing before the age of two has no predictive accuracy at all for adult intelligence. At three and four prediction becomes slightly positive, but the coefficients are so small as to make it quite useless for all practical purposes. Altogether, intelligence testing before the age of six, or five at the earliest, is a practice that should be discouraged as being likely to raise false hopes and fears without being able to give accurate support for them. At the other end of the scale, it seems reasonable to conclude from the evidence that after the age of fifteen or sixteen, there is considerable predictive accuracy in the results of intelligence tests, even over a period of thirty or more years. It is estimated that correlations in the neighbourhood of ·8 can reasonably be expected over such a period after adolescence has been reached, unless there is physical injury to the central nervous system.

Is it possible to rationalize these findings and arrive at some kind of descriptive hypothesis? Anderson has shown that the following ideas will provide a reasonable framework for observed results. Let us regard a child's ability at a given age as a kind of fund containing so many pounds or dollars. Throughout childhood, as intelligence develops, so money is added to the fund, and when adolescence and adulthood are reached the fund is complete. Suppose also that we can measure with complete accuracy the amount of ability the child possesses, or, in terms of our analogy, the amount of money in the fund. Then the hypothesis that the I.Q. remains constant demands that the amount of money paid into the fund each year (the increase in ability of the child) should form a constant proportion of the total already in the fund. Thus, the child with 20 units would add 2 units, whereas the child with 60 units would add 6, and the child with 120, 12 to his existing store.

An alternative hypothesis would be that the increments each year are uncorrelated with the existing fund, that in other words a child with a small fund may have a larger increment in a given year, and a child with a large fund may have a smaller increment. This apparently is what happens, and accounts for all the observed results. When the child is very small the fund, as it were, is very small too, and the increment in absolute size may be as large as the fund, but if the two are uncorrelated, then obviously we cannot from knowing the size of the fund at the age of two, say, predict what its size will be at the age of three, when a large increment of unknown amount has been added to it. As the child grows up the absolute size of the fund increases and the relative size of the increment becomes less and less important. By the time adolescence is reached, the fund is complete and no increments are added to it. Consequently, prediction of adult intelligence become more and more correct as the child gets older because its fund of ability will overshadow in importance the relatively small increases which occur during the last few years.

It follows from these considerations that existing intelligence tests, all of which are based on the assumption of constancy of the I.Q., may be extremely good measures of intellectual ability at the time, but they will be rather poor predictors of future success when given to young children. The obvious deduction to be drawn from this fact, surely, is that if we wish *both* to know the present ability of the child *and* to make a prediction about his future ability, then we cannot rely on one test only but must rather give two tests, one to establish the size of the fund, the other one to try to measure the probable size of the increments.

This is quite a difficult problem. To estimate the present intelligence of a child all we need to do is to measure him and compare him with other children of his own age. To make a ten-year prediction, however, would require at least a ten-year follow-up of a whole group of children, all of whom would have to be measured at the beginning and at the end of this period. This is clearly a much more difficult proposition administratively, and a much more costly one financially. However, it has been done, and the results are quite clear. Items in the original intelligence test which are rather good measures of the status of the child at that time are not good measures for the prediction of his later status, and vice versa; items which are poor measures of his present status may be very good measures of his future status. It is established, therefore, that we can construct tests for the prediction of the intelligence of a child in, say, ten years time, but these tests will differ considerably from those now in use, which are far more effective in telling us about the child's intellectual ability at the present moment. The constancy of the I.Q., therefore, is something of a myth, and if taken too literally it is seriously misleading. Prediction in this field is a little more difficult than it seemed to the early enthusiasts, and much more detailed research would be required before we can say with any degree of confidence what the I.Q. of little Johnny will be when he grows up, or whether Nellie will really be in the mental defective range when she reaches womanhood.

It would be easy to exaggerate the force of these objections. Present-day intelligence tests are obviously quite satisfactory for prediction among adults and also for older children. It is only for the younger children from six to ten, say, that they are not very adequate, and for those below six that they are almost entirely useless. In spite of these deficiencies it may be interesting to see with what success it has been possible, in at least one study, to predict the future of a large group of highly intelligent children. In estimating the success of the twenty-five-year follow-up study carried out by Terman and his associates, at Stanford University, it should always be borne in mind that the tests used by them were among the earliest devised and quite inferior in many ways to more modern tests. Also, they are subject to all the difficulties and complications I have just dealt with. Nevertheless, in spite of all these handicaps, the reader may be surprised to see to what extent even the crude tools of one quarter of a century ago succeeded in giving an accurate forecast of the future of this large group of highly gifted children.

Essentially the problem that Terman put himself was this. What are the physical, mental, and personality traits that are characteristic of intellectually superior children, and what sort of adult does the typical gifted child become? By means of various procedures, almost 1500 children out of a school population of about one quarter of a million were found whose I.Q.s placed them in the top 1 per cent of the population, practically all of them having I.Q.s of 140 or above; the brightest child was a girl with an I.Q. of over 200. A good deal of information was secured on all these children. Parents filled out a twelve-page home information blank, dealing with developmental history, circumstances of birth, early feeding, age of walking and talking, illnesses, nervous symptoms, home-training, and so forth. A similar school information blank was filled out by the child's teacher. A one-hour medical examination was given, covering vision, hearing, nutrition, posture, teeth, heart, lungs, neurological condition, and so on. Thirty-seven anthropometric measurements were also carried out, and a three-hour battery of school achievement tests given. Character tests, interest blanks, records of all books read over a period of two months, and home ratings made by field workers completed the picture.

Although both sexes had an equal chance of being chosen, boys exceeded girls in the ratio of 115 : 100. Terman convincingly rules out the possibility of bias in the selection of subjects to be tested. The probability that there exists a true average superiority of boys in the intellectual functions tested is fairly reliably excluded by the large amount of comparative work that has been done, and the most likely possibility is that boys are more variable with respect to intelligence than girls, producing more very bright and more very dull specimens. This hypothesis is supported by investigations carried out by Thomson in Scotland, embracing whole age groups. Consistently the boys there showed greater variability than the girls. The well-known fact that more geniuses and more mental defectives are male than female might also be supposed to support this argument, although there are obvious historical and social reasons which might explain these facts equally well.

Results of the physical measurements and a medical examination contradict a widely held view regarding highly intelligent children. This view is sometimes known as the 'compensation' hypothesis – in other words, the intelligent child, favoured as it is by intellectual ability, is supposed to be handicapped in other ways; he is depicted as being undersized, sickly, hollow-chested, stoop-shouldered, clumsy, nervous, tense, bespectacled, and over-serious. The less intelligent child, on the other hand, is supposed to compensate for his dullness by qualities of character, health, and body build, which make him superior in these respects to the gifted child. The facts summarized by Terman conclusively contradict this hypothesis. The gifted children as a group were often superior to the best standards for American-born children, both in height and weight; lung capacity, breadth of shoulders, and muscular strength all showed them to be superior to the average child. With respect to health, also, the gifted were superior, while the incidence of nervous habits, tics, and stuttering was about the same for them as it is for the generality of children of corresponding age. These facts fit in with a larger pattern, indicating that instead of a law of *compensation*, we are dealing with a law of *correlation*; children of superior intelligence tend to be superior also with respect to almost all the other desirable qualities which were investigated by Terman.

School achievements of the gifted group were also well in excess of their peers. On the whole, the gifted child's educational achievement was 44 per cent above his norm, or, to put it in a different way, the average gifted child's school knowledge was on a par with that of a strictly average child whose age was 44 per cent greater. As regards the interests of the gifted child, they are much more extensive than those of the average child for intellectual interests, somewhat greater for social interests, and almost identical for activity interests.

Various objective tests of character and personality were given to the children, and they were also rated by their teachers on a variety of mental, social, and moral traits. Practically all the ratings showed the gifted children superior to the average. This was particularly true of volitional traits such as will-power and perseverance, desire to excel, self-confidence, prudence, and forethought, and, to a lesser extent, of emotional traits such as sense of humour, cheerfulness, optimism, and permanence of mood, and moral traits such as conscientiousness, truthfulness, sympathy, tenderness, generosity, and unselfishness. Social trait ratings often showed the gifted child superior in the fields of leadership, popularity, freedom from vanity, and fondness for large groups.

Support for the accuracy of the ratings comes from some of the objective tests. Thus, it was found that 67 per cent of the gifted children were superior to the average child with respect to emotional traits as rated by the teacher, and exactly the same proportion equalled or excelled the scores of control groups on a test of emotional stability. Other objective tests showed the gifted child to be superior in many other ways. As compared with unselected children, these highly intelligent boys and girls were less inclined to boast or to overstate their knowledge; they were more trustworthy when under temptation to cheat; their reading preferences, character preferences, and social attitudes were more wholesome; on the whole set of character tests, the gifted child of 9 years tested as high as the average child of 12.

After six years a follow-up was undertaken, the most important outcome of which was the fact that the composite portrait of the group had changed only in minor respects. As a whole, the group was still highly superior intellectually, the boys having dropped slightly in I.Q. and the girls having dropped somewhat more, a regression effect towards the mean which might have been expected on purely statistical grounds. School work was still at an exceedingly high level, and again the gifted group was superior on the average to unselected children of corresponding age with respect to the physical, mental, and personality traits investigated.

Various other follow-up investigations were undertaken, the latest of them a quarter of a century after the first study had been made, and the group with an average age of 35 can now be assessed with respect to adult achievement. Findings are in many ways similar to those of the earlier work carried out when the subjects were still young. We may start with the most objective type of data, namely, physical measurements, and find that gifted men average 5 ft. 11 in. compared with an average of 5 ft. 8 in. for the United States Army draft selectees, and 5 ft. 9 in. for unselected college men. Gifted women also are taller than unselected women in the United States, the figures being 5 ft. 5 in. as compared with 5 ft. 4 in.

General health, although less directly susceptible of measurement, also appears to be good in the gifted group, and Terman concludes by saying that 'the gifted group is probably at least equal or superior to the generality in respect to general health, height, weight, and freedom from serious defects'.

Of more interest, perhaps, than figures with respect to physical health are figures with respect to mental health. As a further ramification of the 'compensation' hypothesis it is often said that the highly intelligent are more susceptible to neurotic and other mental disorders; the well-known saying that genius and madness are closely allied is still frequently trotted out as a statement of fact, in spite of the complete absence of evidence in its favour. On the basis of their case histories, the men and women in the gifted group were rated for general mental adjustment. There are three categories: (1) satisfactory adjustment; (2) semi-maladjustment; and (3) serious maladjustment. The subjects in category (3) were subdivided into (3a) those without psychosis and (3b) those with psychosis, the criterion for classification under the latter heading being a history of mental breakdown serious enough to require hospitalization.

Sex differences were small, and consequently the sexes were combined by Terman, who found that 81 per cent showed satisfactory adjustment, 15 per cent semi-maladjustment, 3 per cent serious maladjustment without psychosis, and 1 per cent (more accurately 0·81 per cent) serious maladjustment with psychosis. These were the ratings in 1940; by 1945 the proportions of cases in category (3) had risen to 4 per cent and 1·29 per cent respectively.

Comparative figures are difficult to obtain and are available only for the incidence of insanity. In both 1940 and 1945 comparison of the gifted subjects with expectation tables based on the general population of that age indicated that 'for the sexes combined the incidence of insanity for gifted subjects was very slightly below the expectancy for the generality'. Terman states that 'for all grades of mental maladjustment, including category 3b, there is a surprisingly large proportion of gifted subjects who have markedly improved or entirely recovered. It is suggested that superior intelligence may have been a factor in such improvement.' This statement is not based on any comparative figures and the reader is referred to the chapter on 'The Effects of Psychotherapy' for evidence to show that such rapid recovery is a rule rather than an exception, so that we may regard Terman's statement with respect to the superior recovery of highly intelligent people as not being supported by the facts. Terman found no correlation between the mental adjustment rating and childhood I.Q., but did find a slightly inverse relationship between the incidence of maladjustment and the amount of education.

We may now turn to results of intelligence tests applied to

these subjects when they had reached the age of about 30 on the average. A comparison of I.Q.s is extremely difficult because of certain obvious statistical considerations. An I.Q., as defined by the ratio of mental age divided by chronological age, only makes sense with children whose mental age increases *pari passu* with their chronological age; it is clearly inapplicable at later ages when mental age remains stationary, i.e. after sixteen, or begins to decline, say, after forty. Again, while well-standardized tests are available for young children – tests which will extend them to the full, however intelligent they may be – there is a dearth of such tests for adults, and those that exist are not well standardized on a random sample of the population. All these difficulties can be overcome, however, by means of statistical devices which I shall not discuss in detail here. Suffice it to say that Terman's estimate of the I.Q. of his subjects in adulthood is near the 134 mark, thus giving an apparent drop of 17 points in I.Q. from the average of the group in childhood.

Terman considers three explanations for this drop: the first is errors of measurement; the second is a failure of the two intelligence tests used in childhood and adulthood respectively to measure exactly the same functions; and third, maturational changes and environmental and educational influences. He estimates that the first two of these factors probably account for about half of the apparent drop, leaving perhaps nine or ten points to be accounted for in terms of maturational changes or environment. 'Probably the true net drop, beyond that due to errors of measurement and failure to test the same functions, is somewhere between five and ten points.' These, of course, are average results, and individual children showed much greater changes either up or down the scale than can be found on the average. By and large, however, it can be seen that the original test was not quite unsuccessful in forecasting the ultimate adult intellectual status of the children.

Nor can it be said to have failed altogether in predicting educational achievement. Approximately 90 per cent of the gifted men and 86 per cent of the gifted women entered college, and 70 per cent and 67 per cent respectively graduated from college. These figures are about eight times as high as those for the general population in California. The average grade in college of these men and women was superior, but not always as high as might have been expected from a group of such outstanding intelligence. Those who graduated from college had earned slightly higher scores on their childhood intelligence tests than had those who did not graduate from college. Slightly greater I.Q. differences were found between those who made an outstanding record at college and those who did average, or rather poorly.

Some interest attaches to the occupational status and the income of the bright group as compared with the average samples. Of the gifted, 45 per cent were rated as 'professional workers' compared with the Californian average of 6 per cent; 26 per cent in the professional and higher business groups as compared with 8 per cent for the total population. At the other extreme, 6 per cent were in the skilled trades and minor clerical and business occupations as compared with 32 per cent for the Californian average. Less than 10 per cent in the highly gifted group were found in the slightly skilled trades and other occupations requiring little training or ability, which account for 18 per cent of the Californian average. Thus, about eight times as many of the gifted are found in the professions as could be expected by chance. The gifted subjects also compared very favourably with other college graduates, 71 per cent of the gifted, and approximately 55 per cent of college men in general being classed in the two top grades of the professional ladder. 'The conclusion is that the gifted men, both college graduates and nongraduates, were filling positions of responsibility and exercising leadership to a reliably greater extent than the generality of college graduates.' As regards unemployment, it was found that less than 1 per cent of the gifted men were unemployed in 1940, as compared with 11 per cent of employable Californian males.

The men in the various occupational groups were compared on childhood I.Q. and on adult I.Q. The differences on childhood I.Q. are very slight, average scores being 153·2 for the professional, 152·6 for the semi-professional and higher business, and 150·3 for clerical, skilled-trade, and retail business employees. The remaining low-level categories, taken together, gave a mean of 146·8. The adult intelligence test was much more closely related to occupational classification, mean scores decreasing as we go from the top professional to the other groups. This finding, of course, is in line with the view that intelligence tests are less accurate in prediction than in contemporary measurements of intellectual competence.

What is true of the men was also found true of the women. There was little or no relationship between occupational status and childhood I.Q., but considerable relationship between adult intelligence test score and occupational status, the women in the higher professions and in college teaching being markedly superior. Other professions, such as social work, librarianship, nursing, writing, and so forth were second; school-teaching third; and office work and housework lowest of all.

The earned income of the gifted men and women was higher than that earned by the generality of college graduates of corresponding age, whose earnings in turn were considerably greater than those of a random sample of Californian men and women. In 1940, the median earned annual income of the gifted men between 30 and 39 years of age was almost exactly £1000, which is about £100 above the income of average college graduates. By 1945, a considerable improvement occurred and it was found that incomes of £2500 were eight times as frequent among the gifted men as could have been expected by chance. Incomes of £2000 were earned by about half the gifted men; this amount is earned by only about 7 per cent of the generality of United States families.

There appears to be no doubt that the gifted men and women occupied very much better jobs and earned far more

4

IS OUR NATIONAL INTELLIGENCE
DECLINING?

FOR the past twenty years there have been heard rumblings and cries of alarm and despondency from responsible psychologists who have maintained that the average intelligence of this nation, as well as of most other Western nations, is declining. This claim is based on a remarkably simple chain of deductions. In the first place, it is asserted that intelligence is largely an inherited quality. In the second place, it is known that those who are more intelligent tend to have fewer children than those who are less intelligent. If this trend were to continue over a long period of time it would follow that those genes which are the hereditary determinants making for high intelligence would be 'bred out' of the population stock, and a gradual decline of intelligence would be inevitable. Evidence is sometimes presented to show that this decline has already set in; thus, it is asserted that the number of mental defectives has increased in recent years. These arguments cannot be dismissed lightly, because they are buttressed by large numbers of experimental investigations; if they be true, they obviously raise a problem compared with which the dollar gap and the threat of inflation are small inconveniences to be shrugged aside as of no ultimate importance.

But before coming to any despondent conclusions, let us examine the facts, or even more important, perhaps, let us examine precisely what the implications of these facts may be. The first point in the argument relates to the inheritance of intelligence. There have been many debates on this question among psychologists, and many of the arguments that have been presented are clearly inconclusive. Early workers used to quote, for instance, the case of an American soldier who begot one child by a mentally defective prostitute, another by his legal wife. Both had progeny, and while on the normal mother's side the children and their offspring became normal, God-fearing Americans with a sprinkling of very successful business men and professional men, the children of the illegitimate union and their offspring tended to be dull, criminal, and, on the female side, prostitutes. Many of them were mentally defective. Such family trees have been offered as evidence of the inherited nature of intelligence, but quite apart from the fact that it is impossible to go back over the centuries and certify the soldier's illegitimate spouse as mentally defective in the absence of a proper examination, and quite apart from the fact that many errors are likely to be made in the tracing of a family tree of this type, it is surely obvious that those who believe that intelligence is determined by environment would find as much evidence for their belief in this story as do those who believe that intelligence is determined largely by heredity. It has gradually become recognized that the fact that parents and children are alike with respect to intelligence has no relevance whatsoever to the question of whether intelligence is inherited or not; it can be explained equally well by hereditarians and environmentalists. We must, therefore, look for more cogent evidence.

I shall not examine in detail all the various methods which have been suggested for this purpose, because many of them are almost as faulty as the 'family tree method'. I shall only deal with those which are convincing to even the most sceptical. The first method to be enumerated then is the so-called twin method. Here, nature performs for us an experiment which would be beyond the ingenuity of human devising. There are two types of twins, one type arising from the splitting in two of the fertilized female ovum, both parts developing into separate and independent human beings; these are called identical twins because their heredity is completely identical in every particular. The other type of twin arises because, by accident, two female ova happen to be present in the womb and are fertilized by two separate male spermatozoa, thus giving rise to two separate and independent human beings, who are no more alike than are siblings born of the same parents at different times. In other words, their heredity is only about 50 per cent alike. These twins are fraternal twins and they may be of the same sex or of different sex; identical twins, of course, are always of the same sex.

It is possible, although often difficult, to tell whether a given pair of twins is identical or fraternal. Examination of blood groups, of finger prints, and of various other physical similarities may decide with certainty that a given pair of twins is fraternal, and the same methods can make it almost certain that a given pair of twins is identical, although there is always a chance, though only a remote one, that fraternal twins may resemble each other quite accidentally in all the particulars investigated, and thus be diagnosed as identical.

The argument from twins rests essentially on the fact that the two twins, whether they be identical or fraternal, tend to be treated very much alike in a given family. They receive the same degree of intellectual stimulation, they tend to go to the same schools, they have available the same books for reading, have the same friends, talk to the same people, and so forth. The argument, therefore, can be presented in the form of a simple equation. Differences between identical twins must be due to environmental influences. Differences between fraternal twins are due to both environment and heredity. If inheritance played no part at all in the determination of intelligence, then obviously environmental influences would be the only ones differentiating identical twins from each other. In other words, the differences between identical twins should be as great as those between fraternal twins. The more important inheritance becomes, however, in determining the intelligence of the children, the greater should be the differences between fraternal twins as compared with identical twins. We can establish the similarity between sets of twins by means of what is called a coefficient of correlation, which varies from *zero* for no similarity at all to *one* (unity) for complete identity. When we measure the intelligence of identical and fraternal twins (taking care to use only same-sex fraternal twins in order to make the sample more comparable with that of identical twins) we find that the correlation between identical twins is about ·95, while that between fraternal twins is about ·65. The correlation between one identical twin and another is just about as high as the correlation between a given child who is tested today and the same child tested again next week; in other words, identical twins brought up together are about as alike as it is possible to be. Fraternal twins fall considerably short of this identity and it follows quite inevitably that we must attribute to inheritance a very strong influence indeed in the determination of intelligence. It is possible to calculate roughly the amount of contribution which inheritance and environment, respectively, make in this case, and there is some agreement that the percentage contributed by heredity is around the 80 mark, leaving some 20 per cent to be determined by environment. I shall discuss later whether this is a reasonable statement to make; I shall now go on rather to a second method of proof.

This is the so-called orphan method. In the case of twins we dealt with a sample where heredity is identical; in the case of orphans, we are dealing with children where environment is kept as identical as possible. Anyone who has ever seen the typical orphanage institution will remember with some horror the complete identity of living conditions, food intake, schooling, and general treatment, which perhaps inevitably is inflicted on the children. If we take an orphanage where the children have all spent practically their whole lives in the institution from a very early age onwards, then we should be able to predict, on the basis of the environmentalist hypothesis, that all the children should be practically equal in intelligence because their environment has been as exactly equal as human ingenuity can make it. This identity of environment applies particularly, of course, to the intellectual side because all the children have available the same books, the same periodicals, the same teaching, and the same companions. If, therefore, environmental differences are responsible for producing intellectual differ-

ences between children, then here, with identical environment, we should have children differing very little from
each other, if at all. If, on the other hand, intelligence is due
largely to hereditary causes, then one would expect a good
deal of variety in the intellectual achievements of the children. Some would still be bright, intelligent, and successful,
others dull, stupid, and at the bottom of the class, with the
majority somewhere intermediate. When we compare the
actual spread of intelligence in an institution with the spread
of intelligence encountered outside orphanage walls, we
find that the difference is either very small or non-existent.
In other words, children within the orphanage differ almost
as much from each other as do children on the outside. This
result is extremely difficult to reconcile with an environmentalist hypothesis and strongly reinforces the arguments
from the twin method.

A third method of proof depends on a phenomenon which
is known always to accompany inheritance, but practically
never environmental influences; that is the phenomenon of
regression. It was noted originally by Galton, who found
that the sons and daughters of tall parents tended to be tall,
but not quite as tall as their parents, while the sons and
daughters of very short parents tended to be below average
in height, but not quite as much as their parents. In other
words, there was a tendency for exceptionally tall and exceptionally short parents to have children who 'regressed'
to the average of the total population; to put it differently,
they were intermediate in height between their parents and
the average height of all Englishmen or Englishwomen, as
the case might be. This phenomenon of regression has been
found since in every case where inheritance plays an important part, and it is found particularly strongly in the case
of intelligence.

We may note it, for instance, in comparing the average
intelligence of parents of a certain social class or occupational category with that of their children. The average I.Q.
of members of the higher professional and administrative
classes is in the neighbourhood of 150; that of their children

is slightly in excess of 120. The lower professional and technical executive groups have I.Q.s in the neighbourhood of 130; their children tend to be in the 115 region on the average. Highly skilled and clerical groups average I.Q.s around 118; their children around 109. Skilled workers average I.Q.s of 108; their children 104. At the other end of the scale, institutionalized adults have I.Q.s in the neighbourhood of 55, whereas their children go up to around 70, on the average. Casual workers have I.Q.s near the 80 mark, whereas their children average around 90. Unskilled labourers will be found to have I.Q.s, on the average, of 86, whereas their children will average six points higher. Semiskilled workers' I.Q.s will average 97; that of the children 98. I have purposely taken regression as shown by social classes because this makes the phenomenon more vivid, but exactly the same can be observed, of course, if we take people of widely different intelligence from within the same social class.

Now this phenomenon of regression would be extremely difficult to explain in terms of environment. What the environmentalist maintains essentially is that a child's intellectual abilities are determined by the intellectual stimulation, the teaching, and the thousand and one environmental influences which impinge on him during his formative years. If that were true, we would expect children in the higher professional and administrative classes, who received the best possible kind of training, who had ample intellectual stimulation, and whose cultural background is as good as it can be made in our society, to be at least equal and probably superior to their parents, many of whom, in turn, did not have these advantages. But in actual fact we find a catastrophic fall in the intelligence of the children as compared with their parents, a fall, be it noted, which in many cases leads to great unhappiness and disappointment of expectation in the parents, who expect that the environmental advantages which they can afford to give their children would lead to corresponding increases in ability and intelligence. At the other end we would expect that casual workers and institutionalized parents, who give as non-stimulating and poor an environmental background to their children as can well be imagined, would have progeny even lower in intelligence than themselves, but again this is not so. Miraculously, the children are conspicuously brighter than the parents!

Up to a point, of course, the question is somewhat paradoxical. We tend to think of heredity as an agency which causes parents and children to be alike, yet this is, if not a wrong, yet a one-sided view. Parents and children only share a common heredity up to a point. Beyond that a child's heredity is determined in large measure by factors handed on through the parents but finding no expression in them. In other words, what the child inherits from his parents may and often does make him *unlike* his parents.

This fact also lies at the basis of another proof, which is important as it deals with a frequent objection to the use of intelligence tests as a whole. It is said that these tests are so dependent on environmental factors, schooling, intellectual stimulation, and so forth, that they naturally favour certain social classes and put others at a disadvantage. On this environmentalistic hypothesis we would expect a very high correlation between intelligence test results and social class. This, however, is by no means the case. Correlations in this country and in America only run in the neighbourhood of ·3, which means, roughly speaking, that social class determines intelligence test score only to the extent of about 10 per cent. Such a low correlation between what is undoubtedly the most powerful environmental influence in our society today and intelligence test results, indicates a very definite fallacy in the environmentalist's hypothesis because it leaves some 90 per cent of the total variability in intelligence unaccounted for. This argument is frequently put in a less rigorous and more impressive anecdotal form by referring to children of outstanding intelligence born to mentally defective parents, or to mentally defective children born to extremely brilliant parents. These discrepancies arise too frequently to be disregarded and it is very difficult to see how they could possibly be explained in terms of environmental influences; there is no difficulty, of course, in accounting for them in terms of hereditary determination. Yet another way of putting the same argument is by referring to the often demonstrated fact that differences in intelligence between members of the same social class are very much greater than differences between the averages of different social classes; this fact again is impossible to account for in environmentalistic terms.

One further proof to indicate the relative influence of heredity and environment relates to the intelligence of foster children. Here we have a case where heredity in the shape of the real mother influences the intelligence of the child in one direction (such mothers are nearly always dull and frequently mentally defective), while environment in the shape of the foster-mother influences it in the opposite direction (foster-parents are usually chosen for being of above average intelligence and for being able to give the child a good environmental background). We can correlate the child's intelligence after he has been in the foster-home for a number of years with both his natural mother and his foster-mother and see which of these two he resembles more closely. Unfortunately this type of experiment is extremely difficult to control adequately. In the first place there is the difficulty that the child's father is usually unknown and that, therefore, his intelligence cannot be assessed. Frequently the father may be a member of the higher professional or commercial groups, thus handing on to the child probabilities of high innate intelligence; this factor may counterbalance or even override the low intelligence of the mother and give a fortuitously high correlation between the child's intelligence and that of the foster-parents. Even where the father is known, he often refuses to co-operate and have his intelligence tested, so that the same problem arises again, although not in so acute a form, as a reasonable estimate may sometimes be made even without the necessity of a formal test.

An even worse difficulty arises from the habit of many agencies to indulge in what they call differential placement.

In other words, children who are known to be of relatively good heredity or who impress the agency as being bright and intelligent are given to foster-parents who themselves are highly intelligent, whereas infants who appear rather dull or who are known to be of poor heredity are handed to the less desirable foster-parents. This procedure also would result in a spurious correlation between the intelligence of the child and that of the foster parent. When these facts are borne in mind the results of such investigations, while they cannot be said to be conclusive, nevertheless show in most cases that a sizeable correlation still exists between the intelligence of the child and that of his natural mother, indicating the influence of heredity. Most studies also find correlations, sometimes of considerable size, between the intelligence of the child and that of the foster-parents; these correlations cannot be so easily interpreted because, as I have pointed out above, they may be due to the influence of environment, but they may also be due to other causes which are difficult or impossible to control, and which would exert a spurious influence on the correlation between child and foster-parent.

The last argument I wish to discuss derives from animal experimentation and will certainly not be regarded as conclusive by those who hold the view that human intelligence is not continuous with animal intelligence in any way. While few biologists would hold such an anthropocentric view, it is possible to maintain that results derived from animal work must be submitted to specially careful scrutiny before being admitted as evidence for human inheritance. With this proviso in mind we may then quote the studies of Tryon who attempted to breed bright and dull strains of rats in the laboratory. His procedure was an extremely simple one. He used a maze-running test in which the rat has to learn to select the correct turnings in a complex maze which he has to run from beginning to end to obtain the reward. Rats differ considerably in their speed of learning and their ability to eliminate false turnings, and in many ways this test resembles one frequently used for human children in the clinic – the so-called Porteus Maze test – where the child has to trace his path through a maze with a pencil. Tryon selected the most intelligent and the least intelligent of a group of rats on the basis of their maze performance, and then interbred the individuals in these two groups separately, thus getting the beginnings of a bright and a dull strain. He continued this process, always taking the individuals who did best from the bright strain and interbreeding them, and taking the individuals who did worst from the dull strain and interbreeding them, until after seven generations there was hardly any overlap in the performance of the two groups, practically all the 'bright' animals doing much better than practically all the 'dull' animals. In other words, this is a direct proof that intelligence (if we can identify the quality underlying success in this maze-running test as intelligence) can be bred for and is therefore an inherited quality.

What do all these experiments prove? The evidence is sometimes summarized by saying that intelligence is determined by heredity in human beings to the extent of 80 per cent. This is a completely meaningless statement, unfortunately, and for it to mean anything it requires considerable re-wording. In the first place, it is not intelligence we are concerned with but rather variability of intelligence. It is obvious that intelligence as such, or the possibility of intelligent action, is completely inherited. The difference between a human being and a slug or a stone is completely due to hereditary influences, but it is not this absolute standard which characterizes all humans with which we are concerned; it is rather the differences found between one human being and another which we wish to account for. We must therefore substitute the word 'variability' of intelligence for 'intelligence' in our definition if it is to have any meaning at all.

Secondly, we cannot reasonably speak for human beings as a whole, because the relative importance of heredity and environment depends very much on the particular conditions of the particular group one may be talking about. The statement that a given trait is hereditary does not mean that it is not subject to environmental modification. Different genes (the carriers of hereditary determination) vary widely in their responsiveness to environmental conditions. There is, for instance, a *Giant* gene in the fruit fly which causes it to be about 75 per cent larger than the normal individuals, but only when abundant food supply is available; when the larvae are reared on a starvation diet, *Giant* flies are indistinguishable in size from their normal messmates. Other flies possess a gene for *abnormal abdomen* but they only exhibit this abnormality if reared in a moist culture medium. It can be seen, therefore, that in any one environment (abundant food supply, moist culture medium) heredity determines completely the *Giant* size or the abnormal abdomen of these flies, and we would say that the influence of heredity in causing variability along these lines in flies is about 100 per cent. In a different environment (reduced food supply, dry culture medium) we would come to quite a different conclusion.

To apply this discussion to the field of intelligence, it seems very likely that in a country where there is almost complete equality of educational opportunity, the influence of heredity on intellectual differences would appear very much more marked than in a country where there was a very marked disproportion in educational opportunity. The figure of 80 per cent therefore might be a rational estimate for England or America but might be a very misleading one for China or Japan. This argument may be seen even more clearly in the case of a physiological variable such as height, where there can be no argument about the method of measurement. Differences in height are undoubtedly determined largely by heredity. In an environment where there is enough food, and to spare, for every child without exception, height will be determined by hereditary conditions to the extent of almost 100 per cent. In another country, where there is abundant food for some but where many others are reduced to a starvation level, the influence of heredity on final height may be reduced to 80 per cent or even 60 per cent. We are always dealing with an interplay of heredity and environment, and as we change the contribution of the one, so the contribution of the other will change; there is no meaningful final definition which will sum up the relative contribution and interaction of these two. All we can do is to give an estimate of a very rough and ready kind for one particular set of people, living under one particular strictly defined set of conditions. Under another set of conditions the figures may be quite different. Consequently, we would have to qualify the estimate of 80 per cent by stating that it applied, if at all, only to present social and educational conditions in this country and in the United States, and that it would probably give quite an erroneous idea for most other countries.

We might thus arrive at a more cautious conclusion by saying that in this country, at the present time, differences in children's ability to do well on standard tests of intelligence are determined to a much greater extent by hereditary than by environmental causes, and that progressive equalization of educational opportunity and a progressive lessening of differences between social classes are likely to increase the importance of hereditary causes and decrease the importance of environmental ones. Conversely, it is likely that environmental causes play a considerable part as far as many other nations are concerned, and that the greater the educational and social inequalities within a given group, the greater is likely to be the environmental effect on the results of intelligence tests. There are probably few psychologists who would not agree with some such formulation as this.

We must now turn to the second set of facts relevant to our general problem, namely the alleged difference in fertility between the bright and the dull. I shall only quote one study, carried out by R. B. Cattell on 3734 children, some of whom lived in town, others in country districts. Giving an intelligence test to these 10-year-old children, Cattell grouped them according to their I.Q. and ascertained the total number of children in the family for each of the children tested. Results were as follows. In the families of children with a tested I.Q. of above 130, there were on the average 2·35 children (in the town) and 1·80 children (in the country). For the children with I.Q.s between 120 and 130, the numbers were 2·92 and 2·31 respectively. Going down the scale, we find next that for children of I.Q. 110–120, the figures in town and country, respectively, were 2·76 and 2·62. Children of I.Q.s 100–110 come from families having 3·00 and 3·27 children respectively, whereas those with I.Q.s between 90 and 100 come from families having 3·60 and 3·72 children respectively. Going down now to children of I.Q.s between 80 and 90, the numbers are 4·13 and 4·21, and right at the bottom, among the 70–80 I.Q. group, the number of children per family is 3·93 (in the town) and 4·72 (in the country). Summarizing these figures, we may say that the very dull families have a reproduction rate almost twice as high as the very bright. It should be noted that in this calculation no mention is made of those men and women who have no children at all, and who are often of a high intelligence; school teachers and professional women come to mind immediately as examples.

It cannot be said that this correlation between number of children and lack of intelligence is one determined entirely by social class, for while it is true that the so-called working-class groups tend to have more children than the middle-class groups, it has been shown that within a uniform social group (coal miners actually working at the coal face) the more intelligent again tended to have fewer children than the less intelligent. We may therefore accept this tendency as an indisputable fact; the correlation between intelligence and lack of fertility is not very high (·2) but it has appeared in so many well-controlled and well-executed studies that a reasonable doubt about its existence is no longer possible.

Given these two facts, firstly, that intelligence is inherited, secondly, that the more intelligent have fewer children, is it possible to deduce that the average intelligence of the nation is decreasing, and if so, is it possible to give any kind of estimate of the decrease? Thomson has carried out a well-known experiment on the Isle of Wight in which he attempted to obtain direct evidence for this decline. Testing 1084 children of the age of 10 (practically all the children of that age group on the island), Thomson ascertained the number of children in the families of the boys and girls tested. In the table below are given the number of families having any given number of children, and also the average I.Q. of the children coming from families of varying size.

A	B	C
	No. of children	
No of families	*in families*	*I.Q.*
115	1	106·2
212	2	105·4
185	3	102·3
152	4	101·5
127	5	99·6
103	6	96·5
88	7	93·8
102	8+	95·8

It will be noted that in this table too, as the number of children goes up the I.Q. goes down.

To come now to Thomson's ingenious argument. If we assume that the child tested is representative of the average of his brothers and sisters, we can derive two estimates from our data. One is the simple average I.Q. of all the children tested. As these are all 10 year-olds, we can be pretty certain that each child has come from a different family, and consequently, this figure will give us an idea of what the intelligence of the children of the Isle of Wight would be if each family had one child, i.e. if there was no tendency for large family size to be associated with lack of intelligence. This figure is 101·04. We can also derive a figure from this table showing us what the intelligence of Isle of Wight children is, based on the actual facts of large families being more frequent in the lower I.Q. range. This I.Q. figure comes to 98·98, and the difference of 2·06 I.Q. points may be taken as an estimate of the loss of I.Q. in this generation due to differential fertility of intelligent and dull parents.

There are many other estimates based on different sets of figures, some of which are in excess of that suggested by Thomson's results, while others are slightly below it. Thomson's estimate may perhaps be accepted as representative of what psychologists working in this field have considered reasonable. If we can assume this estimate to be correct, and if we can assume decline to continue until the end of the century, we would find that the number of children of scholarship standard would have approximately halved, whereas the number of feeble-minded would have approximately doubled. The general I.Q. level of the population would have been lowered by some five points on the average. These are extremely serious consequences which might spell the death of Western civilization if they were to come to pass. How far then can we trust the figures presented?

One great drawback in the argument is the fact that we know very little about the mode of inheritance of intelligence. Psychologists often take a somewhat simple view of hereditary mechanisms, which does not accord well with modern knowledge, and it cannot be stated too emphatically that no rational prediction is possible without much more definite knowledge on our part of the exact mode of transmission of intellectual ability. Penrose, for instance, has shown, using an admittedly very unlikely model, that the ascertained data do not necessarily contradict the possibility of a stable equilibrium with respect to the intellectual standards of a population. Inferential arguments in science, particularly when they are not based on exact knowledge of the mechanisms involved, are always dangerous and frequently wrong. This does not prove that no deterioration is taking place, but it should make us cautious in accepting it as an established fact.

The second point which is often overlooked is that hereditary determination deals with individual differences, i.e.

D

with the variability of the total group. The rise and decline of intelligence of the population is concerned rather with an absolute standard. These two propositions are not identical, although they are apparently mixed up in the argument. It has been found, for instance, that there is a negative correlation in schoolchildren between stature and family size, short people breeding faster than tall ones. This would lead one to believe that in view of the fact that stature is strongly influenced by hereditary factors, the inhabitants of Toronto, where these measures were taken, would be getting shorter and shorter. In actual fact, measurements of schoolchildren there have shown that the opposite is true and that the mean stature of succeeding generations in Toronto is increasing.

This fact can be duplicated in the field of intelligence also. Both Thomson and Cattell have reported repetitions of surveys conducted some 15 years ago, in which the same tests, or similar tests, were given to groups of children from the same parts of the country. These extensive studies, as well as one or two others from the United States, fail to reveal any decrease in intelligence; if anything, they would seem to show a slight increase. Can this fact be taken as an indication that the hypothesis of national decline in intelligence can now be dismissed? Unfortunately, the data cannot really be regarded as conclusive, or even as very relevant. In the first place, it is well known that test sophistication, i.e. familiarity with tests, can raise a child's score several points. There is no doubt that test sophistication has increased considerably during the past 15 years in the population studied, and consequently we might expect the increase in score due to test sophistication to more than counterbalance the very slight fall to be expected on the basis of the hypothesis under investigation.

There is some direct evidence that this is not an unreasonable assumption. Thomson found much larger rises in test scores in districts where intelligence tests had been used to a considerable extent than he did in districts where little use had been made of them. Coaching may also have played a part; Vernon has shown that many of the tests used in schools are very susceptible to coaching, and there is no doubt that many educational authorities in recent years have resorted to 'intelligence test coaching', which might be expected to raise the average scores of children tested now as compared with previous years. Test sophistication and coaching, however, are only one aspect of the problem. Another aspect which is not covered at all by these investigations is related to the fact that both the Thomson and the Cattell investigations deal with children, thus leaving out of account completely the unmarried and the childless; these relatively large groups might change the predicted effects profoundly and thus explain the actual findings. On the whole, then, these direct experimental enquiries contain too many unknown factors to make it possible to base any firm conclusions on them. They do not support the original hypothesis, but it cannot reasonably be said that they contradict it either.

What conclusion may we derive, then, from our data? It seems clear that we are faced with a problem which may be of very great seriousness indeed. As the maid said when she found a fish in the milk, there is such a thing as circumstantial evidence, and while it is not conclusive, it cannot be disregarded. It seems reasonable, therefore, to ask that the Government should support a large-scale, long-continued experimental enquiry which would settle this question once and for all. Such an enquiry would, of course, have to avoid the inadequacies pointed out above. Difficulties arising from coaching and test sophistication, for instance, could be overcome by intentional coaching of children up to the point where no improvement in their intelligence test scores could be found. A really determined effort to design an adequate research project along these lines would, I believe, find no insuperable obstacles in its way, and in view of the seriousness of the problems, the cost of such an enquiry would seem to be trifling compared with the enormous importance of the results. Social science is often reproached for not giving conclusive answers to problems such as the one discussed in this chapter. The fault usually lies not in the ingenuity of social scientists, who can set up the required experiments quite easily; it lies rather with a society that refuses even the very small financial support required before any such experiment can be carried out. At a time when hundreds of millions are spent on advances in the physical field, social science should not have to adopt a begging attitude, where the sums involved are minimal compared to the social importance of the problem.

PART TWO

VOCATIONAL PSYCHOLOGY

5

FROM EACH ACCORDING TO HIS ABILITY

WHILE in some ways this old socialist slogan is as meaningless as most slogans, it does apparently express a deep-seated aspiration, shared by many people. The assumption underlying it, namely, that different people have different abilities, and that in an ideal society each person would be called upon to contribute work of a kind he was particularly qualified to do, certainly appears to be a valid one in the light of modern psychological research. On this fact have been based the practices of occupational selection and vocational guidance, which play such a large part in modern industrial psychology.

A few examples may serve to illustrate the wide differences in ability which occur in almost all industrial occupations. Among bottom scourers, for instance, it has been found that the production of the better workers is consistently twice that of poorer workers. While the number of bottoms scoured by a good worker might amount to 500 or so a day, others only average 250 or thereabouts. A similar ratio between good and poor workers obtains in the weaving industry. In one study, the total number of yards of cloth produced from the warp was measured, and from this and various constants, the average rate of production in picks per minute obtained. Variation among workers ranged from the rate of 62 picks per minute to 130 picks per minute. The first weaver's hourly earnings were less than one half those of the second weaver's, and from the employer's standpoint the second loom earned over twice as much profit as the first, and also over twice the sum to meet the overhead charges in the same time.

In both our examples, the ratio of best to worst has been roughly at that of 2 : 1. This appears to be a figure found in many investigations. Hourly piecework earnings of hosiery makers, pounds of women's hose produced per hour by knitting-machine operators, earnings of taxi-cab drivers working under similar conditions, all have shown this ratio of the most to the least efficient. Other figures indicate considerably greater individual differences; thus, among spoon polishers, the most efficient work at over five times the rate of the least efficient. On the whole, there appears to be considerable agreement among industrial psychologists that in individuals ordinarily regarded as normal, the most gifted will be on the average between three and four times as capable as the poorest.

This conclusion should always be understood of course to refer to one kind of activity only. The person who shines in one activity may be a complete failure in another, and mediocre in a third. Correlations of success in different activities are relatively slight, indicating that the varying industrial occupations require rather different types of ability, and that it may be extremely important for a given individual to know just what type of activity he himself would be best suited to carry out. That is the point of view of vocational guidance; given the individual, what advice should he be given with respect to his vocational choice? Knowledge of the worker's ability is equally important to the industrialist, whose production will be considerably increased by employing people whose abilities are in line with the job which they are doing. That is the point of view of occupational selection; given a job, which of many applicants is best suited to do it?

In dealing with this problem, there is no necessary assumption that the underlying abilities with which we are dealing are innate. A good case could probably be made out for the hypothesis that the greater portion of individual differences, so far as the requisite industrial abilities are concerned, is in our society due to hereditary rather than to environmental causes. However, such a demonstration is not really required in order to establish the desirability of vocational guidance and occupational selection; the fact that very marked differences exist among individuals is sufficient proof of the need for such selection procedures, regardless of the question of how these differences came about.

It should also be noted that so far we have been dealing essentially with abilities of a rather low order. There is good reason to assume that the more complex an activity, the greater will be the difference in ability between the best and the worst. Tennis or chess, for instance, are activities vastly more complex than polishing spoons; there is very little doubt that the differences between a good and a poor tennis or chess player are vastly greater than the differences between a good or a poor spoon polisher, or bottom scourer. Even wider, one might surmise, are differences between a poor physicist and an outstanding one. As, however, selection procedures in our society are largely restricted to the simpler and more elementary types of jobs, and as I shall deal in another chapter with University selection, I shall here confine myself entirely to industrial jobs of the kind outlined.

Granted that it is desirable to select people for a given type of work in line with their abilities, and possibly with their temperament, interests, and personality generally, we may ask how such selection takes place in the majority of cases. The answer appears to be that nearly always such selection is based on interviewing. A great deal of work has been done on the employment interview in its various aspects, and a brief review of this evidence may indicate the reasons why psychologists have almost universally favoured some kind of objective test procedure over ordinary interviewing processes.

One of the earliest investigations of the interview is reported by Binet, the creator of modern intelligence tests. Three teachers interviewed the same children and estimated the intelligence of each. These estimates were based on the results of an interview conducted by each teacher as he saw fit. Binet reports two outcomes of this experiment which have since been verified over and over again. Each interviewer was confident that his judgement was right. Each interviewer disagreed almost completely with the judgement of the other interviewers. Both of these results are of great importance. The first one explains why, in spite of all the factual information regarding its inadequacy, the interview has remained the firm favourite of most people who have to select personnel for industrial and other purposes. The interviewer becomes convinced that the picture he builds up of the interviewee's personality and ability is a correct one, and in the absence of any challenge to this opinion, and particularly in the absence of a follow-up procedure which will force him to pay attention to his numerous failures, the interviewer becomes more and more convinced of his God-like omniscience and ability. Time and time again does one encounter the individual who admits all the evidence about the inadequacy of the interview but stoutly maintains that he or she is the one outstanding exception to this general rule, and that his or her opinions are almost invariably correct. (Needless to say, experimental studies of such individuals fail to disclose any greater ability to forecast success and failure among them than is found among other people.)

The second point is important because it gives us a method of investigating the interview which is not dependent on long-term follow-up studies with respect to the validity of the interview prediction. If interviewers make accurate predictions then it should be possible over the years to accompany their choices through their chosen occupations and find out what proportion of them succeed and what proportion fail. This is a laborious, long-term procedure fraught with many difficulties. A much simpler deduction to test is the following. Given that interviewers are able to predict accurately the future success of the interviewee, then interviewers should agree with each other.

If interviewers disagree, then clearly they cannot all be right, and if the disagreement is fairly complete, as it so frequently is, then they must practically all be wrong, with one or two possible and unlikely exceptions. This method of assessing the *validity* of the interview by studying its *reliability* has been used very widely and nearly always with identical results, as we shall see.

Reliability and validity are technical terms relating to any kind of psychological measurement. If measurement is 'reliable' then we get consistent results on repeating the measurement process. Interviewers are 'unreliable' because there is no such consistency from the rating of one interviewer to that of another. A measurement is 'valid' if it measures accurately whatever it is supposed to measure. Clearly a measure cannot be 'valid' without being 'reliable'; it can, however, be 'reliable' without being 'valid' by measuring consistently and accurately something irrelevant to the criterion which is to be predicted. Height can be measured with great reliability but it is not valid as a predictor of success in most industrial occupations.

Binet's experiment was conducted in the laboratory rather than in relation to industry. The first industrial study appears to have been carried out by Scott, who had six experienced personnel managers interview 36 applicants with respect to their sales ability. The applicants had to be ranked in order of excellence with respect to their suitability for the position, and the results showed wide disagreement amongst the ranks assigned each applicant. As Scott says, 'In the case of 28 of the applicants, these six managers disagreed as to whether the individual should be placed in the upper half of the group or in the lower half of the group.' This study of reliability suggested that predictions based on the interview would show little validity, and in another study, Scott had 13 executives rate the sales ability of 12 men and compared these ratings with the results of an interview prediction. The average correlation between performance as rated and interview prediction was little better than chance. In yet another study by Scott, 20 sales managers and three personnel research men each interviewed the same 24 applicants. Again, there was a great deal of disagreement among the raters.

One of the most famous studies in this field, which has been quoted again and again, was carried out by Hollingworth. Twelve sales managers, all experienced in personnel selection, interviewed 57 applicants independently and each according to his own style. Again, the applicants were to be ranked according to their suitability for the position, and again each applicant's rankings showed wide variations according to the interviewer. One applicant, for instance, was rated sixth by one sales manager and fifty-sixth by another. Another applicant was rated first by one of the judges and bottom by another!

It would be pointless to go through the several hundred studies which have been done in replication of these experiments. There is practically unanimous agreement regarding the unreliability and lack of validity of the interview. Certain reports appear to give some evidence in favour of the interview, but when looked at critically it is usually found that there are serious faults to be found in the procedure. In one study, for instance, Clark had two investigators interview students and make predictions of their scholastic performance. These predictions were found to be reasonably accurate. However, the interviews were conducted late in the semester and the students were asked 'how they were getting on in their work'. Thus the students would know quite well what their scholastic standing was, and the interviewer's 'estimate' was little more than an echo of the student's own appraisal of himself.

The very strong evidence that the interview by itself is an inadequate method of determining a person's ability to do a certain job has led to a certain revision of the claims made for it. It is frequently said nowadays that the interview should not be used as an alternative to tests of ability but rather as a supplement; it should serve as a means of carefully synthesizing the data into an evaluation for prediction of over-all ability, proficiency, or potential job success. In this it would be regarded as an alternative to a method which would recommend itself to the statistically trained psychologist, namely, that of formulating a mathematical equation based on the observed predictive accuracy of each isolated test.

The hypothesis on which this use of the interview is based is not an unreasonable one, but there is considerable evidence now to suggest that here also the interview fails to do what it is intended to do. Some of this evidence is reviewed in another chapter, so I shall rest content with quoting just one investigation which made a direct comparison between the statistical and the interview approach. In this, the same set of tests was given to large groups of candidates. Half of the candidates were selected on the basis of a statistically weighted average of their test scores, the other half were selected by interviewers who had available to them all the test scores but who could supplement these by their own enquiries and who could assign as much or as little weight to the test information as they liked. Contrary to expectation, the ratings which took into account all the information obtained in the interview, as well as the test scores, did not predict as well as the test scores alone. Test score prediction was over 30 per cent better than prediction based on test and interview. On the basis of a large number of similar investigations, dealing altogether with almost 40,000 men, it was concluded that 'The improvement in predicting . . . success by having in addition to test scores an interviewer's evaluation of experience, interest, and personality, is relatively small and may well be negative.' Here also, then, we must conclude that the interview is an almost complete failure and that the time devoted to it as far as accuracy of prediction goes is wasted. The interview, far from increasing accuracy of prediction, may actually lessen it.

A third use of the interview appears to be more promising, although it is relatively restricted in its function. I remember giving a lecture on the interview to a group of industrialists, one of whom approached me afterwards and said that while he was very interested in hearing about the uselessness of the interview, he had ample evidence that it could be very successful indeed. I asked him for his evidence and he proclaimed, with great pride, that about ten years ago he had picked his secretary in spite of very poor scores on all the selection tests 'and now', he added triumphantly, 'she is my wife!' There is no doubt that for jobs which require personal contact as an important ingredient, it may be desirable for the individuals concerned to meet, if only in an informal or formal interview, and that test scores alone do not act as a substitute in predicting how one person will get on with another in personal inter-relations.

This view has been put with particular force by a group of psychologists responsible for the selection of officers to be retained in the post-war American Army. They proceeded on the assumption that if an interview was to be included in the process, it should make a 'distinctive' contribution. By 'distinctive' they meant that the interview should concern itself with something that could not be measured better by other techniques. It was agreed, therefore, that intelligence, education, various personality traits, and experience would not be given consideration in the interview. Nor would the interview concern itself with the integration of these various factors as such integration would be performed better by statistical techniques. All that remained after the interview had been stripped of those functions which could be better performed by other methods, was 'social interaction', that is to say, the ability to deal with people. The assumption was that by assigning a specific and unique purpose to the interview, a better measurement of social interaction could be obtained since no time and energy would be lost in irrelevant questioning or evaluation. Results seem to bear out this hypothesis because very high reliability and surprisingly high validity are reported.

While these results are interesting and important for a general appraisal of the interview as a selection instrument, they are not really relevant to most industrial purposes, as personal relations do not play an important part in most of these. The selection of foremen and other supervisors might, with advantage, be enriched by selection procedures assessing their 'social interaction' ability, but for most jobs, ability on the job is far more important than social interaction, and as regards ability on the job, there is very little doubt that interviewing is an extremely inefficient method which cannot rationally be defended.

If we leave out the interview, therefore, we are left with psychological tests as predictors of vocational ability. Large numbers of these tests have been constructed and used, and many studies are available to show how much value can be placed on them. The criteria used for assessing success on a job differ widely, of course. They may be concerned with quantity or quality of output, the amount of spoiled work, the number of accidents, the number of breakages, length of service or stability on the job, rate of advancement, earnings, and various other factors. Sometimes a rating constitutes the criterion, but this is not usually as accurate and objective as the criteria mentioned before.

The procedure followed in the construction and validation of a series of tests for the selection of workers for a certain job can best be followed by taking a number of examples and discussing these in detail, rather than by an abstract discussion of the various steps gone through. I have taken my examples largely from the older literature because long-continued follow-ups are available to show that the results are not merely a flash in the pan but can be reproduced year after year with constant success. I have not selected particularly successful studies but have tried to choose some which would be representative of the whole run of selection procedures when done by a competent investigator. The reader will find no difficulty in generalizing the rather detailed examples given to other occupations and jobs of which he has greater knowledge.

The first example deals with the selection of electrical sub-station operators. Economy in the distribution of electric current calls for the transmission of high voltages which are reduced at electrical sub-stations before being delivered as current to the consumer. High-voltage current is received in the sub-station along a number of lines from generating stations; after being stepped down, the current is then transferred to individual consumers over a large number of circuits. A great deal of equipment for transforming and regulating voltages is included in these lines and circuits, as well as a great number of recording meters, relaying and other protective devices and rotative equipment. Manipulation of numerous switches is involved in the operation of this equipment, and the manipulation of these switches, the reading of the meters, and maintenance of the station and its equipment are the chief duties of the electrical sub-station operator.

The chief responsibility of the operator is to avoid errors in switching. It does not need much imagination to see that the consequences of such an error may be disastrous. The unexpected failure of lights or power equipment in a hospital, particularly during an operation, may be fatal. Many industrial operations depend on uninterrupted processes, and the entire product or even the machinery used at the moment of current failure may have to be written off. In addition to such inconveniences and losses and possible damage to the very expensive equipment in the sub-station itself, errors may lead to the injury of the operator or to actual loss of life. Job training, of course, is given to all sub-station operators, but nevertheless, it was found that the number of errors made was far too large to be considered satisfactory. Consequently, Viteles, one of the best known industrial psychologists in the United States, was called upon in 1927 to make a thorough analysis of the occupation of sub-station operators and to suggest tests for the selection of competent men.

The first step taken by Viteles was to make a thorough analysis of the activities involved in sub-station switching. A detailed study, carried on over a period of several months, suggested the following main abilities as necessary for satisfactory operation. In the first place, Viteles put the 'ability to learn and to recall in proper order the complex series of switching operations with which the operator must be that the number of serious accidents had decreased from 1·6 to 1·1, and of minor accidents from 42 to 29 per one million kilometres. There was also a decrease of 50 per cent in the length of training required, and a marked reduction in the use of current and the cost of repair. It has been estimated that the introduction of psychological procedures saved an amount of twelve million marks in one year.

Similar results were obtained in Paris, where, subsequent to the introduction of psychological tests, the percentage of streetcar and bus drivers dropped for incompetence either during or subsequent to training was reduced from 20 to 3, representing an annual economy of 150,000 francs (at a time when the franc was still in a favourable position on the world markets!). Drivers hired after the introduction of the selection procedure were responsible for 16·5 per cent fewer accidents than those hired before. This represents an annual saving of 130,000 francs per annum.

It is not always possible to predict exactly what will be the qualities required in a given job. It might be surmised, for instance, that a quick reaction-time would be useful in taxi-cab drivers. It was found, indeed, that drivers with the greatest number of accidents had the slowest reaction-time on a performance test. However, men with the fastest re-action-time also tended to have a great many accidents. The interpretation may be that those who are very quick are likely to take chances because of over-confidence, thus inviting accidents. Whatever the interpretation, an empirical study is always required to show whether or not the original psychological hypothesis on which selection tests is based is correct or not. Given such proper validation, however, there is no difficulty in constructing selection batteries for almost any kind of a job. Taking as an example the selection of taxi-cab drivers, Snow has shown that when drivers are tested and rated as satisfactory or unsatisfactory, the average number of accidents per man in the unsatis-factory group was 1·00 and in the satisfactory group it was ·20. Almost twice as many men in the unsatisfactory group had accidents compared with the others, and over three

familiar'. Next, he put 'accuracy in following directions and in employing knowledge of sub-station operation in switch-ing and blocking'. Then came the 'ability to comprehend readily instructions given either verbally or in writing'. After that 'persistence in keeping at a problem until it has been solved, or until the operator has satisfactory reason for believing that the problem cannot be solved by methods at his disposal'. Hardly less important was the fifth point – 'judgement and analysis in solving a new problem, e.g. in locating and remedying trouble'. Next came the 'ability to give coordinated attention to a number of different opera-tions or things at the same time; to spread attention over the details of a blue print, over the correct switching handle, ammeters, etc.' Last came the 'ability to carry in mind the location of equipment in substations and an image of wiring arrangements, etc.'

In the case of emergency conditions, Viteles concluded that the outstanding qualities needed for the continuance of safe and accurate operation were temperamental in nature. Ability to resist fear was put high in the list because in sub-station operations the effect of fear is generally displayed in an immediate loss of accuracy, an increase in the time taken to clear up trouble, and in a general loss of certainty and reliability which may extend over a considerable period of time following the onset of the fear-producing stimulus.

On the basis of this analysis, Viteles made up two sets of tests to examine as far as possible the mental abilities and temperamental traits necessary for safe and accurate sub-station operators under all conditions. The first set of tests was largely of the pencil-and-paper type, dealing with intelligence, mechanical aptitude, and the like. The second series consisted of four performance tests designed, in part, to resemble the switching operations required in the station operator's work, and giving scores to measure the candi-date's ability to follow directions, to learn instructions, and his persistence against monotony and physical fatigue.

Having decided on the tests to be used, Viteles proceeded to show that they were reliable, i.e. that in repeatedly testing the same people, each subject would make roughly the same score on subsequent occasions as he did on the first occasion. He then proceeded to test the validity of the tests. As a first step he took 84 operators, each of whom had been working on the job for over a year, and divided these into three groups, designated as best, average, and poorest, respectively. The three groups were practically identical with respect to age and length of service, and it was found that the ratings agreed well with the actual number of errors made by these men, 23 per cent of the best, 52 per cent of the average, and 77 per cent of the poorest group being involved in errors during a given period. On 30 September 1928, the poorest operators were responsible for eight times as many errors per man as the best operators, and for three times as many errors per man as the average operators. The ratings may therefore be considered as reasonably valid.

The selection test battery was next given to all three groups of operators, and considerable differences were found. The poorest group had an average score of 54, the average group a score of 69, and the best group a score of 81. Seventy-five appeared to be a critical score for selection with this battery. If this score had been used in the hiring of operators on whom the study was done, only 8 per cent of the poorest operators would have been hired, whereas 71 per cent of the best operators would have been employed.

Having thus obtained evidence that test scores were significantly related to performance of the job, selection of sub-station operators was from then on based on test performance. Tests were put into operation on 1 April 1928. The net result has been a marked decrease in operating errors. During 1926, 1927, and 1928, the number of errors was 36, 35, and 35, respectively. Immediately after the introduction of the selection procedure the number of errors for 1929 dropped to 20, for 1930 to 18, for 1931 to 12, and for 1932 to 4. Introduction of the selection procedure, therefore, had reduced errors to about 10 per cent within less than five years. Considering the great expense to the community involved in each error, the small sum of money required for the study and the implementation of the selection procedure was thus amply justified.

The tests used by Viteles were largely standard tests available commercially. For certain purposes, however, industrial psychologists make up tests which, in their opinion, embody many features of the job for which selection is to be done. An example of this is a rather complex test of driving ability. In this, the applicant is seated in front of a reaction stand which has two independently movable handles, and two foot pedals. Various visual and auditory stimuli are given in random order, and he has to react to each of these in a specified manner by pulling one or both of the handles and by pressing down on one or both of the pedals. Distraction signals are occasionally introduced to investigate to what extent they will impede his reactions. When this test was given to drivers known to be safe, they were found to be greatly superior to other drivers known to be frequently involved in accidents. Consequently, the test was introduced as a routine device for hiring drivers in Milwaukee, and a follow-up showed that the number of men discharged because of accidents decreased from 14·1 per cent in 1924 to 0·6 per cent in 1925. Apart from this considerable reduction in accidents it was also found that there was a marked reduction in turnover, 75 per cent remaining in service, as compared to 62 per cent prior to the introduction of the test.

It should not be imagined that work along these lines has been done exclusively in America, and my next two examples will be given from studies carried out on the Continent. Berlin tramway drivers were selected by means of a series of tests, some of which resembled the one just described. Comparing a group of apprentices hired without the psychological examination with another group who were tested before selection, it was found that those who had not been examined had 50 per cent more accidents than those who had passed the psychological test. Comparing the number of accidents after the introduction of the testing procedure with the number of accidents before, it was found

times as many had over two accidents in the unsatisfactory group.

All our examples so far have been taken from the industrial and transportation fields. Other examples come from office occupations. O'Rourke, for instance, made up a test for predicting efficiency in the general activities of typists and stenographers. Of those having the highest scores, 99 per cent were rated above average in efficiency; of those having the lowest test scores, only 4 per cent received such a rating. The same psychologists devised a series of tests for the selection of mail distributors and showed that whereas in pre-selection days 50 per cent of employees surpassed a given criterion, 93 per cent did so after the introduction of the tests. Where before the introduction of the test 25 per cent had been rated as poor, none were so rated after the selection procedure had been introduced.

These are all relatively old reports taken from American practice and Continental work; the reader may be interested in the results of similar work carried out in Britain during the war, where personnel selection procedures were used on a very large scale. Of most interest, perhaps, are figures showing comparisons between the number of failures in groups selected by means of psychological methods and in groups selected by other methods and trained simultaneously. As Vernon and Parry point out in their book on *Personnel Selection in the British Forces* from which these figures are taken, 'the respective failure rates . . . showed great improvement attributable to personnel selection'. Thus, of drivers selected by the old method, 30 per cent were failures; of those selected by the new method, only 14 per cent failed. Among clerks, the respective figures are 11 per cent and 4 per cent. For wireless operators they are 7 per cent and 0.5 per cent. For special operators, the largest of the group studied, the failure rate under the old method of selection was 60 per cent, under the new method it was only 7 per cent!

Special interest was shown in the selection of tradesmen and mechanics, where it was possible to compare the failure rates on training courses of some 10,000 army tradesmen selected by four different procedures during four months of 1942. Those nominated by C.O.s or technical officers had a failure rate of 19·2; those nominated at their own request, one of 19·6; those called up by the Ministry of Labour as semi-qualified tradesmen, one of 19·4. The failure rate of those selected by psychological procedures was 11·1.

Similar figures can be quoted from the other services. The failure rate among naval mechanics and fitters dropped from 14·7 per cent to 4·7 per cent. What is possibly even more important, the introduction of psychological methods not only reduced the failure rate but also extracted a much larger proportion of trainees from available naval recruits without denuding other mechanical branches, which were also making large demands at that time.

It would be pointless to multiply instances, all of which show improvements of between fifty and several hundred per cent. Nor can one go through the thousands of published reports dealing with selection work without coming away with the firm conviction that where psychological selection procedures are introduced by competent psychologists, spectacular improvements in performance and considerable reduction in failure rates can be confidently expected.

This result of the application of psychology to industry is not really surprising. Individual differences in ability to perform a given job are so wide, and the number of abilities called for by a specific job are so narrow, that even with a relatively simple and non-analytic method, success is almost inevitable.

The position is very different when we turn from occupational selection to vocational guidance. Here we do not have to select the most promising candidates from a large number of applicants to carry out a specific job; we have to predict for a given person which of many thousand different jobs he might be best suited for. This is very much more difficult, for obvious reasons. Instead of being able to test for the presence of qualities needed for one job, we must now assess the relative presence or absence of abilities involved in a large number of jobs, thus multiplying the amount of testing required a thousandfold. Instead of dealing with a specific job, about which it is easy to acquire information, we deal with a whole congeries of different jobs masquerading under the same name. A surgeon, a G.P., a consultant in psychiatry, a medical historian, the editor of the *Lancet*, and the head of the L.C.C. medical services, all come under the general heading of 'doctor'. Nevertheless, their occupations, and therefore, presumably, the abilities needed are as diverse as is conceivable. The term 'secretary' may refer to someone carrying out a highly confidential and qualified job, requiring great intelligence and initiative; it may also refer to a girl whose time is spent almost entirely on gossip and making tea.

Even if all available jobs could be neatly catalogued with specific requirements, nevertheless our knowledge of the abilities and temperamental traits relevant to success in any of these occupations is still so much lacking that, without very large-scale research, predictions would mostly be impossible. We have information on some twenty or thirty out of the many thousands of jobs between which a choice has to be made, and there is no reasonable prospect of adding to this number to any considerable extent in the near future.

Perhaps one of the main reasons for this comparatively undeveloped study of vocational guidance as compared with industrial selection is the fact that while occupational selection more than pays for itself – in all the examples given, the immediate financial return to the Company initiating the investigation more than paid for the whole enquiry in less than one year – there is little immediate financial gain for anyone in vocational guidance. It pays for itself in terms of individual happiness and productivity, and therefore, presumably, in greater social usefulness of the person successfully advised, but such long-range considerations seldom play a rôle in our social and political thinking, and such work as has been done in this field has been undertaken almost exclusively by private organizations like the National

Institute of Industrial Psychology, which are not subsidized by the Government.

In spite of the difficulties attending vocational guidance, there is good evidence that, even in its very early stage of development and in the absence of much desirable knowledge, it does have potentialities far beyond what one would have imagined. I will only quote one example, the Birmingham Vocational Guidance Experiment, in which 1639 children were followed up over a period of two years, and 603 of them over four years. Half of these, the experimental group, had been given guidance along psychological lines, the other half, the control group, had only received advice at ordinary employment agencies. Various criteria were used to judge the efficacy of the advice, such as employers' ratings, and the length of time during which positions were held. We may divide both the experimental, psychologically guided group, and the control group into two parts – those who took jobs in accordance with advice, and those who took jobs not in accordance with advice. Taking the psychologically guided group first, we find that at the end of two years, 90 per cent of those in 'accordance' jobs were satisfied with their jobs, whereas only 26 per cent of those in 'non-accordance' jobs were. At the end of four years, the percentages were, respectively, 93 and 33. Thus, of those who followed the psychological advice about three times as many were satisfied as of those who did not follow the psychological advice.

The position is quite different in the control group, where of those who followed the advice, 64 per cent were satisfied with their jobs after two and after four years, whereas of those who did not follow the advice, 76 per cent and 78 per cent were satisfied. Thus, if anything, the children who followed the employment officer's advice were less satisfied than those who did not !

Findings relating to the retention of jobs were similar. In the experimental group, those in 'accordance' jobs retained their first job for over two years in 60 per cent of the cases, and over four in 46 per cent of the cases ; percentages in the 'non-accordance' jobs were 11 and 11 respectively. In the control group, the figures for 'accordance' jobs were 37 per cent and 27 per cent for two and four years respectively; for 'non-accordance' jobs they are 33 per cent and 26 per cent respectively. Thus, there is practically no difference in retention of jobs in the control group between 'accordance' and 'non-accordance' boys and girls; there is a very large difference in the psychologically guided group. This experiment, carried out under the auspices of the National Institute of Industrial Psychology, was done some twenty-five years ago. Its findings have been largely neglected by society until World War II, when vocational guidance and occupational selection came together in the Forces Personnel Selection work.

A brief word may perhaps be said about one unique feature of this work. In occupational selection, the person devising the selection procedure is usually indifferent to the fate of those who are turned away. In vocational guidance, the guidance expert is concerned with placing his particular client in the type of work best suited to his interests and abilities. In the Armed Forces, however, we have a position rather different from that obtaining in either case. We are dealing with what a physicist might call a 'closed system'. We must find employment for all men and women who have been called up; we cannot throw the least able on the scrap heap of unemployment. At the same time, we cannot carry out a selection procedure based on the demands of one particular job in isolation from all others. If that were done, we would denude many other important jobs of those who are well qualified for them, an event which occurred quite frequently in the early days of the war, when some arms or units employed selection procedures, thus obtaining all the well-qualified recruits, while others were left with what remained.

It thus became essential to have a very carefully balanced system, in which the abilities of all the recruits and the demands of all the different sections of the Army had to be brought into line and a compromise reached in which a balance was preserved between all these contending forces. The successful achievement of such a balance on the basis of complex statistical computations is perhaps the outstanding success of British industrial psychology during the war years. It seems possible that we are going in a direction in which we will more and more regard society as a 'closed system' and in which we will try to effect the best possible compromise between the varying abilities of different individuals and the industrial needs of the society. The haphazard work of the labour exchanges would then become much more informed and reliable, and we would obtain a population at once more productive and more contented in their chosen profession.

I am not advocating this particular course, or even prophesying it. There are many obvious difficulties and objections of a social and political nature which the scientist is not particularly well qualified to discuss. Dealing only with the facts, there remains no doubt, on the basis of the evidence, that a great improvement could be made in production by the use of suitable selection procedures. These selection procedures are socially and politically neutral. They might be used by a tyrant to increase the efficiency of his slaves; they may be used in a free democracy to lead to greater productivity and happiness. A good deal of rethinking of many industrial problems will undoubtedly be required if psychological selection methods are to be used in this country on any large scale. It seems difficult to believe that society will refuse the beneficent power which modern science has placed into our hands because of fear that that power might be abused.

6

THE USE OF TESTS IN STUDENT SELECTION

UNTIL fairly recently the problem of student selection has not been a very serious one in Britain. There has, of course, always been some degree of conscious selection, but this has been in terms of voluntary limitation rather than necessary exclusion, and little dissatisfaction was felt by those concerned in this process. The major agent which determined selection was apparently income, and as this is relatively objective and easily measurable, the system worked fairly well within the social and ethical limitations of this particular philosophy.

In the United States there has always been a much greater pressure on the part of young people to be given opportunities for higher education, and, of course, the number of University students has for quite a while been almost ten times as high proportionately as in Britain. It may be partly for this reason that the problems of selection have been faced much earlier and in a much more realistic fashion by the Americans. However, in recent years the same problems have arisen in Britain too, and most Universities nowadays have between 2 and 100 applicants for each place. (It is almost impossible to give any exact numbers as many students, wise in their generation, apply to several Universities at the same time.) Particularly in the medical schools pressure is considerably in excess of the number accepted. This situation shows no sign of improving and for many years to come we shall be in the position of having to carry out some process of conscious and deliberate selection among those wishing to enter our institutions of higher learning.

It is not the purpose of this chapter to argue about the desirability or undesirability of having to carry out student selection procedures. It can be argued that everyone, regardless of ability, temperamental qualification, or any other consideration, should be allowed, if he so wishes, to continue his education up to the point where he feels that he has reached the highest point of self-fulfilment. It is argued by others, perhaps more cogently, that limitations of intelligence make it impossible for the great majority to benefit from University studies and that to combine in the same class persons of considerable ability with others of below average intelligence would make a farce of any kind of advanced teaching. This question need not be debated, simply because in our lifetime there is no possibility whatsoever of achieving a position where more than a small fraction of those wishing to partake of the fruits of higher education will actually be able to do so. Economics is a hard taskmaster, but in this case, at least, it clearly tells us what the limitations are within which we have to consider our problem.

In the first instance, we may well ask what the selection procedures are which at the moment determine the fate of many thousands of our most capable and intelligent young men and women. No proper survey has been done, but it is safe to say that, in the majority of cases, interviews based in part on past achievement, headmasters' recommendations, and so forth, are the basis of acceptance or rejection. In the course of a somewhat cursory investigation, I have come across evidence of other criteria, such as the quality of the candidate's handwriting, which were used by some people in authority as sufficient evidence for rejection; I do not think, however, that in the majority of cases such completely unsatisfactory and non-valid methods are being used. One thing is safe to say, however, and that is that no British University at the moment is making use of psychological tests to help in the selection of students. This fact is somewhat surprising in view of American practice, which relies to a large extent on the use of such tests, and it will be the main task of this chapter to investigate the degree of validity of current procedures as compared with psychological tests.

Before we do so, however, let us for a few moments look at the results of current procedures in Britain. Basing my calculations on published evidence obtained at various Universities, I calculate that the average I.Q. of students lies somewhere between 125 and 130, with wide differences between different colleges and possibly also between different faculties. Students in the medical faculties, for instance, tend on the average to be inferior with respect to intelligence to students in the faculties of Arts and Sciences; students taking Mathematics and Philosophy tend to be superior to students taking History and English, and so forth. Arguing from the known distribution of intelligence in the population and the number of students attending Universities, it can be shown that little more than half of those whose abilities would enable them to benefit from a University education are actually reaching the University; this argument may be inverted to read that a large number of students are receiving University education whose actual intelligence is inferior to that of men and women not attending University. If only the most intelligent were admitted to University, then the *lower* limit of acceptance would be somewhere in the neighbourhood of an I.Q. of 135; a comparison of this figure with the present *average* intelligence of, say, 127, indicates the failure of the Universities to attract and select a large number of highly intelligent students.

American figures are, of course, quite different. The average intelligence quotient of students there is in the neighbourhood of 110, which means, among other things, that about one quarter of the student population there is of below average intelligence. There are, in fact, colleges in the United States where the average intelligence of the student body is below the average intelligence for the whole country! It need hardly be said that these figures have no relevance to the standards obtaining at the well-known American Universities, such as Harvard, Yale, Princeton, and so forth; the intellectual standing of students there is on a par with the English average. Up to a point, the lower intelligence of American students reflects their larger number; it is impossible to increase a student body tenfold without a considerable lowering of the average I.Q. In part, it reflects the American tendency to see a University, not so much as a scholastic institution, but as a continuation of high school which has social functions quite separate from those of higher learning. These figures are mentioned because they indicate that procedures which may work perfectly well in the United States may not necessarily work well in Britain and that no easy analogies can be drawn where conditions are so different.

Bearing in mind this warning, we may first of all look at the results of American experiments. Attempts were made early in the century to use psychological tests as measures of students' intelligence; unfortunately, these early measures were based on inadequate hypotheses and showed no degree of correlation between success at University and success on the test. In the main, these early tests were of a physiological nature, based on hypotheses linking intelligence with speed of reflex activity and other neural manifestations which we now know to be only slightly, if at all, relevant to our problem. The construction of intelligence tests for use with the Army, however, made available to Universities measures of intelligence of a less physiological nature, and these new tests were applied in great profusion to many hundreds of thousands of students. A whole flood of reports was issued by psychologists in various Universities and by now there are several thousand papers describing the results of this work.

By and large, the findings are remarkably unanimous. Students as a whole do very much better than non-students on intelligence tests. Students who do well in their studies usually do better on intelligence tests than do students who fail or just manage to pass their examinations. The success of a student in his final examination can be predicted with considerable accuracy on the basis of his performance on an intelligence test given at the time when he enters college. The accuracy of the predictions made varies widely from one institution to another. In some cases it hardly exceeds chance, in others it almost reaches perfection. There are several reasons for these discrepancies which are rather instructive.

In the first place, colleges differ in the degree of homogeneity of their student body. In some cases an extreme variation in intelligence can be observed among students; in other cases all students tend to cluster closely round a common average. Prediction is obviously easier and more accurate when there is great variability; it is much more difficult when students are very similar with respect to the trait which is being measured. A second point related to the first concerns the degree to which the University accepts the verdict of the intelligence test. Some Universities, while administering tests, pay no attention to the results in their selection procedure, but use the scores for other purposes, such as advising students with respect to the kind of courses they should take, and so on. Other Universities rely heavily on the results of intelligence tests. Most steer a middle course between these two extremes. Prediction will usually be most accurate in cases where no attention is paid to the results of the intelligence test because, in that case, the dull and the intelligent alike will be admitted to the courses, and the student body will be very heterogeneous. If great reliance is placed on the results of the intelligence test, heterogeneity will be reduced and predictive accuracy within the accepted group will fall. It is possible to make statistical allowances for these two facts and thus compare different colleges on a more even footing.

A third point relates to the type of examination which determines the student's final degree. Objective-type examinations, which have become more and more widely used in the United States, usually show higher correlations with the predictions made on the basis of intelligence tests than do the essay-type examinations still almost universally used in this country. In part, this may be due to the fact that the objective type of examination in many ways resembles the intelligence test and that, therefore, the two may have some specific aptitude in common which has been called, in a somewhat uncomplimentary way, 'bittiness'. In each case, the student has to produce a large number of quite specific answers in a short period of time without linking up his knowledge into any kind of structural whole.

This possible disadvantage of the objective-type examination should be contrasted with the disadvantage of the essay-type examination, which is our fourth reason to account for observed differences in accuracy of prediction. It will be clear that accuracy of prediction cannot, by and large, be superior to the reliability of whatever is predicted. In other words, if the examination itself is very unreliable, then not even a perfect measuring instrument could give very accurate forecasts. Now essay-type examinations are known to be very unreliable; results depend on the personality and the prejudice of the examiner to such an extent that if the same set of papers were to be marked by two different examiners, quite different results would be obtained. There have been several empirical enquiries into the reliability of essay-type examinations, and the universal finding has been that while agreement between examiners is better than what one would expect by chance, it is not so far above chance as to make the results a good indication of the candidate's ability. In one such study, for instance, the same essay in a bunch was graded by different examiners as constituting a clear failure, an average pass, and a first-class piece of work, deserving of distinction! In another study, the chief examiner, somewhat exasperated by the low quality of the essays he was confronted with, wrote down what he considered to be an example of how the work should have been done. This essay accidentally got mixed up with the others and was promptly failed by some of his fellow-examiners!

Most of this work, admittedly, has been done with school-children rather than with University students, but few experienced examiners would claim reliabilities anything like as high as those achieved by objective tests, and the total reliability of the examination varies widely from college to college, depending on the capacity of the examiner for objectivity, his integrity, the number of papers he has to judge, and various other factors. On the whole, the evidence seems to show that in a well-run essay-type examination, the reliability of the final grade is indicated by a correlation of about ·8; in a poorly run examination, it may be as low as ·6, or even lower. These values, accordingly, set a limit to the accuracy of prediction possible; even a perfect measuring instrument could not predict the success of an examination any more accurately than the set of marks given by examiner A can predict the set of marks for the same papers given by examiner B. It is well to bear in mind this very real drawback of the essay-type examination when comparing it with the putative drawbacks of the objective-type examination; fortunately, again, we are not called upon to pass judgement here, because, from the point of view of selection, the type of examination adopted may be regarded as given.

A fifth variable which is important is the time allowed the psychologist to carry out his investigations. If all the testing has to be done within one hour, it is unreasonable to expect forecasting accuracy to be as good as when he has four or five hours to carry out his investigations. The time element quite frequently is a crucial one, particularly when anything more than a very rough estimate of intelligence is wanted; differential forecasting, i.e. prediction that candidate A would do well on the Arts side but poorly on the Science side, while candidate B may succeed in the Medical faculty but not in Arts or Sciences, can only be made on the basis of lengthy, time-consuming procedures.

The last variable affecting accuracy of prediction, and in some ways the most important, is the technical competence of the investigator. I have sometimes heard testing procedures condemned by people who have had actual experience with them, only to find on closer investigation that the testing was done by someone not acquainted with the proper procedures, ignorant of the precautions to be taken, and incapable of using the complex and elaborate statistics required to do the job well. It is an error to assume that anyone with a degree in psychology can institute and carry out a selection procedure. Experience and very special qualifications are required, and the amateur has no part whatever to play in this field. Before condemning any kind of selection procedure, it is important to see what the expert can do with it. To base rejection on incompetent, amateurish work cannot be justified.

If we consider only studies in which the investigation was carried out competently, the statistical treatment was adequate, and other conditions reasonable, we find that the data from one study tend to be very similar to those of another, and that, on the whole, they leave no doubt whatever that tests can predict reliably and reasonably validly future performance of University students. This is true in the United States; can it be said to apply in Britain also? Comparatively few investigations have been done here, unfortunately, but what has been done already is sufficient to indicate that essentially the same considerations apply here as in the United States. Here also a forecast based on intelligence tests predicts with reasonable accuracy the final standing of the students in their examinations. The accuracy of prediction, as might have been expected, is a little lower here because of the greater homogeneity of the student population, but the difference is not very marked, and may, for practical purposes, be disregarded.

How do the actual figures of 'test-forecasting' in Great Britain compare with current interview procedures? One excellent long-term study carried out in London compared the forecasting accuracy of the usual procedures, i.e. interview, précis, and essay, with that of a battery of selection tests. Available to the interviewers were the candidate's paper qualifications and entrance examination results. The main object of the interview was to assess the candidate's suitability to pursue a course of study, special consideration being given to the factors of general intelligence, previous education, training, and experience, interests and motivation, and personality and character. The interviewers were as experienced and competent people as are usually chosen for this type of work, and there is no reason to assume that they would be inferior to interviewers at other institutions.

The result of comparing the interview results with the intelligence test are interesting and similar to what American practice had led one to expect. The interview failed completely in predicting success, whereas the intelligence test prediction was reasonably adequate. Two interesting points arise from this. In the first place, the interview tended to correlate negatively with intelligence tests; in other words, the interviewers tended to select if anything the duller candidates. In the second place, the material on the candidate's paper qualifications and entrance examination results, which was available to the interviewers, would by itself give relatively good prediction of final examination standing; if anything, therefore, the interview *decreases* the accuracy of prediction from what it would have been if judgement had been based on these qualifications alone. The data from this English study then are in complete accord with American experiments; interviews are practically useless for the purpose of predicting success or failure of University students, whereas intelligence tests provide predictions which are reasonably accurate and reliable.

The point is sometimes made by opponents of testing procedures that intelligence is not the only factor which is important in University students and that character and personality play a decisive part. This is probably true. The conclusion is sometimes drawn, however, that for this reason interviewing is superior to selection by means of tests. This deduction, of course, does not follow, because it makes three assumptions, none of which is supported by facts. The first assumption is that interviewers are able to assess with any degree of accuracy the person's character and personality. I have summarized the evidence on this point in another chapter and will not do so again here; no one who has examined the literature can have the slightest doubt that the interview as a clue to personality qualities is extremely unreliable and almost entirely lacking in validity. Different people interviewing the same candidate frequently come to completely opposing conclusions, and their conclusions seldom agree with objective facts. This unwelcome home-truth is

E

difficult to accept by most people, who pride themselves on their insight into human nature and their interviewing ability. Nevertheless, if we want to base our conclusions on facts rather than on emotions, we can hardly reject out of hand the unanimous evidence of countless well-executed studies. It follows that even if character and personality are important, nevertheless the interview would not be a proper method of assessing them.

A second point is that no reasonable person would reject an instrument which can help in one direction because that instrument is not so useful in others. We make use of a hammer in spite of the fact that we cannot use it as a saw or for measuring the strength of an electric current; it is difficult to see why we should reject intelligence tests because they measure intelligence rather than various other qualities which may also be important. After all, few people would deny that intelligence is one essential attribute of a good student; it is not necessary to claim that it is the *only* important attribute in order to make out a good case in favour of intelligence tests. The evidence is quite conclusive that a person scoring below a given level on an intelligence test has almost no chance whatsoever of succeeding in his University studies; it is cruel to him to permit him to make the attempt and fail, just as it is cruel to the more able person whose place he takes in the University, and who is thus prevented from making use of his ability. There is no claim in this, of course, that the possession of high intelligence assures a student of success; it is much easier to predict failure than success because a low score on an intelligence test indicates absence of an ability which is absolutely essential if the student is to pass his examinations. A high score indicates merely that he possesses sufficient ability to pass if he chooses to apply himself to his studies. There may be many reasons which are difficult to foresee which may make it impossible for him to live up to this promise. He may have to spend a good deal of time earning his living and thus not be able to study properly; he may have a nervous breakdown and have his anxiety and emotional upsets interfere with his work; he may run away with his Professor's wife and be ignominiously suspended from the University. All these things have happened and have kept highly intelligent students from passing their degrees. Consequently, no one would claim infallibility for the forecasts made on the basis of intelligence tests; all that is claimed is that they measure with reasonable accuracy one of the important elements which make for success.

The third point that should be stressed is that there are available now methods for measuring certain traits of personality and character which are important in success and which, when combined with knowledge of a candidate's intellectual ability, make forecasts considerably more accurate. Traits such as persistence, interest, level of aspiration, and emotional instability can now be measured with fair accuracy, mainly by individually applied tests, but also by group tests, and in several investigations such group tests have been shown to predict success at reasonable levels of accuracy. It has been shown, for instance, that the successful student is persistent, emotionally stable, and has levels of aspiration not too far removed from reality; the unsuccessful student of similar intelligence lacks persistence, is unstable, and his levels of aspiration are unreasonably high or low. These tests are still in their infancy and considerable improvements can be expected in the near future; nevertheless, even in their present state they predict success at a very much higher level than interviews do, and may therefore be regarded as complementing the purely intellectual type of test on which the measurement of intelligence is based.

Looking at the facts then, in an unimpassioned way, we find considerable evidence showing that interviewing procedures possess no reasonable forecasting accuracy as far as scholarship is concerned, that intelligence tests do possess such forecasting efficiency, and that recent developments indicate that tests of personality and character are already in a position which allows us to make relatively successful predictions.

Why then are these tests not used in British Universities? The main arguments, as far as I have been able to discover, are the following: In the first place, it is said that intelligence tests, and any other type of test, are not infallible; forecasts are not 100 per cent efficient, and consequently if decisions are based on them, these tests may often be wrong. This argument is indisputably true; it does not seem to me, however, that one can draw from it any conclusion regarding the use of tests. Admittedly, testing procedures are fallible, but the proper standard against which to compare them surely is that presented by other fallible selection procedures rather than that of perfection. There is no doubt whatsoever that in the selection problem, which conditions beyond our control have forced upon us, errors will be made; we will accept students who will turn out to be failures and we will reject others who might have made a useful contribution. The system in force at the moment has been shown quite clearly to be faulty, and to be based on methods which do not give forecasting accuracy significantly different from what one would have obtained from simply tossing a coin in deciding to accept or reject a given student. Intelligence tests, while far from infallible, can do considerably better than this. I have calculated that where under present conditions the failure rate in a University is 15 per cent, the use of tests could reduce the failure rate to something like 2 per cent or 3 per cent, provided that the same examination standards were kept, and assuming a selection ratio, i.e. a ratio of applicants to vacancies, roughly similar to that obtaining at the moment. Along similar lines it can be calculated that the number of people obtaining first class degrees could easily be doubled, again assuming that standards remain the same. There is no implication in all this that the new procedures would render selection foolproof, or that errors would not be made; the only claim, and this is based very firmly on factual results of scientifically controlled studies, is that the number of errors would be considerably smaller than it is at the moment.

There is also another point relevant here, namely, that

procedures which to begin with are subject to error can only improve by constant use, by following up erroneous predictions to see why an error was committed, and by trying new methods for improving their forecasting efficiency. There is little opportunity for British psychologists to acquire experience in this field and to improve their methods in the absence of University support. One or two enquiries, notably that set on foot by the Nuffield Foundation, can be quoted as exceptions to this general rule, but by and large it remains true that those who refuse to allow selection tests to be administered in our Universities because they are subject to error are thereby making it more difficult to eliminate these very errors.

The second argument frequently advanced has already been dealt with at some length. It relates to the putative qualities of character and personality, which the ideal student is supposed to possess in addition to, or sometimes independently of, intellectual ability. This argument is difficult to counter because it is based on a hypothetical view of human nature and interviewers' abilities which are never subjected to critical and experimental scrutiny. As I have pointed out above, the evidence seems to be fairly conclusive that whatever these alleged qualities of character and temperament may be, the interview is not an efficient method for assessing them with any degree of accuracy.

A third argument takes exception to the atomistic and statistical nature of a selection procedure based entirely on tests. It is maintained that many students would dislike having their future decided on the basis of mechanically derived scores treated in terms of statistical functions and worked out by calculating machines; this impersonal method would, to them, lack the personal relationship which exists in the interview. Experiments suggest that students who are accepted find a lot to say in favour of the procedure which has given such acceptable results; if selected by interview they regard the interviewer as a highly competent, sagacious person who has succeeded in divining the hidden gold in their souls and the unlimited potentialities inherent in them. If the selection has been by means of objective tests they marvel at the cleverness of the investigator who could measure with such precision their undoubted intellectual abilities. If they are rejected, however, they tend to feel that the interviewer was a malignant old fool whose prejudices made it impossible for him to give them a fair hearing, and whose lack of insight into human nature was only paralleled by the obtuseness of his understanding. As for the test, of course, there could be no doubt that it had no relevance to any genuine intellectual qualities and was merely a parlour game which would not be taken seriously by any reasonable person. It seems, therefore, that concern with the feelings of the student should not be an overriding consideration, particularly when the students are informed of the facts, as undoubtedly they should be, before being subjected to any selection procedure.

In any case, few people suggest that selection should be based entirely on the results of a single test, or even a battery of tests. These should form an important part, but only a part, of the total selection procedure, which should take into account all information about the candidate which may be obtained from his credential file, his headmaster's report, a medical investigation, and an interview in which all these items of information could be integrated. An important part of the whole procedure, of course, would be a detailed follow-up, i.e. it would be necessary to find out the actual predictive accuracy of all these various items of information, so that in future years more weight could be given to the best predictors and less weight to the less reliable kind of information.

It will be clear that this work could not be done on a small, part-time basis by people not really expert in the field. Test construction, particularly when new tests have to be produced every year, is a difficult and time-consuming job, and in the United States organizations have been set up which undertake this work for a whole group of Universities. The same might be essential in this country because few Universities could support the necessary research and development work of their own accord. Administrative difficulties may be considerable, but in the interests of prospective students no effort should be spared to make available to them the best possible selection service.

So far I have only dealt with the use of intelligence tests for the purpose of selection. It would be quite erroneous to imagine that this is the only, or even the main, use to which the data obtained can be put. In a recent large-scale investigation of American University practice it was found that, on the average, each University made about five different uses of test results. The following are only a few of the many possible ways in which these results have been used. In the first place, students working below expectancy, i.e. whose work was not up to the standard indicated by their intellectual abilities, can easily be located, and it has been shown that counselling service, given to such students, leads to marked improvement in their work. Secondly, University teachers and administrators are frequently faced with requests for advice on the part of students wishing to specialize. Such advice can be given much more adequately when objective facts regarding the student's intelligence, interests, and personality are known from a properly carried-out testing programme. At the moment such advice is almost entirely subjective and often bears little relation to reality. A third area of usefulness relates to decisions regarding post-graduate work which often have to be made, and to advice regarding the choice of a profession once University training is over. The excellence of the work done by the student during his studies will, of course, determine recommendations and suggestions to a large extent. Quite clearly, these can be made more relevant still by taking into account the actual capacities of the candidate. The same success in college may attend the persistent efforts of the less intelligent as well as the sporadic efforts of the very bright; knowing both degree of success and amount of ability present gives a more complete picture to the instructor than would either alone.

In some American Universities, it has been found

advisable to use intelligence tests not as an entrance qualification but rather to take those students who made low scores on their tests and discuss their results with them in great detail, pointing out the degree of probability of success and failure associated with a score of this type. In this way, many prospective students who would have been ill-fitted to the intellectual endeavour required of them, and who would have been rated after one or two years as hopeless failures, have been enabled to come to a rational decision and withdraw their application. In thus helping them to avoid a useless struggle, the tests serve an exceedingly important function; in many ways, some such voluntary principle of selection may be more appropriate in certain circumstances than a more mechanical one enforced by the ruling body in the University. Indeed, the facts presented in this chapter only go to show that intelligence tests are extremely useful predictors of achievement; just how they should be used in the setting of any particular University depends on factors which it would be difficult to discuss here because they are too specific to admit of easy generalization. American Universities certainly show little uniformity in the use they make of intelligence test results. This is all to the good because it is essential that in the early stages of the development of a technique uniformity should be avoided and as many different types of experiment as possible carried out so that new and better methods should take the place of others which are inferior to them.

To conclude, it seems to me that the case for the introduction of selection procedures by properly qualified psychologists is unanswerable. Mistakes would no doubt be made, but it is safe to say that they would be fewer and less serious than those which are being made at the moment. In addition to helping with the selection of students, test results could be used in many other ways to assist the University and to help the student with his problems. There have been no factually supported objections to the use of tests, but there has been an almost unending stream of evidence to indicate the many uses to which they can be put. It has been said that most scientific inventions take fifty years from the time of their discovery to the time when they are passing into practical use. It is now almost fifty years since intelligence tests were first introduced and shown to be valid and useful methods of measurement, so perhaps we may take this as a good omen for the future!

7

ASSESSMENT OF MEN

THERE exists an erroneous impression that methods of selection based on psychological tests are relatively new. This is almost certainly not true; stories of both sensible and absurd methods of selection can be found in the histories of many countries. Perhaps one of the oldest is to be found in the Bible, where Gideon is reported to have used a two-stage selection procedure in his war against the Midianites. The first method used was a kind of psychiatric screen based largely on reports of anxiety and depressive features. Apparently, a proclamation was read out to the effect that 'Whosoever is fearful and afraid, let him return and depart early from Mount Gilead.' The effect appears to have been quite remarkable because 'there returned of the people twenty and two thousand; and there remained ten thousand'.

This is a more severe reduction in numbers than would be tolerated by most modern commanders. However, Gideon went on to put into effect a second stage, consisting of a psychological performance test. This is most easily described by quoting the Bible directly :—

'And the Lord said unto Gideon, The people are yet too many; bring them down unto the water, and I will try them for thee there; and it shall be, that of whom I say unto thee, This shall go with thee, the same shall go with thee; and of whomsoever I say unto thee, This shall not go with thee, the same shall not go.

'So he brought down the people unto the water: and the Lord said unto Gideon, Every one that lappeth of the water with his tongue, as a dog lappeth, him shalt thou set by himself; likewise every one that boweth down upon his knees to drink.

'And the number of them that lapped, putting their hand to their mouth, were three hundred men: but all the rest of the people bowed down upon their knees to drink water.

'And the Lord said unto Gideon, By the three hundred men that lapped will I save you, and deliver the Midianites into thine hand: and let all the other people go every man unto his place.'

Gideon's test, as we may perhaps call this procedure, differs in its whole set-up and conception from those used in the selection of students and of workers, as discussed in previous chapters. However, it is similar in many ways to tests and procedures advocated by certain modern schools which believe that orthodox methods of selection take too 'atomistic' a view of human nature, and that we must substitute what they call a 'holistic' outlook. This view deserves closer scrutiny.

In selection work, the assumption has usually been made that a given job requires abilities A, B, and C, character traits X, Y, and Z, and a temperament of type α. Consequently, we devise tests for these various abilities and traits and select those people who have the highest scores on the relevant tests. This assumption has been hotly disputed by German military psychologists, whose conceptions are based on quite a different way of looking at human nature. Believing that analysis into abilities, traits, and such like disrupts the 'total personality' of the candidate, they have tried rather to observe the candidate's behaviour in a complex situation to arrive at a kind of 'holistic' appraisal of his reactions, and to make their forecasts and base their selections essentially on this general impression rather than on any numerical and quantitative test results.

The situations used by these German military psychologists were sometimes odd and often ingenious. For instance, a candidate would be required to pull a strong metal spring as hard as he could. The stronger he pulled the stronger and more painful would be an electric current going through his body. While he was exerting himself in this way, a hidden camera would take photographs of his facial expression. His performance would not be judged on the actual amount of pull exerted, but rather on his total behaviour, including his facial expression. The hypothesis on which a test of this type is based is not in itself an unreasonable one; there was, however, one crucial point which German military psychologists failed to take into account. A hypothesis is not proved to be correct because it appears to be reasonable; what is required is a follow-up study to show that the people who are picked out by the selection procedure are in actual fact superior to those who are rejected by it. This was never done by the Germans, nor by the Japanese, who in some ways followed similar methods, and consequently little can be said about the usefulness of these methods. We do know that many of them are extremely unreliable, i.e. that two people observing the same situation would disagree to a considerable extent in their judgement, and it is a well-known axiom in statistics that unreliable data cannot be valid.

Be that as it may, the English War Office Selection Boards took over the principles on which the German methods have been based and adapted them for use in this country. The results achieved by these 'W.O.S.B.s' will be discussed later on in this chapter; they are mentioned here primarily because they in turn had their methods and principles taken over and used by a selection agency in the United States, set up by the Office of Strategic Services. This Office, which will be familiar to many readers from a number of films featuring its exploits during the war, is a kind of mixture of M.I.5, Hercule Poirot, and Bulldog Drummond. Faced with the task of recruiting a large number of people for a variety of purposes requiring the highest degree of morale, mental preparedness, intelligence, integrity, and courage, the O.S.S. decided to entrust the selection to a group of psychologists who set up a number of selection camps, only one of which will be described in detail here. These psychologists took over the holistic ideas of Simoneit, whose *Wehrpsychologie* had inspired the German selection methods and the British W.O.S.B.s. The actual procedures used can best be followed by describing the sequence of events which a candidate would go through from his first contact with the selection agency until his final fate was pronounced.

Each candidate was interviewed in Washington, told that he would be subjected to a selection procedure, and also that during that procedure he would not be known by his own name, but would be *incognito*. He had to choose a name, make up a life history, and never reveal his true identity. He was then asked to remove all his outer clothing and was issued with Army fatigues and various other items of clothing which would obliterate all visible social and educational differences between the candidates. He was then, together with others, taken to the assessment camp where he would arrive early in the evening. He was welcomed and fed in the dining-room, where he would mingle freely with the other candidates, as well as with members of the assessment staff (of whom there were about as many as there were candidates in each batch).

After dinner, a number of paper-and-pencil tests of intelligence and personality were given, as well as a detailed personal history questionnaire. Last of all, he was given a test of observation and inference, which rather resembled a well-known party game. He was taken to a room, told that it had been occupied by a man who left a number of belongings behind him, and asked to reconstruct this person's physical appearance, his character and personality from these items. Then he was left to go to sleep, ready for the trials of his first day.

During the morning, a 'leaderless group' situation would be presented to groups of four to seven candidates at a time. They would be led to a shallow, narrow little rivulet, the banks of which were about eight feet apart. On one bank was a heavy rock, on the other a log. There were trees on the sides of both banks, and on the side where the group stood there were a number of boards, none long enough to reach from bank to bank, three lengths of rope, a pulley, and a barrel with both ends knocked out. They were told that in front of them was a raging torrent such that it was impossible to rest anything on the bottom of the stream. They were supposed to have come back from a mission in the field and be faced with the task of transferring a delicate range-finder, skilfully camouflaged as a log, to the far bank, and of bringing back a box of percussion caps, camouflaged as a rock, to the other side. They were told they could make use of old material lying around. No leader was appointed because it was the express purpose of the test to see whether any natural leaders would emerge.

Behaviour differed widely. Some made inappropriate or inadequate suggestions, others talked a good deal but were not listened to by the rest of the group, others yet showed a capacity for getting their ideas executed. The group was observed by psychologists who rated their behaviour in terms of energy and initiative, effective intelligence, social relations, leadership, and physical ability. Once a man had emerged as a definite leader in the group, he might be told that he had just been shot by a sniper and the group, leaderless again, had to carry on without him and throw up another leader. Other similar tasks were arranged to serve as duplicates, all of them involving physical activity. On another occasion, later in the programme, a leaderless group situation would be arranged depending more on intellectual factors, such as, for instance, a discussion on a pre-selected topic, where again the group had to come to a decision and where, during this discussion, evidence was collected regarding the emergence of leadership qualities and other important traits.

A little later, each candidate separately would be faced with a rather different type of test. Ostensibly, this was a test of the candidate's ability to direct two helpers in building with him a frame structure out of simple wooden materials. He would be shown the materials, the task would be explained to him, and then the staff member would call over two men working in the field. In actual fact, these two men were junior staff members who had been instructed not to disobey orders and to carry out whatever directions were given them explicitly, but who, within the bounds of this ruling, were to present the candidate with as many obstructions and annoyances as possible. These two members traditionally assumed the names of Kippy and Buster. Kippy always acted in a passive, sluggish manner, doing nothing at all unless specifically ordered to. Instead he would stand around, often getting in the way, either idling with his hands in his pockets, or concerned with some insignificant project of his own. Buster, on the other hand, was aggressive, forward in offering impracticable suggestions, ready to express dissatisfaction, and quick to criticize what he suspected were the candidate's weakest points. There are innumerable ways in which one can frustrate an officer in charge of a situation like this, and Kippy and Buster exploited them all to the full. Never in the history of the project did anyone succeed in building the model with their help in the time allotted!

Again, the behaviour of the candidate would be observed in detail; whether he lost his temper and struck his subordinates, whether he became moody and gave up, whether he tried to do the job himself and got rid of his two doubtful assistants, or whether he tried to humour them and jolly them along.

Interviews, memory, mechanical comprehension, and various other tests followed, until in the evening the stress interview was staged. This was designed primarily to test the candidate's capacity to tolerate severe emotional and intellectual strain, a strain created by rapid and merciless cross-questioning under disagreeable conditions with the aim of detecting flaws in a story which the candidate had been given only a few minutes to make up. The candidate would go into a small room where he would find a note telling him that a night watchman had found him going through some papers in a file marked 'Secret' in a Government office in Washington. He was not an employee of the agency occupying the building; he had no identification papers whatsoever on him; he would be questioned in a few minutes about his presence there, and he was to make up a cover story giving a plausible and innocent reason for his actions. He was also to be careful not to reveal his true identity but to stick to the assumed one under which he was known throughout the assessment period.

Having been given twelve minutes to make up his story, the candidate was taken to a basement room where he found himself facing a spotlight strong enough to blind him for a moment. The room was otherwise dark. Behind the spotlight sat a scarcely discernible board of inquisitors. The candidate had to sit down so that the full strength of the beam of light was focused directly on his face, and he would then be submitted to a gruelling, searching, and highly disagreeable cross-examination. Regardless of his performance, he would be told at the end that he had done poorly and that he had failed this test. This would be a serious affair for the candidate, of course, as the test had been built up previously as playing an important part in his acceptance.

Immediately after the stress interview, the candidate reported to another member of the staff elsewhere in the building. There he was cordially greeted and made to feel at ease in the company of a sympathetic listener. The main aim, however, of the interview was to make the candidate 'break cover' and reveal his true identity to the deceptively cordial staff member.

On the second day there would be an assigned leadership test in which every one of the candidates in turn undertook to be the leader, as well as a variety of observation, interrogation, terrain, 'aptitude', and other tests; also included in the day's work would be an obstacle course. Various other tests of one kind or another filled the rest of the day, and on the morning after, all the candidates would be addressed after breakfast by the Director of the project and then sent back to Washington. Interspersed with the various tests which have been mentioned there were lengthy and confidential interviews, during which candidates were allowed to reveal their own identity and which served the purpose of furnishing the interviewer with an overall picture of the candidate's personality.

A considerable number of observers took part in the

tests, interviews, stress situations, and other activi-
d an attempt was made to integrate their conclusions
some kind of personality description. Again, the atom-
approach was eschewed and no attempt was made to
each person to rate the interviewees on each of a number
f personality traits. Rather, an attempt was made to get
agreement among all the assessors in terms of a generalized
personality description on which would then be based the
recommendation regarding that particular candidate.

It is very difficult to find evidence regarding the usefulness of this procedure. Attempts were made to get ratings
on the recruits' effectiveness from the overseas staff, from
the commanders directly in charge of the men, from returned colleagues they had been working with, and from
reassignment area interviewers. None of these methods were
satisfactory because of the unreliability and lack of validity
of the criteria, and also because of the very large element of
luck which enters into the question of success and failure of
a secret agent. An obviously good candidate may break
down under extreme torture and be counted a failure; a
poor candidate may, through the nature of his assignment,
escape all danger and be reckoned a success. Nevertheless,
in spite of these and many other difficulties, the follow-ups
did show in all cases that prediction had been better than
chance, in some cases a good deal better, and while improved appraisal techniques are certainly urgently needed,
there is little doubt from the published data that, by and
large, the procedure was relatively successful in selecting
men for the Office of Strategic Services.

It is one thing, however, to find a procedure to be relatively successful and quite another to agree with the theoretical bases on which it is founded. It is possible that the
success of the O.S.S. selection procedure may have been due
to the methods and theories used by them. It should be
noted, however, that in addition to what is novel in their
techniques they did make use also of procedures which have
been shown to be valid and useful in other situations, and in
an atomistically oriented programme. Examples are, for

instance, the intelligence and vocabulary tests used [in the] O.S.S. as well as many of the paper-and-pencil tests. [The] degree of success achieved by the selection staff, there[fore] might conceivably be due not to what was new but to w[hat] was old; not to the holistic approach but to the remains [of] the atomistic approach. The reports of the project do no[t] enable one to answer this question. It would have been easy to have made predictions on the basis of each test itself in a numerical manner and to have combined these in a purely statistical fashion so as to obtain a prediction along strictly atomistic lines without interfering with the assessment pro-gramme, and it would have been possible then to compare the effectiveness of the different tests, and also the effective-ness of the two different ways of combining the scores, the statistical, atomistic way, and the holistic, intuitive way. This could have been done, and the answer would have been most instructive. The fact that it was not done indi-cates the impatience with scientific proof and the sovereign disregard of patient verification of theories, which is so characteristic of the intuitive holistic school. Throughout the report, persuasion and appeal to common sense and presumed higher principles are substituted for proof and verification.

Fortunately, it is not necessary to make a decision regard-ing this important point on the basis of such inadequate data. The recent work by Kelley and Fiske on the selection of clinical psychologists has furnished us with the necessary data needed to answer the question of the relative usefulness of the atomistic and the holistic approach. The setting of this particular selection procedure is rather interesting. The American Veterans' Administration, anticipating a huge legacy of neurotic and other mental disorders among war-time soldiers now separated from the Service, set up a large number of hospitals and clinics for their treatment. Staffing became a problem, as not enough clinical psychologists were available, and by large-scale grants and promises of secure positions, the V.A. attracted considerable numbers of psychologists into the clinical field. This faced the Universities with the problem of selection. A small number of places was being competed for by large numbers of well-qualified psychologists. No single University could solve this problem on its own, and consequently a number of them united in order to work out a selection procedure which held out promise in this field.

Wisely, the psychologists responsible for this project did not make any *a priori* decision as to the adequacy of the atomistic or the holistic method of approach; they decided instead to accumulate sufficient data to assess the relative value of both procedures. This decision influenced the whole set-up of their experiment. In some ways, this repeated many features of the O.S.S. procedure, although, of course, there was less stress on physical activities and more stress on mental ones. The 'country house' feature of the O.S.S. and W.O.S.B. procedures was retained, i.e. the segregation in a separate building of a small batch of candidates, together with a large number of assessors, for a period of several days or a week. Also retained was the stress on observational techniques and interviews, as well as on more customary types of objective and paper-and-pencil tests. It would be unnecessarily repetitive to describe in detail the candidates' movements throughout the assessment period; I shall merely describe a few tests which differ in some ways from those already enumerated. One of these was the expressive movement situation test in which the candidate would read a poem, trying to get the feeling which the poet was trying to convey. Then he would be asked to go into another room and express the feeling of the poem without using his voice. Another test would require two students to read through directions which assigned certain rôles to them, such as, for instance, that one of them was a Superintendent of Schools whereas the other one was a teacher in a High School, about whose sexual conduct there had been certain persistent rumours. The Superintendent had called the teacher to his office to talk to him about this and the two students were now to act out the improvised discussion in front of six staff members.

Yet another test was the Block Situation Test, which resembled a game played by a team of four individuals. This consisted of 16 especially cast cement blocks of assorted shapes and colours, all of them extremely heavy. This game required that all of the blocks were to be placed into four groups so that each of the blocks in any group was similar to all of the other blocks in that group. The score in the game was the total number of moves needed to accomplish this objective. Only one block was to be moved at a time, and 30 seconds were allowed for each move. This test resembles the Leaderless Group Test, but lays greater stress on the intellectual side of the task.

While in its general set-up and the procedures used, this assessment programme does not differ to any considerable extent from the O.S.S. one, there was a marked difference between the two with respect to the treatment of the raw data. In the O.S.S. programme there was constant contamination of data from one test with those of another, and of the ratings made by one person with the ratings made by another. This made it impossible to assess the value of any particular test in its own right, but enabled merely a final holistic interpretation to be derived, which had to be accepted or rejected as a whole. In the Kelley and Fiske study, however, predictions were made on the basis of each procedure separately before results were combined in any way, so that throughout the whole course of the experiment, it was possible to see how much each procedure added in forecasting efficiency to what was already known, and thus to compare the holistic with the atomistic type of approach.

It is interesting to consider the views of the assessment staff regarding the probable outcome of the experiment. On the whole, they were convinced that the most useful predictions would be made on the basis of the interviewing procedures, these being the most holistic and flexible instruments at their disposal. Next, they considered, would come projective and other non-quantitative tests, whose purpose is to give an impression of personality. Least important of all, they thought, would be the objective tests and the past academic records of the candidates. In other words, the staff themselves were in sympathy with the aims and outlook of the O.S.S. Assessment Staff, and there can be little doubt that they were among the most competent psychologists in the country to carry out this procedure adequately and to its best advantage. Yet a follow-up of the actual achievements of the candidates, and a comparison of these achievements with the forecasts made on the basis of the various assessment measures used, revealed a picture almost exactly the opposite of what had been expected by the assessment staff. Most important of all and most successful in prediction were the objective tests and the scholastic records of the candidates; least prognostic of all were the projective tests and the interviewing procedures. The holistic approach emerges as a definite failure. The more different impressions and records were put together to produce a recognizable portrait of the person, the less accurate was the prediction based on the portrait. A single paper-and-pencil test which could be sent through the post at a cost of a few pence gave a better prediction than any of the enormously expensive and complicated procedures favoured by the O.S.S. staff.

Was this result completely unexpected? In a way, there is evidence in the O.S.S. report which might have forewarned the enthusiasts advocating holistic procedures. The O.S.S. procedure lasted for three days; in one of their stations, however, it was impossible to carry out a three-day procedure, and consequently a one-day session was substituted for it. In terms of the holistic philosophy, this reduction in valuable material should have led to a decline in the accuracy of forecasts made. In actual fact exactly the opposite was observed. There was a considerable and statistically significant increase in predictive accuracy in the one-day procedure as compared with the three-day procedure. No explanation in terms of different allocation of candidates to the two stations was possible, nor could it be argued that the quality of the assessors was different in the two stations. Consequently, the O.S.S. staff admitted that, in a way, the greater the amount of information they possessed, the less accurate was final prediction. They did not draw the obvious conclusion that this fact is fatal to the holistic outlook, but argued instead that future work might remedy this unfortunate position.

The true facts of the situation seem to be fairly clear, however. The human brain is not a very efficient machine for integrating a large number of different facts. It cannot, in this respect, compete with the calculating machine and the statistician's formulae. It is too easily side-tracked by what are rather unimportant issues; it is too easily influenced by facts which may in themselves be interesting but are irrelevant to the prediction to be made; it cannot evaluate the complexities of a lage number of linear and non-linear relationships all to be combined to give maximum predictive accuracy. It may succeed in giving the assessor a general picture of the person he is dealing with which satisfies the assessor himself, but unfortunately, the picture does not seem to be a true one, nor does it seem to allow for any accurate predictions to be made. Thus, we find in a wider field very much the same type of result which we have already encountered in our discussion of interviewing procedures generally. There is an inverse relationship between subjective feelings of certainty and success of prediction. The more certain a person feels he is right, the less accurate his prediction tends to become. Many people are content to go no further than this subjective feeling of knowledge. If the data summarized so far indicate one thing, it is that some objective measure of validity is absolutely indispensable if we are to avoid error, inaccuracy, and failure in our attempts to form an accurate assessment of men.

Compared with the colourful and perhaps slightly absurd activities of the O.S.S. assessment staff, British practice in officer selection has been rather more staid and conservative. As mentioned before, however, its inspiration came from the same source as that of the American group, and its outlook was no less 'holistic' and opposed to 'atomism' and 'analysis'. Here also we find practice based on firm assumptions, rather than on proof, and a tendency to neglect verification in favour of argument and general impression. A brief account of the origin and later development of the War Office Selection Boards, or W.O.S.B.s as they were affectionately called, may be instructive, partly because of the great social influence these Boards have had, and partly because there is a widespread tendency among business men and industrialists to take over uncritically procedures and methods whose usefulness outside the rigid structure of the Army remains doubtful.

As is so often the case, the only way in which psychology could gain a foothold in an established organization like the Army was through the obvious and catastrophic breakdown of traditional procedures. In the early years of the war, the Army had found its officers from among men who had taken a school certificate, or some higher examination, and who had, at the same time, attended one of the schools providing an Officer Training Corps. Selection was carried out by Interview Boards attached to Army Commands, the technique being that of the simple interview lasting for about twenty minutes. In 1941, however, it became clear that this traditional method of officer selection was breaking down. The failure rate at Officer Cadet Training Units (O.C.T.U.s) was rising to quite alarming proportions, a state of affairs which is wasteful and has a very bad effect on the morale of the ranks, who as a consequence did not apply for commissions in anything like the numbers required. In addition, it was found through psychiatric examination of officers who had suffered a breakdown on service that many of these men should never have been commissioned at all. There was growing public concern about this state of affairs, and questions were being asked in Parliament in ever-increasing numbers.

There are many reasons for this failure of traditional methods; one of these, possibly the most important, could be found in the fact that until that time, officers had come almost entirely from one social class. Methods of selection were based on this fact in the sense that they implied the existence of a social background common to selectors and candidates. Reliance on intuitive judgements based on resemblance of candidates to interviewers probably worked reasonably well as long as this fundamental condition was fulfilled, but as the war progressed the reservoir of candidates of this type became exhausted, and very soon selection boards were faced with candidates whose personality and background were quite alien to the officers who had the task of selection. Under those conditions, traditional methods were inadequate and judgements became based on irrelevant factors. Complaints began to be heard that the Board did not take sufficient time and trouble over each candidate, that the qualities which they looked for and the principles on which they worked were not evident, and that considerations of social class and background unduly influenced decisions.

W.O.S.B.s were set up in the summer of 1942 in order to remedy these deficiencies along the lines already described in this chapter. Most reliance was placed on a variety of standard or 'real life' situations, interviews, and paper-and-pencil tests. The Board sifting the evidence consisted of military people (including the president, a regimental officer with the rank of full Colonel, and a number of officers with regimental experience, referred to as Military Testing Officers), a psychiatrist and a number of psychologists.

W.O.S.B.s thus arose in a crisis situation when traditional methods had broken down, and they were asked to do two things. They were asked to provide the Army with a sufficient number of officers of good quality and they were asked to raise the morale of the Army regarding applications for commissions. Their task was an immense one; an impression of its size may be gained from the fact that during three years about 100,000 applications for commissions had to be dealt with. How did the new methods work?

There is very good evidence to show that the new method was definitely superior to the old. For a short while W.O.S.B.s and Old Procedure Boards were working side by side, and it was possible to follow up the men whom they had recommended for commission. Of those recommended by W.O.S.B.s, 35 per cent were found to be above average; while of those recommended by old procedures, only 22 per cent were above average. The percentage of candidates rated average was almost identical, but those rated below average came from War Office Selection Boards only in 25 per cent of the cases, and from Old Procedure Boards in 37 per cent of the cases. Certain alternative hypotheses suggest themselves which might account for these differences, such as that W.O.S.B.s may have had more and better candidates to choose from, or that they might have accepted fewer of the candidates available, thus sending on only 'safe bets', but the facts do not support these hypotheses, and there appears to be very little doubt that the War Office Selection Boards were substantially better than Old Procedure Boards.

In so far then as its first task, namely, that of supplying reasonably proficient officers was concerned, the W.O.S.B.s may be said to have scored a substantial success. The same may be said with respect to the second objective. The selection procedure was considered fair and adequate by most of those who passed through it, and their reports led to a considerable increase in the number of applications for commissions. Thus, on the whole, we may say that psychological procedures of selection, when called upon to deal with an emergency situation of great importance and social significance, did not fail to reach their main objectives. There are, however, certain doubts regarding a rather different question, namely, whether the procedure used was the best one that could have been used, and whether theoretical assumptions and presuppositions regarding the 'holistic' approach to human personality did not prevent results from being even better. There is considerable evidence that the Boards were very unreliable in the sense that different Boards used different standards, and that a person might be accepted by one Board and rejected by another. In one experiment, two batches of candidates were assessed by each of two Boards. Only in 60 per cent of the cases was there agreement as to disposal. This must be regarded as a very serious discrepancy indeed. In another experiment, it was shown that of a batch of candidates split in two at random, one half of the sample being sent to each Board, 23 per cent were successful at one W.O.S.B., and 48 per cent at the other, a result which reflects the different patterns of judgement existing at the two Boards. Such unreliability is hardly tolerable in selection procedures which decide the fate of large numbers of people. They are concomitants of the insistence of 'holistic' and intuitive methods of appraisal, and it is unlikely that any method relying on human judgement to such an extent can ever be made anything like as reliable and accurate in its results as objective tests and statistical methods of combining data.

The obvious counter-argument to this might be that while objective tests may be more reliable in measuring whatever they are measuring, they could nevertheless be much less relevant to the ultimate issues for which selection is taking place; taking a somewhat absurd example, we can measure height with extreme accuracy and reliability, but such a measure would not be relevant to the purpose of officer selection. There are two answers to this objection. In the first place, it can be shown that objective tests are relevant to the objectives of the selection procedure and may indeed give better and more accurate forecasts than holistic procedures. One such example has already been given in connexion with the work on the selection of clinical psychologists. Another one may be taken from the War Office Selection Board procedures. It was found there that success at O.C.T.U. was predicted better by an intelligence test than by the whole W.O.S.B. procedure! No other examples can be given from the work of these Boards because, like the O.S.S. assessment staff, they pooled all judgements and test results in deference to their theoretical prejudices, thus making it impossible for a statistical evaluation of independent tests to be carried out, and for comparisons to be made between the atomistic and the holistic procedures. However, the evidence already collected and discussed is sufficient to indicate that there is every reason to believe in the relevance of many objective tests to the selection of officers.

In a sense, perhaps, this insistence on rigid methods, experimental validity, and statistical verification of results as opposed to intuitive holism, subjective appraisal, and verification by argument, may appear exaggerated to the reader in view of the fact that, up to a point, the holistic procedures have been shown to work. There is one important point, however, which has hitherto not been considered. When the W.O.S.B.s were set up, personnel was drawn almost equally from military and psychological quarters. Right from the beginning there was opposition in the Army against having non-military persons associated with selection, and, since 1946, the Boards have consisted only of military members, in spite of the contrary advice from all the psychologists and psychiatrists who advise the War Office in these matters. This is almost certainly a retrogressive step and one which is based essentially on the failure of those responsible for the work of the original W.O.S.B.s to provide adequate evidence of validity with which to confront critics. If we do not validate strictly, then we can only offer psychologists' opinions against laymen's opinions, and if the laymen form part of a powerful and well-established system like the Army, their views are likely to prevail. This, then, is one further strong reason for not resting content with subjective impressions and holistic assumptions; when challenged, these fail to provide incontrovertible evidence in favour of the procedures, methods, and policies followed.

The work of the War Office Selection Boards, half-hearted as it was in the acceptance of scientific methods and standards, nevertheless had wide repercussions outside the military field. The Civil Service Commissioners who are charged with the task of examining the qualifications for appointment of all candidates for Central Government posts, including positions in the Foreign Service, decided to adopt the system of 'Country House' psychological examination to their own needs and accordingly called into being the organization somewhat sibilantly called C.I.S.S.B. This formed part of a scheme for selecting men and women for the administrative class of the Home Civil Service and Branch A of the Foreign Service, i.e. Civil Service in the Senior Branch, which is concerned with policy, and the higher stratum of the Foreign Service, which provides the majority of top-ranking diplomats and consular officials. This new scheme involves three stages. The first of these, which eliminates nearly 40 per cent of the candidates, is a general intellectual screening consisting of papers in arithmetic, general knowledge, and general intelligence. Successful candidates go on to the C.I.S.S.B., the second stage, and armed with a recommendation they are then interviewed by a final Selection Board.

During most of its life, C.I.S.S.B. operated at a house within thirty minutes' train journey from London. Three groups of seven candidates each were tested at the same time, and to each group were attached three assessors, two administrative Civil Servants and one psychologist. The testing and assessing programme is a very thorough one, making use of eight kinds of items: a personal history, reports from teachers, Army officers, and former employers, interviews, questionnaires, results of the qualifying examination, intelligence tests, personality tests, and the usual 'real life' situation practical exercises.

These exercises are largely of the type described already but specially slanted to the needs of Civil Service or Foreign Service duties. The candidates are presented with a range of concrete situations, such as might be found in a more complex and technical form in government work. They take place in an imaginary community, which is afflicted with most of the problems, social, political, and economic, which confront British officials today. This setting, about which candidates are briefed from a bulky memorandum in Civil Service style, lends interest and realism to the examination.

Candidates have been followed up over a period of several

years now and it is possible to measure their success. On *a priori* grounds one would have expected comparatively low correlations between forecast and final achievement, if only for the reason that the great majority of candidates are of very high intelligence, so that tests of ability, which are much the best-developed type of psychological test available nowadays, would not be likely to provide good discrimination between them. The facts do not bear out such a pessimistic conclusion. Prediction has been successful to an extent that few psychologists would have believed possible, particularly when it is remembered that the criterion of success in the Civil Service and the Foreign Office is itself a very fallible one. Thus, in this field also, modern assessment procedures have proved their value and have been found conspicuously superior to older methods.

Certain incidental findings relating to C.I.S.S.B. selection procedures deserve some discussion because they are of quite general significance. It is found, for instance, that candidates tend to favour procedures which have high 'face' validity, i.e. which appear to them intuitively to be reasonable and related to the type of work for which they are being selected. They tend to show a certain amount of hostility towards procedures the rationale of which they do not clearly see, and which to them appear unrelated to their future jobs. Much the same is true of high officials, Members of Parliament, and other V.I.P.s, who occasionally visit selection units and favour the selection staff with their opinions. Unfortunately, this 'face' validity of tests shows an almost exact inverse relationship to the actual validity of tests, as shown by their ability to predict final success. Tests showing 'face' validity tend to be not only unreliable but also very expensive and time-consuming; in fact, they seem to account for much the greater part of the total time spent at W.O.S.B.s and C.I.S.S.B.s.

This places the psychologist in a difficult position. At the one extreme he can use methods which have high 'face' validity and will please his subjects, and those who set up the testing procedure and who are ultimately responsible for it to Parliament. The favourable impression created thus, however, is counterbalanced by the fact that the procedures will be almost entirely worthless. At the other extreme, he may use tests and procedures known to be valid and to predict candidates' success with high accuracy. If he does that, however, he will incur the hostility of candidates and the displeasure of those who have called him in in the first place. The idea of statistical and experimental validation of tests and test items is not one which has penetrated to the candidates or the general public, and it appears to be a very difficult concept to put over.

The psychologist usually tries to resolve this impasse by compromise, i.e. by using procedures which are truly valid without appearing to be so, and also procedures which have 'face' validity but whose true value is doubtful. This is probably not too bad when it is done consciously and with full knowledge of how the results should be combined in order to give maximum forecasting accuracy. When, however, as tends inevitably to happen, the psychologist is displaced from the selection organization by laymen who feel that he has done his duty and that they can take over now, without loss of accuracy, then stress tends to be put increasingly on the more popular rather than on the more valid tests, and validities may drop to zero or may even become negative. Selection is an extremely skilled process requiring an unusual combination of abilities ranging from insight and technical knowledge on the one hand to scientific integrity and mathematical sophistication on the other. Slight changes which, to the layman, may appear unimportant, may be reflected catastrophically in falls of predictive accuracy.

This danger is particularly acute when procedures which have been shown to be valid in connexion with the Armed Forces or the Civil Service are taken over into industry or business enterprises for the selection of higher-grade personnel. It is possible that suitable adaptations could be worked out for this purpose, but it is quite certain that without the skilled help of experienced psychologists such an adaptation would be bungled and fail to improve on current methods, poor as these are.

In summary, we may say, then, that when we leave the field of ability and try to assess the much more complex pattern of trends which goes to make up the good officer or the outstanding Civil Servant, our problems become very much more complex. This complexity leads to alternate methods of trying to achieve a solution, dividing those who wish to go on along the customary lines of scientific advance by means of 'atomistic' analysis and experimental verification, from those who feel that 'holistic' intuition and insight freed from the need for verification can alone provide a solution. Experimental data are available to show that both methods are already in a position to improve considerably on older methods, and that the objective tests of the 'atomist' give more reliable and more valid forecasts than the intuitive appraisals of the 'holistic' psychologist, although the latter's procedures tend to have higher 'face' validity. Application of these methods outside the fields of officer selection and Civil Service selection is still a question for the future, but it is already possible to prophesy that only the most stringent regard for rules of scientific procedure is likely to prevent these from becoming merely an expression of 'intuitive' prejudice and subjective bias.

8

WORK, PRODUCTIVITY, AND MOTIVATION

INDUSTRIAL psychology, in so far as it is concerned with the improvement of working conditions, the increase of productivity, and the problems of motivation and incentives, has to live down a good deal of opprobrium attaching to its childhood and adolescent escapades. Under the proud title of 'scientific management', it succeeded in antagonizing workers to such an extent that the 'efficiency expert' is now one of the best-hated figures on the contemporary scene. This hatred is understandable historically; is it an appropriate emotion in the world today, or could it be that we are failing to make use of quite genuine contributions of science to the various fields mentioned?

Scientific management originated in the brain of F. W. Taylor, an American in the best tradition of the English crank. He worshipped 'efficiency' in all its forms, and carried this worship a little further than most of his concontemporaries. He invented the 'overhand' pitch in baseball, which is now standard; he also constructed a spoonshaped tennis racket because he was convinced that this shape was more efficient than the more usual one. Unlike many other cranks, however, he put his theory to the test, and went on to win the American national championships with his racket.

When this apostle of efficiency looked at Industry, he was appalled by the waste and inefficiency he found there. He laid down a three-point plan for improvement, which in essence though not in detail may still be regarded as a kind of industrial psychologist's manifesto. His first point was: Employ only good men. By this he did not mean men who were morally good; although he was a Quaker, he did not try to mix morality and efficiency. He meant men who by inheritance and training possessed the right combination of aptitudes for the job in question. This question of *selection* has been dealt with in detail in the fifth chapter of this book, so that no more will be said about it here.

Taylor's second point dealt with the question of *instruction*. Having selected your men, he said, 'instruct them properly'; what he meant by this we shall see in a minute. His third point dealt with motivation; after selecting and training your workers 'stimulate them by the incentive of higher wages'. Detailed discussion of this point also will be deferred until later; let us only note at this stage that Taylor correctly diagnosed the three main problems of industrial psychology to consist in selection, training, and motivation. While his solution of these problems leaves much to be desired, his formulation is still acceptable.

Being experimentally minded, Taylor tried to prove his point by comparing results achieved by following his ideas with those achieved along routine lines. He got permission from the Bethlehem Steel Company to investigate the process of loading and unloading pig-iron. In the plant which he selected for his experiment, 75 labourers were engaged on this work, shifting about 12½ tons of pig-iron each per day. This was considered a reasonable rate of work, and foremen and officials, when questioned, doubted if it could be substantially increased. Average earnings of the workers were about one dollar and fifteen cents per hour.

Taylor set about his task by following his first maxim – employ only good men. He used as his guinea-pig a Pennsylvanian Dutchman called Schmidt, the choice being governed as much by the strong physical frame of the man as by his cupidity ('stimulation by incentive of higher wage') and his willingness to do exactly as he was told ('instruct them properly'). Taylor then tried all possible variations in methods of loading and unloading pig-iron. He got Schmidt to use large, small, and medium-sized shovels; he got him to carry varying amounts straight from the dump to the freight car, or alternatively to shift the iron in a series of stages. In the end, he got what he was looking for – the most

F

efficient method of carrying out the job. Day in, day out, Schmidt was moving $47\frac{1}{2}$ tons instead of the usual average of $12\frac{1}{2}$; Taylor had put up the productivity of his guinea-pig to almost four times what it had been before. When he communicated this result to the managers of the company, they were incredulous; soon, however, they were convinced of the exciting new possibilities opened up by this young fanatic.

When they applied his methods of selection, training, and 'stimulation' to all their employees engaged on this particular type of job, they found that the total number of men needed dropped from 500 to 140. Wages of those retained went up by 60 per cent, from one dollar fifteen cents to one dollar eighty-five cents per hour. The company saved 75,000 dollars per year, and was firmly convinced of the usefulness of 'scientific management' from then onwards. There was just one snag in all this. Only one person in eight was found capable of working at the pace required; the others were either thrown on the scrap-heap of the unemployed, or else had to find work elsewhere. Small wonder that the workers as a group fiercely resented 'Taylorism', and did their best by means of industrial action to keep his methods out of their workshops. Taylor never understood why he became so unpopular, or why his name became a byword of slave-driving inhumanity; as a pioneer in 'human engineering' he took the point of view that the human being in his work can be dealt with exactly like any other piece of engineering equipment. Modern psychology does not make this mistake any more, but the sins of the fathers are being visited on the children, and to many trade-unionists the industrial psychologist still appears to share the quite unpsychological attitudes of the early pioneers.

Taylor's genuine contribution may be said to have consisted in the discovery of what are called *time-study* methods. If we take any given job, and observe different people going through the required motions, we find a considerable diversity. Some proceed quickly and methodically, arranging their tools appropriately so that they are at hand when needed. Others work slowly and haphazardly, never have their tools ready and in the right place, and generally give the impression of incompetence. Most people are somewhere intermediate between these two extremes. Taylor suggested a detailed study of each particular process, with a view to finding the best method of carrying out the task, arranging the material, and timing the different operations involved. To arrive at this 'best' method, he suggested the following procedure.

First, divide the work a man is performing into simple, elementary movements. Then pick out all useless movements and discard them. Study how each of several workers makes each of these elementary movements, and with the aid of a stop-watch select the quickest and best method of making each movement. Describe, record, and index each elementary movement with its proper timing: establish the percentage of time which must be added to the working time of a good workman to cover unavoidable delays, accidents, interruptions, etc.; find out the percentage of time that must be allowed for rest, as well as the intervals at which rest must be taken in order to offset physical fatigue. These steps Taylor calls the *analytical* work; they are followed by the *constructive* work, which consists in combining the elementary movements into groups, and relating them to the work environment.

Later workers have improved on Taylor's original plan. Gilbreth in particular, another somewhat eccentric psychologist whose life has been portrayed in the film 'Cheaper by the dozen', has made a useful contribution by identifying and naming the most frequently occurring seventeen industrial movement-sets or 'therbligs' as he calls them by spelling his own name backwards. These 'therbligs' – search, find, select, grasp, transport loaded, position, assemble, use, disassemble, inspect, pre-position, release hold, transport empty, rest, unavoidable delay, avoidable delay, and plan – are each given a shorthand symbol, and a process chart is made depicting the exact sequence as well as the timing of these movement-sets. Gilbreth and his wife, who aided him in this work, used modern inventions like high-speed photography and film in their attempts to get a complete record of the exact details of all the work-movements, and materially improved on the rough inspectional method of Taylor.

Do these methods of analysis work? There is little doubt that they do. A few examples must suffice. One study showed that girls folding cloths according to a pattern were making from 20 to 30 motions per piece. Time- and motion-study of their movements reduced this to 10 motions, and increased average production from 150 dozen to 400 dozen per day. Other studies have shown increases in output of 88 per cent in dipping chocolates; 100 per cent in putting paper in boxes of shoe polish; 200 per cent in polishing metals; and 200 per cent also in using the emery wheel in filing spoons.

A more detailed example may give some insight into the exact mode of procedure of the psychologist called upon to deal with one particular job. I have chosen for discussion the classic investigation of bricklaying by Gilbreth. This is one of the oldest trades, and one of the most conservative; in several hundred years there had been little or no improvement in the implements and materials used, or in the methods of laying bricks. Gilbreth, who in his youth had himself been a bricklayer at one time, made a detailed analysis of all the movements involved, as well as of the implements used. He laid down the exact position which each foot of the bricklayer had to occupy in relation to the wall, the mortar-box, and the pile of bricks, so that it was unnecessary for him to take a step or two toward the pile and back again each time he picked up a brick. He investigated the best height for the mortar-box and the brick pile, and followed this up by designing a special scaffold, with a table on it, upon which all the materials could be placed so as to keep bricks, mortar, man, and wall in their proper position. A special labourer was detailed to keep these scaffolds adjusted in height for all the bricklayers, in line with the growth of the wall in height. By this simple device the bricklayer is saved the exertion of having to stoop down to the level of his feet for each brick and each trowelful of mortar, and then having to straighten up again. When it is realized that each bricklayer throughout recorded history has thus lowered his body (weight some 160 pounds, say) down two feet and raised it up again the same distance over a thousand times a day, lifting at the same time a brick weighing about five pounds, the full extent of the saving in energy made possible by this simple invention will be appreciated.

Other improvements included the proper positioning of the bricks, best side up, in special wooden frames, so that they can be picked up and placed directly, without fumbling and turning; proper placement of this 'pack' of bricks exactly where it can be reached with least trouble; special methods of mixing the mortar just right so that bricks could be embedded at the proper depth with a downward pressure of the hand, thus saving time in 'tapping' the brick. Through this very detailed and painstaking study, Gilbreth reduced the number of movements required for laying each brick from 18 to 5. In a demonstration of his method, he compared the number of bricks laid per hour in the execution of a standard task (laying a factory wall, 12 inches thick, with 2 kinds of brick, faced and ruled joints on both sides of the wall) by union labourers trained by him, with the standard older method. Gilbreth showed that his method resulted in 350 bricks being laid per hour, as compared with 120 bricks along traditional lines. It needs little imagination to see the relevance of these findings to the problems of a society like ours which is suffering from a chronic housing shortage and from an almost equally chronic man-power shortage in the building trades.

Yet one more example may be given to illustrate some consequences of psychological investigation not touched on so far. Thompson in his work on the improvement of quantity and quality of the output of ball-bearing inspectors showed that 35 girls could do the work previously done by 120, and that accuracy increased, in spite of the speeding-up of the whole procedure. This is the advantage as seen from the point of view of the firm; how about the girls employed on this work? They average from 80 to 100 per cent higher wages than they had received before; their hours of labour were shortened from 10½ to 8½ per day, with a Saturday half holiday. Also, they were given four recreation periods each day, which made overwork impossible for a healthy girl. From the point of view of the girls, these were decided improvements which more than made up for any possible disadvantages. Thus workers, management, and society all benefited from the change.

All these examples are from very simple motor movements in industry. Quite a different type of activity was studied in another experiment, namely, the speed of reading of university students. One would imagine that university students could read with tolerable expertise, but in actual fact it was found that the great majority read at speeds so slow that there was serious interference with their studies. Unnecessary lip-movements accompanied by a tendency to 'hear' himself reading out the printed words; regressive eye-movements sweeping back over material already read, because it had not been properly comprehended; too frequent fixation of the eye on different parts of each line of print – these and similar easily corrected errors keep many students to reading speeds several hundred or even thousand per cent below their maximum. Proper analysis and training methods were found to be extremely effective in teaching these students to read properly, and accompanying this improvement were considerable gains in academic standing.

Analysis need not confine itself to the simple or complex movements made by individuals; it is often an extremely worth-while job to study the behaviour of groups engaged on a common task. If an individual is not always organizing his movements to the best advantage, it is almost axiomatic that a whole group of individuals will be much less efficient still. The difficulty of such organization is seen clearest perhaps on the football field, where many attempted manoeuvres come to grief because of some breakdown in interaction. An example will make clear the kind of analysis I have in mind in this connexion. It is taken from psychological work carried out by the research section of an army group in a country which shall remain nameless.

It is well known that army drill precedes historically the time- and motion-study methods of Taylor and Gilbreth, and that its purpose is similar to theirs. After a preliminary analysis of the work involved, say, in loading and firing a gun, a decision is made as to the number of people required, and the exact jobs which each of them is to do. This decision is incorporated in the drill manual, and henceforward each gun crew goes through the same series of motions in loading and firing the gun. (That, at least, is the theory!) During the war, an analysis was made of the efficiency of this drill, by having a team of soldiers studied in close detail while they were going through their work. Ten soldiers were required for firing one particular gun according to the regulations, and the exact movements of each of the ten were recorded for each second from the time the first command was given to the end of the exercise.

The results were rather interesting. Some of the soldiers were busy only for a few seconds, and spent the rest of the time standing by. None were working more than half of the time. One soldier did nothing whatever. His task used to be that of holding the officer's horse; the horse had vanished into the limbo of forgotten things, but the drill still required someone to be there to carry out this hypothetical task! Reorganization of the drill showed that it could be carried out by five, instead of ten, soldiers; the most efficient method of firing was found to be one in which two teams of five men each alternated rapidly between firing and resting. Ten men employed in this way were found to give the gun a fire power almost twice what the original single team of ten men had given it.

This true story contains a moral which could be duplicated many times in modern history. Wasteful, old-fashioned methods of carrying out a given operation are likely to be retained unless a special effort is made to discover what goes on, and to improve it. It may often seem to need nothing but common sense to discover and improve upon these ancient habits and methods, but in actual fact the special training of the industrial psychologist enables him to do this type of work much more thoroughly, much more quickly, and with much greater success, than would attend the enthusiastic but ill-guided efforts of the amateur, or the self-styled 'expert' who has merely a nodding acquaintance with modern methods of scientific investigation. Indeed, it is the exaggerated claims of the latter, and his frequent disregard of important psychological variables, which have contributed to the suspicion with which psychology is viewed in industry.

In spite of its undoubted success in increasing productivity, 'Taylorism' has been attacked on several grounds. Some of these objections have been on technical, others on social grounds. To take technical objections first, it has been pointed out that movements are executed in patterns, and that it may be impossible to take the best movements from each of several different patterns and fit them together into a new one; just as a work of art is more than the individual objects depicted, so a total movement sequence has a unity which cannot be broken up into analytic segments. Myers has put this point of view by saying: 'The best mode of carrying out an industrial operation is not derived from a combination of more elementary movements selected from different individuals. Style is all important. An organism is organized; an individual is indivisible, and it is that very interrelation and integration which distinguishes the organism and the individual, let us not say from a machine, but from a mere aggregate of parts.'

Similar criticisms have been brought against the notion of the 'one best method'. A method of carrying out a task which is 'best' for one person may not be equally good for another; individual differences may make this concept of doubtful applicability. Cochet played tennis in quite a different way from Tilden; Perry's game was not at all like Budge's. Is it meaningful to say that by somehow averaging the service of Tilden, the backhand of Budge, the forehand of Perry, and the cool analytical generalship of Cochet, we could build up an ideal 'best' way of playing tennis?

These objections, it will be noted, are theoretical; they would suggest that improvement of productivity along the lines suggested by Taylor and Gilbreth was impossible. Yet the evidence is quite conclusive; apart from the few studies cited above, there are literally hundreds of others, all showing that very substantial improvements can be made through time- and motion-studies. We may agree that analysis can be taken too far, and that other factors should also be taken into account; it is hardly possible to deny the whole weight of the evidence and declare the impossibility of analysis. Few psychologists would endorse some of the exaggerated notions of analysis put forward by the early writers; none would deny that to a considerable degree these methods work.

We come next to the second type of objection, those based on social or political grounds. Workers often object to being treated as objects of study; they resent being made into experimental 'guinea-pigs'. They tend to feel that the result of such studies may be a speeding-up of industrial processes which may be injurious to health, and which will leave them exhausted and too tired to enjoy the increased pay which their increased production may bring them. They sometimes fear that while increased production may be rewarded at the time, the new standard may soon be regarded as average, and wages may be slashed again during the next slump. All these objections are reasonable and may be regarded as the result of bitter experience. Yet they do not really apply to the scientific study of production itself, but rather to the abuse of the results of such study.

This is a much more general problem, of course, which applies equally to all branches of science. Knowledge of bacteriology may result in medical advance or in bacteriological warfare. Knowledge of atomic structure may put at our disposal energy for peaceful purposes, or result in atombomb disaster. The use which society makes of scientific knowledge is determined by social and political forces; in themselves scientific discoveries are neutral. In the hands of a dictator, methods of industrial psychology may be used to increase the productivity of his slaves in order to further evil ends; firmly controlled by the democratic representatives of a free people, these methods may make work easier, more productive, and more rewarding. Greater productivity within a nation may not spell happiness for everyone, but it may dispel clouds of inflation, bankruptcy, and national indebtedness which make happy adjustment for the individual more difficult. The hostility of the worker to all methods whose aim is the increase of productivity is understandable in an exploitive society; where the worker holds the whip-hand through union activity such hostility may be short-sighted and redound to his own disadvantage.

The fact that industrial psychology can be of great use and importance to the worker is brought out most clearly perhaps in a series of investigations conducted early in the century into hours of work. These investigations, which were instrumental in bringing about the change in the length of the working day from 10 hours or more, maintained for 6 full days a week, to 8 hours a day, with a half day off on Saturday, showed conclusively that *average hourly output varies with the length of the working day*. The longer the working day, the smaller is the amount of material produced per hour; the shorter the working day, up to a point, the greater is the amount of material produced per hour. This rule may be generalized to cover the whole working week, as was shown most clearly in some investigations carried out during the time of the First World War in munition factories in this country.

Because of the sudden, desperate need for munitions in the early stages of the war, hours of work in factories were increased well above the usual. Output did not seem to keep pace with expectation, and consequently an investigation was made. It was found that when hours worked were reduced from 58·2 to 50·6 per week, there was an increase in hourly output of 39 per cent, and an increase in total output per week of 21 per cent. Thus reduction in the number of hours worked led to an increase in output. The same was found in another factory, in which women were engaged on the moderately heavy work of turning fuse bodies. When hours of work were reduced from 66 to 48·6 per week, there was an increase in hourly output of 68 per cent, and a 15 per cent increase in total production. These increases did not come about immediately after the switch-over had been made; as Myers comments, 'the human organism, after becoming adapted to certain hours of work, requires time, when that adaptation is disturbed, before it can give its maximal response to improved conditions.'

Over-long hours of work, an almost constant feature of Victorian industrialism, are uneconomical as well as bearing harshly on the worker. It should not be thought, however, that this relation between output and hours of work is a linear one. It has been shown over and over again that there is a point of diminishing return; that if hours are reduced below a minimum of 35 or 40, hourly output not only ceases to rise, but actually begins to fall. This appears to be due to various factors, such as dislocation of the habitual working pace, 'warming-up' time required before getting into one's stride, general mental attitude towards short-time, and various other considerations. This point of diminishing return differs in different industries and different jobs, and also depends on the sex of the operator; proper scientific investigation is needed to decide in each case what is the optimum working time from the point of view of the worker and of the firm, viewed in combination.

Taylor opened up an important field, but he never saw more than a very small segment of it, blinded as he was by his 'human engineering' outlook which left out of account some of the most important variables. As Dubreuil says in his book *Robots or Men*: 'Taylor's genius stopped on the threshold of a new world, of whose importance he was apparently unaware, viz. that of the inner forces contained in the worker's soul, and operating through the infinite powers of internal impulses which can be directed from without only by setting them free.' Recognition of this point of view is closely related to Taylor's third point – motivation through money incentives – and was dramatically forced on industrialists and psychologists alike through the failure of an experiment. This led to a series of classic investigations which take their name from the Hawthorne plant of the Western Electric Company where they were carried out, and are now known collectively as the 'Hawthorne experiment'.

For many years, psychologists had been interested in the improvement of working conditions; the studies on hours of work mentioned above were just one small part of the work carried on under this heading. Conditions investigated included lighting, temperature, humidity, and other physical factors; attempts were made by systematic changes of these variables to determine optimal conditions of work. Measures of output usually indicated that improvement of conditions was accompanied by increased production; these increases were seldom very large, but nevertheless they suggested that physical conditions played an important part in productivity.

The Hawthorne experiment at first followed this pattern, when it was found that increased illumination increased output. When, however, the investigators went on to *decrease* intensity of illumination, confidently expecting a decrease in output, they were startled to find that apparently the change in illumination had brought about a change in the attitude of the workers, so that an increase in effort more than compensated for the deterioration in working conditions. In other words, the fact that the expected decrease in output did not follow deterioration in working conditions suggested that the increase in output which had followed improvement in working conditions might have had quite a different basis from that which had been assumed almost without question, and that further investigation of the workers' motivation might throw some light on this puzzle.

An experiment was accordingly arranged, in which six girls who were employed in assembling relays were segregated in a special *test room* for over two years. They were subjected to a variety of changes in working conditions, and it was found that from the beginning of the experiment to the end the girls showed a steady increase in production. Even in periods when output would have been expected to drop because of deterioration of conditions, increases were manifest. During the period of investigation there was an increase in contentment among the girls, a greater interest in the job and in the working situation, and a reduction in absences of almost 80 per cent. Repeated interviews with the girls and detailed observation led the observers to the conclusion that the increase in output was due to changes in attitude. The girls were consulted before any changes in the working situation were made, their opinions were asked as to the effects of the changes, and they worked under conditions free from hard and fast supervision. They consequently appeared to develop a new social orientation which was the main determinant of their behaviour in the industrial situation, and which was not directly affected by the experimental changes of physical conditions introduced by the investigators.

There is a considerable amount of evidence in the Hawthorne reports, collected by interviews from large numbers of workers in the various departments, that work efficiency and job satisfaction are closely linked, and that attitudes towards the firm are an extremely important factor in motivation. The worker who feels that he is just a cog in a vast machine, who believes that his employers regard him merely as a replaceable part in their programme of 'human engineering', whose only interest in the work is centred on the pay packet, is likely to limit production to the absolutely necessary minimum. The worker who is made to feel that the firm is interested in him as a human being, who believes that his own interests are being considered by the managers, and who can find genuine interest in his job, is likely to strike out for maximum, rather than for minimum production. There may be an important lesson here for those who run the nationalized industries, as well as for those responsible for 'free enterprise'; mechanical efficiency is not enough if it fails to take account of the attitudes of the workers, and if it does not integrate them psychologically with the aims and aspirations of the firm for which they are working. Taylor's contribution, by leaving out the human touch, laid itself wide open to attack; it is only by combining it with a wider interest in the people concerned, and a more human regard for their individual characteristics and differences, that it can possibly be made to fit into our democratic society.

According to this view, Taylor's insistence on economic factors in motivating his workers is very wide of the mark, and other considerations may be much more important. That this is so is shown by various studies, all of which agree that in spite of the unholy alliance between orthodox Capitalism and orthodox Marxism in regarding the economic motive as the strongest, if not the only, force in industry, other, more psychological motives are regarded as more important by the workers themselves. In one typical American study 'opportunity for advancement' was ranked as the most important consideration in evaluating one's job, followed by 'steady work', 'opportunity to use own ideas', 'opportunity to learn a job', and 'good boss', an item which was meant to sum up the psychological attitude stressed on the preceding pages. Next came 'opportunity to be of public service', and only then came the item 'high pay', followed by 'good working conditions', 'good hours', and 'clean and easy work'. These facts speak for themselves.

Nor should it be imagined that they only apply to the United States. Samples of different types of workers were questioned in this country on the importance of various factors in their working lives. Top came 'interest of work', followed by 'prospect of promotion'. 'Security' came next, followed by 'pay' and 'working hours' neck-and-neck. Only very little behind came 'social side of the job' and 'holidays'. Again, therefore, factors other than the economic are considered much more important.

I would not like to give the impression in this chapter that we know all the answers to the problems posed by industry, or that such knowledge as we have can be applied immediately and with unfailing accuracy whenever and wherever trouble arises. Nothing could be further from the truth. We know very, very little indeed of the mysterious forces which shape our conduct, which we refer to as 'incentives' and 'motives', and which politicians and other 'practical' men attempt to manipulate with such little skill and small effect. However, a beginning has been made, and the results of applying such limited knowledge as we have acquired are far from disappointing. The evidence points in the direction of a more equalitarian, democratic organization of industry, a more humanized relationship between managers and workers, and a more psychological, and less economic, approach generally.

The passing of 'economic man' has been noted by many writers in recent years. Not so many have realized that a whole new approach to social and political problems may be in the making, an approach based on factual knowledge of human nature rather than on hypothetical beliefs and preconceived notions. Political parties generally seem to have exhausted the dynamic which once motivated them, and are looking around for new ideas and new conceptions. Might it not be that these new ideas and conceptions are to be found in a realistic appraisal of the potentialities, abilities, attitudes, and motives of the human beings who make up society? Where there is so much agreement among all parties about the *aims* of society, should not the disputes about *means* be handed over to scientific investigation? The solution of social problems can in principle at least be found in the same way as the solution to physical and chemical problems; we do not determine the atomic weight of gold, or the size of the moon, or the spectral colour of hydrogen by a counting of heads, and there appears no ground for assuming such a method to be any more effective in arriving at correct decisions about industrial productivity, or motivation, or other psychological problems. The specious appeal of Communism to many people lies in its apparently 'scientific' approach to social problems; the substitution of genuine science for the bogus rationalizations of doctrinaire decisions which characterize Marxian dialectics may harness much-needed enthusiasm to the cause of modern democracy. The working out of such a programme must inevitably be the task of many brains and will require much theoretical and experimental study; to have indicated the infinite possibilities of such an approach is one of the chief contributions of psychology to modern thought.

PART THREE

ABNORMAL BEHAVIOUR

9

NORMALITY, SEX, AND SOCIAL CLASS

NORMALITY is a term which recurs with disturbing frequency in the writings of psychologists, psychiatrists, psychoanalysts, sociologists, and other people concerned with human behaviour. The reason for being disturbed at the use of this term is a very simple one; 'normality' is one of those words that may mean all things to all men. There is no one agreed definition which might serve to delineate a given segment of behaviour; instead, the term has two main and many subsidiary uses, and the same writer frequently employs it now in one sense, now in another.

Nevertheless, the concepts denoted, however poorly, by this term are so important that a brief discussion may be in order. Two main uses of the term 'normality' will be fairly obvious to anyone who considers the matter at all. We may mean by 'normal' that which characterizes the conduct of the majority of people; this we may call the *statistical* definition of normality. A person of normal height is one who does not deviate very far in either direction from the average. A person who is normal with respect to weight is one who is neither heavier nor lighter than the majority of other people of his own height. This usage of the term is perfectly clear, straightforward, and intelligible. It does, however, present certain difficulties when we consider certain traits such as intelligence, or beauty, or health.

Let us look at intelligence. The statistically normal person is the one whose I.Q. lies near the average; both the mental defective with an I.Q. of 60 and the genius with an I.Q. of

180 are 'abnormal' according to this definition. The statistically normal person is neither beautiful nor ugly; the good-looking girl is as much a statistical abnormality as is a downright ugly one – perhaps even more so. This ambiguity of the term comes out strongest in relation to health. The normal person is one who has an average number of illnesses and fractures and whose life is ended by one of the more common diseases. The person who is completely healthy and lives to a ripe old age, without any kind of physical disease, would be exceedingly abnormal from this point of view.

This is not a usual method of looking at health or beauty or intelligence. We tend to substitute for the *statistical* norm an *ideal* norm. We call a person normal the more he approaches the ideal, whether it be ideally high intelligence, good looks, or uninterrupted health. But the ideal norm may be one which is statistically very infrequent, or which in actual fact is not found at all in the population examined.

Confusion between these two uses of the term is quite common, particularly with respect to mental health. When the psychoanalyst declares that no one is normal, he has in mind the ideal concept of normality. The reader, however, often attempts to understand such a remark in terms of a statistical norm and declares it to be self-contradictory and absurd. The same misunderstanding arises in many other contexts. It is only necessary to keep in mind its semantic roots in order to avoid its obvious pitfalls.

There is a third meaning of the term which has also played an important part in the development of psychology. According to this interpretation, we call normal that which we consider to be *natural*. Thus, we consider it normal for the male to be dominant and the female to be submissive; we consider heterosexual attraction normal, homosexual attraction abnormal. We would hold these views even though it could be shown that in some communities, among the ancient Greeks, say, homosexuality was statistically more frequent than heterosexuality, or that among some nations, say the ancient Egyptians, the women tended to be more aggressive and the males more submissive. Nor would we hold these views because we could say in any absolute sense that dominant behaviour in males was ideal or desirable. Our feeling would be rather that biologically nature has created men and women to act in certain ways and that, quite regardless of statistical or ideal norms, behaviour in accordance with these putative aims was normal and behaviour counter to these putative aims was abnormal.

The tendency to regard certain forms of conduct as natural and biologically innate is not logically absurd. It seems to be based in many cases, however, on an erroneous identification of that which is natural with that which is current in our society. This tendency to regard as natural (instinctively innate) that with which we are familiar is brought out very clearly in certain animal studies. We regard as instinctive and natural, for instance, the behaviour of cats who catch and kill mice and rats and feed on them. We may not regard this as ideal behaviour – in many cases we disapprove of a well-fed cat killing birds and other animals for no apparent purpose – but we regard this behaviour as innate and therefore natural and normal. Yet the evidence is fairly conclusive that it is nothing of the kind.

Kuo, an American psychologist, brought up kittens in a diversity of different conditions. Having separated them from their mothers he fed some on milk and slops in complete isolation, others he fed on meat, while yet another group was brought up together with young rats. Other groups, brought up on milk and slops, or on meat, were allowed to see rats and mice running around the room outside their cages, and a last group was brought up in the usual way by their mothers. At the end of the upbringing period, he observed the behaviour of each cat when left alone with a number of rats. The behaviour of cats in the different groups was strikingly different. Those brought up in the ordinary way killed and devoured the rats without exception; those at the other extreme, who had been brought up in isolation and fed on slops and milk, showed no tendency at all to catch, kill, and eat rats and mice; the other groups occupied intermediate positions, but with a strong tendency to react in an abnormal, unnatural way, i.e. not to regard the rats as food. Repetitions of the experiment have confirmed the essential correctness of Kuo's point, namely, that this particular activity in the cat is not instinctual, innate, and therefore natural, but is an acquired habit which can very easily be eliminated by suitable training.

Perhaps equally impressive is evidence given by anthropologists from their studies of various tribes. Let us take the almost universal assumption (universal, that is to say, in our particular culture) that men are dominant and aggressive, whereas women are submissive and peaceable. This pattern, however, appears to be far from universal. Among the Arapesh, a mountain-dwelling people in New Guinea, we find that both men and women show what we would call feminine traits. This group appears to have outlawed competition, aggressiveness, and dominant behaviour, and to have replaced these with mutual trust and affection. There is very little stress on age or sex differences in their society, which comes as near, perhaps, as any to the ideals of a classless society. Even the children's games are non-competitive and any fights which arise are immediately broken up by adults. Observers frequently refer to the Arapesh as 'one big happy family'.

At the opposite extreme, take the Mundugumor, a cannibal tribe in New Guinea. There, both men and women show what are considered masculine traits. They are ruthless, violent, domineering, aggressive, and ready to fight at the slightest provocation. Right from the beginning the child is born into a hostile world, weaned early, treated to blows, and often killed by the mother, who shows no signs of that hypothetical maternal instinct which we consider so natural and normal a feature of femininity.

An actual reversal of sex attitudes is found among the Tchambuli. Here the woman is the dominant, impersonal, managing partner and the man the less responsible and emotionally dependent partner. It is the woman who makes the sexual choice; it is the man who is chosen. Women get along well with each other; men are 'catty' about other men, suspicious, and distrustful. Because of their dependence on the women for security the men are shy, sensitive, and subservient; they engage in artistic and other 'feminine' activities, such as dancing, weaving, and painting. Many other examples could be given of behaviour patterns, which to us appear quite unnatural and abnormal but which, nevertheless, appear to enjoy stability and make possible a life not noticeably inferior in happiness and contentment to our own.

These examples show how very relative the concept of normality, whether in the statistical or in the natural sense, really is. Ultimately, it would seem that the natural meaning of the term 'normal' can be reduced to the statistical; we regard as 'natural' that which occurs so frequently in our society as to be practically universal. Sometimes, of course, we may be mistaken in our assessment as to the frequency with which certain forms of conduct occur; Kinsey, for instance, found that over 30 per cent of his male subjects had indulged in active homosexual practices at one time or another, a figure certainly well beyond what most people would have guessed.

From the scientific point of view, animal and anthropological studies are quite convincing proof of the relativity of many of our standards of normality. Many people, however, tend to reject them in a somewhat wholesale manner by saying that what may be true of animals and the 'heathen Chinee' does not really concern our civilized society very much. Consequently, I will give one further example of the relativity of our concepts of normality by comparing groups taken from within our own society. In view of the great complexity of modern cultures, it will be essential to go into far more detail here than was required in connexion with the anthropological and comparative evidence; the reasons for this will become apparent soon.

The example I have chosen is taken from the Kinsey report on 'Sexual Behaviour in the Human Male', and deals with the sexual practices of middle-class and working-class groups in America. There is little doubt that a similar study, if carried out in this country, would reveal similar differences, but in the absence of experimental proof for this assumption, it may be wise to remember that this study was carried out in the United States, and that the detailed figures, even if they can be accepted as representative of sexual behaviour over there, cannot necessarily be transferred directly to English conditions.

Kinsey's interest was essentially in human sexual activity. This he defines in a very down-to-earth way, which has been criticized by psychoanalysts and others, who attempt to trace the vagaries of the sexual impulse into the most remote corners of our behaviour. Such objections may indicate possibilities for further study; they are hardly relevant to the monumental work done by Kinsey along his self-avowed restrictions. His concern is essentially with those sexual activities of an individual which culminate in the event which is known as orgasm, or sexual climax. According to him, there are six chief sources of sexual climax. 'There is self-stimulation (masturbation), noctural dreaming to the point of climax, heterosexual petting to climax (without intercourse), heterosexual intercourse, homosexual intercourse, and contact with animals of other species. There are still other possible sources of orgasm, but they are rare and never constitute a significant fraction of the outlet for any large segment of the population.' Kinsey refers to these six types of sexual satisfaction as 'outlets' and his studies are mainly concerned with their incidence in various samples of the population.

All his data were collected through first-hand interviews of which some 12,000 had been held prior to the publication of his book, and of which about 5,300 were used in his actual computations.

The accounts dealing with Kinsey's method of making contact and of carrying out the interviews are of absorbing interest. Interviews included a list of professions as varied as bootlegger and psychiatrist, prostitute and clergyman, gambler and lawyer, editor and pimp. The interview itself appears to have been a somewhat gruelling experience,

judging by Kinsey's own summary, with rapid-fire questioning, cross checks on accuracy, and the habit of placing the
burden of denial on the subject. Kinsey believes that the
interviewer should not make it easy for his subject to deny
his participation in any form of sexual activity. 'It is too
easy to say "No" if he is simply asked whether he has ever
engaged in a particular activity. Consequently we always
begin by asking *when* they first engaged in such activity.'
This, as he points out, places a heavier burden on the individual who would like to deny his experience, and since the
form of the question makes it apparent that the interviewer
would not be surprised if the interviewee had had such an
experience there is less likelihood of it being denied.

Kinsey took the task of preparation for the interview very
seriously, even to the extent of inventing a special coded
system of writing down the answers which would guarantee
secrecy, as no one except he and his co-interviewers were
familiar with the system. He went as far as to learn the
sexual vocabularies of the various groups he was dealing
with, believing that it is necessary to comprehend the whole
range of possible techniques in each possible type of sexual
behaviour, and that for most of these types, as well as for the
hundreds of possible positions in intercourse and the scores
of varying techniques in the homosexual act, there exist
specialized terms which the interviewer must know if he is
to understand and obtain reasonable co-operation from his
subjects.

The total data obtained in these interviews were broken
down according to sex, race, cultural group, marital status,
age, educational level, occupational class, occupational
class of parent, rural-urban background, religious adherence, and geographical origin. Statistics are then presented
in detail for the various constituent groups. As our interest
will be mainly in the comparison between middle-class and
working-class subjects, the other breakdowns will only be
mentioned where they appear relevant. Kinsey defines
social level partly in terms of education, partly in terms of
the type of work the person is doing, but as the two types of

classification give essentially identical data, there is little point in going into the details as to which is used in any particular comparison.

Kinsey summarizes his conclusions in the following words: 'The data now available show that patterns of sexual behaviour may be strikingly different for the different social levels that exist in the same city or town, and sometimes in immediately adjacent sections of a single community. The data show that divergences in the sexual patterns of such social groups may be as great as those which anthropologists have found between the sexual patterns of different racial groups in remote parts of the world.'

Having quoted the conclusions, let us now turn to the evidence. As regards the total number of outlets of sexual climaxes per week there appears to be no very considerable difference between the different classes, although there is, of course, in all classes a natural decline from a maximum of about five per week at the age of 16–20, to something like two per week at the age of 40–45. There are, however, marked differences among the social classes with respect to the proportion of the different types of sexual outlet recognized by Kinsey. His main comparisons are between the college-educated group, the high school group, and the elementary school group (i.e. those who never enjoy any form of secondary education), and his findings will be summarized by taking each outlet in turn. As an example let us take his unmarried 16–20 year-old group, as these men may be taken as typical of the many others for which data are provided.

In this group masturbation provides 29 per cent of all outlets for the elementary school group, 37 per cent for the high school (secondary school) group, and 66 per cent for the college group; nocturnal emission provides 5 per cent of all the outlets for the elementary school group, 6 per cent for the high school group, and 16 per cent for the college group; the figures for petting to climax are respectively 2 per cent, 3 per cent, and 5 per cent. In all three outlets, therefore, the college group is consistently more active, the high school group intermediate, and the elementary school group least active. This is reflected in the totals. Masturbation, nocturnal emission, and petting to climax account for 87 per cent of all the sexual outlets in the college group; they account for 46 per cent of all sexual outlets in the high school group; and only for 36 per cent of all sexual outlets in the elementary school group.

The picture is quite different in the other three types of outlet. Two of these are relatively unimportant. Sodomy (intercourse with animals) accounts for 1 per cent of sexual outlets in both the elementary and the high school group and is not represented at all in the college group; homosexuality accounts for 7 per cent of sexual outlets in the elementary school group, for 11 per cent of outlets in the high school group, but only for 2 per cent in the college group. Much more important is pre-marital intercourse, which Kinsey divides into intercourse with companions, i.e. with girls of the same social status as the interviewee, and intercourse with prostitutes. Figures for intercourse with companions and prostitutes respectively are 51 per cent and 6 per cent in the elementary school group; 39 per cent and 3 per cent in the high school group; and 9 per cent and 1 per cent respectively in the college group. Altogether, pre-marital, homosexual, and animal intercourse account for 65 per cent of all sexual outlets in the elementary school group; 54 per cent of all sexual outlets in the secondary school group; but only 12 per cent of all sexual outlets in the college group.

The main difference will be seen to be between the college and the non-college groups. Almost 90 per cent of all college students' sex outlets are provided by masturbation, nocturnal emission, and petting; only about 10 per cent by direct intercourse. About two-thirds of the outlets of the non-college group are provided by direct intercourse. These figures show a very marked difference in behaviour patterns between the two groups. However, these data, interesting as they are, are only part of the evidence; we must also be concerned with the conscious evaluation of these various outlets by middle- and working-class groups respectively, and the degree to which they are considered 'normal'.

At lower social levels Kinsey found that masturbation was looked down upon as abnormal, a perversion, and an infantile substitute for socio-sexual contacts. Most lower level boys masturbate, but seldom have more than a few experiences before stopping abruptly and immediately after their first experience of heterosexual coitus. This view of masturbation as a perversion is often bolstered up by rationalization to the effect that masturbation does physical harm. The attitude of the lower class towards masturbation is similar to that obtaining among some primitive peoples – not involving moral values as much as implying amusement and contempt of the social incapacity of the individual who has to resort to self-stimulation for his sexual outlets. Among college students, masturbation is not regarded as exactly desirable or commendable, but is accepted as being less immoral than heterosexual extra-marital contacts.

Divergent as attitudes of college and non-college interviewees are with respect to masturbation, the greatest difference arises with respect to petting and extra-marital relations. In the college group, sexual morality lays great emphasis on the preservation of the virginity of the female, and to a somewhat lesser degree that of the male also, until the time of marriage. 'The utilization of pre-marital petting at this level is fortified by the emphasis which marriage manuals place upon the importance of pre-coital techniques in married relations; and the younger generation considers that this experience before marriage may contribute something to the development of satisfactory relations. Petting thus is a compromise based on the acceptance of a code (the avoidance of pre-marital intercourse, the preservation of one's virginity), which is of fundamental importance in the *mores* of the upper social level.'

Non-college groups, and particularly the lowest educational levels, do not share this strong taboo against premarital intercourse, but rather accept such intercourse as natural, inevitable, and desirable. Their taboos are directed against any substitutes for simple and direct coitus. Petting involves a variety of techniques which are quite unacceptable to lower levels and which are regarded as immoral perversions, unnatural, undesirable, and abnormal. The question of morals does not, on the other hand, enter very much into their consideration, and pre-marital intercourse particularly is more or less taken for granted. As Kinsey points out: 'So nearly universal is pre-marital intercourse among grade school groups that in two or three lower level communities in which we have worked we have been unable to find a solitary male who had not had sexual relations with girls by the time he was 16 or 17 years of age.'

The pattern set by pre-marital intercourse is in many ways followed after marriage in extra-marital contacts. In the lower social levels, extra-marital intercourse is widely accepted as natural and usual and begins almost from the day that marriage is contracted. Gradually, as the years pass, extra-marital intercourse becomes less and less frequent. The course of events is quite different for the college trained man. Having exercised his restraint in homosexual relations for a number of years, he carries over this restraint into the marriage relation and tends to have a relatively small number of extra-marital relations. (In fact, because of this restraint, he may have great difficulties in developing satisfactory sexual relations with his wife and may, and frequently does, carry over habits of masturbation even into the marriage relation.) As the years go by, however, extra-marital relations become more numerous among the college-trained men until they reach a peak at the 50-year and over level.

Thus the trend is directly reversed when we compare upper- and working-class groups. The upper-class groups start out with restraint and adherence to ideals of virginity and monogamy, and tend to drift away from these ideals in later life to extra-marital relationships. Working-class males tend to start out with a contempt for the ideals of monogamy and virginity and have large numbers of extra-marital affairs. As they get older, however, they tend to approach more and more in their conduct the ideals they did not themselves share in their youth.

It is not, however, in the main the figures, interesting as they are, which throw a good deal of light on the different conceptions of 'normal' sexual behaviour held by middle- and working-class people; it is the expressed views of Kinsey's interviewees regarding their attitudes towards various sexual practices which are so enlightening. As our first example we may take the attitude towards nudity. The wide differences in tolerance among different nations regarding feminine nudity are well known; Kinsey points out that similar differences exist between different classes in the same society. Thus, nudity is considered almost an essential concomitant of intercourse among practically all college-trained males, who find it difficult to comprehend that anyone should regularly and as a matter of preference have intercourse while clothed. On the other hand, among those with the least amount of education, those who favour nudity in intercourse constitute an actual minority. Nudity by them is regarded as far more indecent than intercourse. Kinsey mentions the case of one highly promiscuous male who had had intercourse with several hundred girls and who emphasized the fact that he had never turned down an opportunity to have intercourse except 'on one occasion when the girl started to remove her clothing before coitus. She was too indecent to have intercourse with!'

Different attitudes regarding extra-marital petting have already been mentioned; these apparently carry over into married life, where the college-trained male, persuaded by marriage manuals that the female needs extensive sensory stimulation if she is to be brought to simultaneous orgasm in coitus, indulges in lengthy petting activity. There is a minimum of such sexual play at the lower levels, where many consider that intromission is the essential and the only justifiable activity in a 'normal' sexual relation. It is interesting to note that from preliminary figures on the sexual behaviour of women, Kinsey concludes that in spite of the adherence of the upper-level males to marriage manual recommendations, satisfactory orgasm is achieved more frequently by lower-level females.

Kissing as an erotic technique is very much more widespread among the middle-class groups but is regarded with some distaste among lower-class people. Deep kissing is almost universally prevalent in the college-educated group where its sanitary implications do not appear to present any obstacle to its acceptance. 'This group accepts mouth contacts in its erotic play although it objects to the use of a common drinking glass. On the other hand, the lower-level male considers such oral contacts to be dirty, filthy, and a source of disease, although he may drink from a common cup which hangs on the water pail, and he may utilize common utensils in eating and drinking.'

The two classes again show a marked difference in their attitude towards variation of position in intercourse. The most common upper-level variant with the female above the male is considered a veritable perversion among people of lower social levels.

There is one interesting point which Kinsey brings out rather clearly. It is that males who are moving from one social class into another, either up or down, tend to adopt the sexual practices of the class into which they are moving, rather than those of the class which they are leaving behind. This shows how complex the pattern of determinants of our conceptions of 'normality' really is; they obviously cannot be deduced in any simple and straightforward manner such as a counting of heads, or by a consideration of some abstract ideal.

I have given a rather extensive discussion of the concept of 'normality' and tried to show, as clearly as possible, that in this sphere also the principle of relativity reigns, and that there are no firm absolute ideals which determine behaviour even within one single, fairly closely-knit society. This does not mean that there do not exist religious and other groups which hold very firm opinions as to what the social norms should be or ought to be; it is merely that in actual fact, no such universal norms of behaviour do exist. Once this is realized important consequences follow from it in the field of clinical work, social service, and legal practice.

Essentially what happens in these three fields is that upper-class males and females lay down the law, or try to advise and help people from the lower social classes. 'Wherever professionally trained persons try to predict the behaviour of lower-level individuals, conflicts are likely to arise because of these diverse sexual philosophies.' In clinical practice, for instance, among physicians, psychologists, psychiatrists, nurses, psychoanalysts, marriage counsellors, and others, therapy, advice, and help in the sexual sphere are based essentially upon concepts of marriage and sexual conduct which agree with the norms obtaining among the upper social levels from which the practitioner comes, but which may be quite inappropriate to the norms of the social level of the person to whom the advice is given. It is easy to imagine the effects of advice at a marriage-counselling clinic, which emphasizes the need for prolonged pre-coital play, variety in techniques, stimulation before sexual union, some delay after effecting such union and then, in the end, orgasm which is simultaneous for the male and the female. Adequate as such a pattern may be in the counsellor's own group, it would certainly be considered abnormal and perverse among a large portion of the population to whom the advice is addressed.

Schoolteachers and others in social service are faced with similar problems. Kinsey quotes the case of an unmarried college graduate teacher who, when faced with the fact that one of her boys had had intercourse with one of the girls in the class, recommended the boy's expulsion from the school, resulting in public disgrace for both the boy and the girl. More appropriate action might have been taken had the teacher realized that more than one fourth of the other boys in the class had had similar sexual experiences.

It is, however, particularly with respect to laws governing sexual behaviour that lack of realism is particularly prominent. Kinsey estimates that if existing laws regarding sexual behaviour were strictly enforced, more than 95 per cent of the total male population would be in prison. 'Only a relatively small proportion of the males who are sent to Penal Institutions for sex offences have been involved in behaviour which is materially different from the behaviour of most of the males in the population.' If the law were thus enforced in all its majesty, 5 per cent of the population would maintain the other 95 in enforced idleness!

Fortunately, the contact between the law and the people is mediated by policemen and others whose upbringing is more in accord with the *mores* of the working-class groups than it is with the college-trained law-givers. Thus, laws against pre-marital intercourse are rarely enforced because it is difficult for a policeman to feel that a crime is being committed when he finds a boy involved in the kind of sexual activity which was part of his own history of growing-up, and which he knows to be all too common in the histories of a great majority of adolescents in his community.

There is one other group who may be recommended to ponder deeply the implications of the various conceptions of what is normal and what is natural. That is the group of people who write books on the future of marriage and issue recommendations regarding improvements in the functioning of this sacred institution. Having perused two-score at least of such books, many of them by eminent statesmen and philosophers, I have come to the conclusion that they are based almost entirely on the assumption that the whole population is made up of individuals with an I.Q. of at least 180, all highly educated, adhering to certain ethical conceptions of unparalleled loftiness, and all resembling the author like an unending collection of monozygotic twins. It would be amusing, were it not so tragic, to realize that these are serious attempts to come to grips with a serious problem. How can we even begin to say what should be until we know in great detail just what is and how it has come about? Comparative studies of different nations, different classes within the same nation, and even of animals are essential before any reasonable proposals can be put forward in this extremely difficult field.

It is doubtful if this learned display of accumulated wisdom gets us very much further than the famous quatrain which W. James wrote down during a drug-induced dream. Experimenting with various methods of influencing consciousness, this famous philosopher several times dreamed during these states that the secret of life had been imparted to him, only to find that upon waking he had forgotten it again. He resolved to write it down immediately, and succeeded in doing so. When he woke up he hurriedly picked up the sheet of paper, and found that the secret of life, as written down by him, amounted to this:

> Higamus, Hogamus,
> Woman is monogamous;
> Hogamus, Higamus,
> Man is polygamous.

He was somewhat disappointed, although it is difficult to see why. There is probably more truth in this verse than in most philosophical writings.

The real danger of the marriage reformers is not that there is any likelihood that their proposals might be accepted; even college-trained males in our society usually know enough about life to realize the utter futility and impossibility of these proposals. What is frightening is rather the tacit acceptance of reviewers and public alike that no factual data, no extended experience in the field in question are required from those offering blue-prints for the future of marriage. Even the Royal Commission on this subject has followed the same procedure, calling for expressions of opinion and attitude by large numbers of people and various interested groups rather than appointing a staff of research sociologists, psychologists, and psychiatrists to go into the various problems, assemble the evidence known from the literature, elaborate hypotheses, and carry out research to test these hypotheses. Where so much human happiness is at stake it would seem that the very small amount of money required for some permanent research institution devoted to the exploration of human sexual behaviour, whether normal or abnormal, should not be begrudged.

10

THE EFFECTS OF PSYCHOTHERAPY

THE incidence of mental disorders in modern life is truly frightening. Few people quite realize the implications of recent trends. Approximately half of all hospital beds in Great Britain and in the United States are given over to patients suffering from mental disorders. One person in 35 will be certified mentally ill some time during his life. Among the literate white induction examinees in the American Army, 14 per cent were rejected for psychiatric reasons; to this should be added the very large number who suffered a nervous breakdown during the war. About one quarter (some put it as high as 50 per cent) of those who visit their G.P. for ostensibly physical ailments are found to suffer completely or mainly from mental illnesses. No wonder that the problem of cure and alleviation of these disorders occupies a prominent place in modern medical practice.

Certain methods, while effective up to a point, are ruled out in modern democratic countries for various reasons. For instance, it has been observed that when neurotics enter a concentration camp many of their symptoms tend to vanish; the immediate fear of death overrides the anxieties and hysterical defence mechanisms of the neurotic. There is probably a marked positive correlation between incidence of neurosis and the material welfare of a country; in the United States it has become almost fashionable to have some form of neurotic disorder, and an upper-middle-class person is quite looked down upon if he cannot speak of 'his psychoanalyst' as having advised this, that, and the other.

Up to a point, of course, it is difficult to estimate the amount of neurosis existing in a country apart from the efficiency of the medical service; in a backward country, neurotic disorders may go completely untreated, or be diagnosed under the heading of some physical disorder and

G

thus create the impression that there is less neurosis there than in other countries where medical men are more alert to this type of illness. This makes any kind of accurate comparisons of one country with another, or of trends within one country, extremely difficult.

However that may be, there can be no doubt whatsoever about the magnitude of the problem. Many people tend to look at it from the wrong point of view. They tend to regard neurotics as being in some way qualitatively different from themselves just as, say, a person who has a broken arm or a cancer is qualitatively different from the person who has not. This is a pre-scientific way of looking at the problem, reminiscent in some ways of the exploded notion in the intellectual field that people are either geniuses, or mental defectives, or normal, i.e. that they fall into one of three separate categories which do not overlap in any way. We now know that this is untrue and that intelligence is a continuous variable ranging from the lowest mental defective to the highest genius. In a similar way, the neurotic is not a thing set apart from the rest of humanity; he is simply located at one end of a continuous distribution ranging from the extremely stable, emotionally mature person through the average to the immature, unstable, potential neurotic. Given a sufficient stress, most people will tend to break down and develop neurotic manifestations; the person at the immature, unstable end of the continuum is liable to break down under very slight provocation, whereas the person at the other end of the continuum would be able to stand almost incredible stresses before giving way.

It follows from this that people suffering from neurotic disorders of various degrees of severity are part of the general population, rather than being segregated into institutions, and extensive investigations leave little doubt that in an average sample of the 'normal' population some 10 per cent would be found to be suffering from debilitating emotional disorders, with another 20 per cent or so suffering from the milder forms, which may, nevertheless, cause them to make frequent visits to their G.P., and which will interfere with the efficiency of their social, marital, and work adjustments.

These are the facts regarding the size of the problem. Can psychotherapy do anything to alleviate the suffering caused by neurotic disorders of one kind or another? Psychotherapy may be defined as a systematic and persistent exploration of a neurotic patient's mental processes by verbal means in order to help him toward better personal and social integration. There are two major forms of psychotherapy, the Freudian or psychoanalytic, and the more or less eclectic methods used by non-Freudian psychiatrists. Both are being used very extensively indeed. From the hundreds of thousands of patients being treated each year one would expect that detailed results of the efficacy of these various forms of treatment would now be available. A survey of the literature discloses a number of interesting facts.

There are a fair number of reports by hospitals and private psychiatrists giving data on follow-up investigations of their patients. Usually the outcome of the treatment is stated in terms of 'cured', 'very much improved', 'improved', and 'not improved', although other terms are sometimes used. In the majority of cases there is little attempt by the authors to define exactly what they mean by these terms, and the judgement as to which term is applied to the patient is exceedingly subjective. This point should be noted carefully because it indicates that these judgements can only be accepted with great reservation.

However, taking them at their face value, we find considerable agreement among the average percentage rates of recovery given by the various authors. Those using eclectic methods of treatment report that about two out of three tend to recover or improve. Those using psychoanalysis report recovery or improvement only in about half of their cases; this is in part due to the fact that a large proportion of patients receiving psychoanalytic treatment tend to break off treatment and must therefore be counted as failures. If these cases are omitted, the percentage of cures and recoveries attributed to psychoanalysis is similar to that given for eclectic treatment, i.e. about two out of three. These figures look promising; the neurotic who comes for treatment certainly appears to have a very good chance of recovery.

There is one difficulty, however, in accepting these figures as proof of the efficacy of psychotherapy. Implied in the methodology of these studies is the ancient fallacy of *post hoc ergo procter hoc*; the improvement follows the treatment and is therefore attributed to the treatment. This assumption is certainly fallacious, at least in part; spontaneous recovery from neurotic disorders is observed quite frequently. Any mental hospital with a long waiting list finds that neurotics who have been asked to wait six months or more for treatment will write at the end of the six months' period that they do not need treatment any more as they have recovered sufficiently without it.

Consequently, what is needed is obviously a control group, that is to say, a group of patients not treated by psychotherapy but in other ways similar to the neurotics who did receive treatment. This control group would then furnish a base-line against which to compare the recovery rates of the experimental group, i.e. those receiving the eclectic or psychoanalytic treatment. Unfortunately, none of the psychiatrists and psychoanalysts reporting on the results of their treatment have included such a control group; consequently, we must fall back on two studies which have to serve as a base-line for our appraisal. The first of these studies makes use of the amelioration rate in American State Mental Hospitals for patients diagnosed under the heading of neurosis. Patients in these hospitals received no psychotherapy but merely custodial care. Occasionally, a very slight degree of psychotherapy was given to them in the Reception Hospitals, but this is not sufficient to be included in our definition of 'systematic and persistent exploration'. There are some objections to the use of the figure as an estimate of 'spontaneous remission'. In the first place, psychoneurotics are not usually committed to State Hospitals unless they are in a very bad condition indeed.

Overcrowding and lack of funds thus restrict admission to the most severe cases of all. Secondly, people who go to State Mental Hospitals are usually of a lower economic, educational, and social status than are patients in the type of hospital to which members of our experimental group are admitted. Thirdly, the fact that a patient is discharged from a State Mental Hospital as cured is not necessarily equivalent in meaning to his being discharged as cured by a private physician; standards at the State Hospitals are probably less severe than those of Private Hospitals. With all these qualifications in mind, we may note that the percentage of cures, or improvements, in this population is again of the order of two out of three; if anything it is slightly higher than that found for patients receiving psychotherapy.

The other base-line estimate which we have available is, perhaps, rather more trustworthy. This was derived from 500 disability claims due to psychoneurosis treated by G.P.s throughout the United States of America. These cases were taken consecutively from the files of the Equitable Life Assurance Company, and the people concerned had all been ill of a neurosis for at least three months before claims were submitted. They could fairly be called 'severe' since they had been totally disabled for this three months period, and rendered unable to carry on with any occupation for remuneration or profit for at least that time. These patients were regularly seen and treated by their own physicians with sedatives, tonics, suggestion, and reassurance; no psychotherapy was attempted. Repeated statements by their physicians, as well as independent investigations by the insurance company, confirmed the fact that the patients were not engaged in productive work during the period of their illness. During their disablement, they received disability benefits; this fact of disability income may have actually prolonged the total period of disability and acted as a barrier to incentive to recovery. As the author of the report from which these figures are taken remarks, 'One would, therefore, not expect the therapeutic results in such a group of cases to be as favourable as in other groups where the economic factor might act as an important spur in helping the sick patient adjust to his neurotic conflict and illness.'

The cases were all followed up for five years or more, and often as long as ten years after the period of disability had begun. The following criteria of recovery were used; they are much more explicit and at least as stringent as those used by most psychiatrists and psychoanalysts in their work: (1) Return to work, and ability to carry on well in economic adjustments for at least a five-year period; (2) Report of no further or very slight difficulties; (3) Making of successful social adjustments. It was found, using these criteria, that 72 per cent of the patients recovered after two years. Another 10, 5, and 4 per cent, respectively, recovered during successive years, so that altogether 90 per cent recovered after 5 years. Taking the two-year period as the most reasonable for comparative purposes, we find again, therefore, that in this sample also, two out of three neurotics recovered without benefit of psychotherapy.

This control group too is, of course, far from perfect. We cannot be sure that the cases considered were identical with those making up the experimental group. On the other hand, this control group complements the other one because now we are dealing with entirely voluntary, unhospitalized patients, coming from a relatively high socio-economic stratum, the majority being executives, teachers, clerical workers, and professional men. In a way, therefore, the deficiencies in the two samples cancel out and the fact remains that both give identical figures for spontaneous recovery.

We thus find that among neurotic patients being treated by psychoanalytic or eclectic psychotherapy, about two out of three recover. Similarly, among neurotics treated by their G.P. along non-psychotherapeutic lines, or obtaining simple custodial care, again two out of three improve. It is difficult to interpret these results as supporting in any way the hypothesis that psychotherapy has a beneficial effect. These are the facts: it would be easy to take them too seriously and conclude that psychotherapy had no effect at all. It would be equally easy – and equally wrong – to discard them altogether by saying that the data here summarized are too faulty to deserve serious consideration. The data are faulty, but they are the only ones in existence; if we are to look for any justification for modern psychotherapeutic practices, it is to them that we must look, and if we do that the conclusion is inescapable – not that they prove psychotherapy to be valueless, but rather that they fail conspicuously to show any positive consequences to follow its use. It is still possible that more adequate research may disclose such effects, but until such research has been carried out, we must surely conclude with the old Scottish verdict of *not proven*.

It may be interesting to consider how such more adequate research would have to be carried out. First and foremost, of course, we must insist on the provision of a control group, i.e. a group selected on the same basis as those receiving treatment but left without treatment for a given period. This requirement is basic, but it often arouses objections based on ethical principles. Can we justify the withholding of therapy, however insecurely it may be based, and however little we may know about its effects, from the person who is actually suffering at the moment? The dilemma thus created is a very real one, but the answer, fortunately, can be given without having to come to grips with it. Most hospitals have a long waiting list in any case, so that large numbers of people desirous of treatment are not, in actual fact, receiving it. All that the rigours of the experimental method would require, therefore, would be – not the condemnation of people who would otherwise have been treated, to a long period of non-treatment, but rather a selection, according to sampling principles, from among those who would not have been treated in any case for a long time, to serve as a control group. It is difficult to see any objection to this procedure on humane grounds, and surely on humane grounds there is little justification in arousing hope and causing people to spend much time and money on treatment procedures the effectiveness of which is unknown.

Granted, then, that we have an experimental group, who are to be given psychotherapy, and a control group, who are not, both selected in such a way as to be equal in age, proportion of males and females, educational background, socio-economic status, and, if possible, type and severity of disorder, we would subject both groups to a searching personality investigation by means of psychological and physiological test procedures. We would also obtain self-ratings from them with respect to a variety of relevant traits, and we would obtain objective information regarding their behaviour from relatives, ward sisters, and others in constant contact with them. After the experimental group had been given treatment, both groups would again be investigated along the same lines, and differences between them noted as being presumably due to the effects of psychotherapy.

As a next step, the control group would now receive psychotherapy and be investigated again at the end of that period, comparing changes made during this treatment period with changes taking place in the same group during the non-treatment period. Last of all, both groups would be followed up over a period of years to study the long-term effects of treatment.

In this brief sketch, I have passed over rather lightly what is perhaps a crucial point in such a study, namely, the accurate assessment of personality and personality changes without which the whole research would be valueless. Change in the patient may take place in a variety of different fields, and it is important to study all of these before drawing any conclusions. Thus, a patient may feel very much better but become an intolerable nuisance to his relatives; this is often alleged to happen after operational interference with the frontal lobes. It is impossible, therefore, to give an overall estimate of recovery; what is needed is a much more detailed investigation of precisely what changes have taken place. Self-ratings and observance of social behaviour are relatively easy to obtain in principle, although the detailed arrangements may require a good deal of technical skill; it is when we come to personality changes that a certain amount of ingenuity is needed.

The almost universal practice hitherto has been to have these qualities rated by the psychiatrist in charge of the case. There are many weighty objections against this practice. In the first place, these ratings are known to be highly unreliable in the sense that two different persons making the ratings, both being equally competent and knowledgeable, will often disagree to a considerable extent. But a rating which is not reliable cannot be valid and we cannot base our conclusions on unreliable and invalid data. In the second place, the psychiatrist treating his own case is emotionally involved in the success or failure of his treatment, or at least this possibility cannot be ruled out. Assessment must be free from the possibility of unconscious distortion of this type. It follows that we must find some alternative method of personality assessment. Probably the most objective and most valid type of assessment in this situation would be by means of objective tests. These tests are relatively unfamiliar to most people not directly working in this field, and a few words must therefore be devoted to a discussion of the rationale underlying them.

What do we mean when we say that a person is anxious? We mean that he blushes easily at the slightest provocation, his heart begins to race, his hands may tremble, his mouth goes dry, his digestion is affected, and various other physical phenomena of one kind or another will be evoked in him with great ease. These are the objective facts to which we may refer; we find that by and large they tend to accompany verbal reports of apprehension, unreasoning fear, depressive tendencies, and so forth. There is a close relationship between the mental reports of anxiety and the physical signs, just as there is a close correspondence between a verbal report of feeling hot and the physical measurement given by a thermometer.

When we compare two groups of people, one of which

quite obviously is in a highly anxious state, the other one quite obviously in a cool, calm, and collected frame of mind, we can show fairly easily that these two groups differ with respect to many objective measurements based on the physiological signs mentioned above. Thus, if we measure the heart-beat of people in the two groups under resting conditions and suddenly fire a blank cartridge into the air, there will be a much more rapid acceleration of heart-beat in the anxious than in the non-anxious group, and the return to normal will be much slower in the anxious group. Similarly, if we take a measure of muscular tension in these two groups, while the members are engaged on some kind of stress-producing mental work, we will find much greater muscular tension in the anxious than in the non-anxious group.

Alternatively, again, we may pass a slight electric current through the palm of our subject, registering the resistance offered to its passage through the skin. This resistance changes with emotional excitement, and if we ask our subjects an embarrassing question, or tell them to put their hands in a bowl full of ice-cold water, or warn them that they will receive an electric shock presently, the decrease in the resistance of the skin of the anxious group is very much greater, and the resistance takes very much longer to return to the normal state, than does that of the non-anxious group.

These are only some of the objective ways in which such a trait as anxiety can be measured. Another method which has become more and more important in recent work is by way of conditioned reflexes. Most people nowadays are familiar with the principle at least of the conditioned reflex. Offer a piece of meat to a dog and he will salivate. Ring a bell without showing the meat and the dog will not salivate. If, then, over a period of time you always ring a bell before giving the dog the meat, you will find that in the end the dog salivates when you ring the bell even without being given any meat. The unconditioned stimulus – the meat – by being constantly associated with the conditioned stimulus – the bell – has apparently transferred its power to evoke the response – salivation – in the animal to the conditioned stimulus.

In the human being, conditioning is rather more difficult to establish. The two most widely used methods are the eye-wink reflex, and the so-called psychogalvanic reflex. The eye-wink reflex occurs naturally when a blast of air is directed at the eye. This eye-wink can be measured exactly, either by taking a continuous film of the movement of the eyelid, or by attaching a thread to the eyelid which activates an ink-writing pen moving over the surface of a paper-covered rotating drum. By always ringing a bell before applying the blast of air, it is possible finally to obtain the eye-wink reflex as a response to the conditioned stimulus – the bell, even when the unconditioned stimulus – the blast of air – is omitted.

The psychogalvanic reflex has already been mentioned; it is the decrease in the resistance of the skin to the passage of an electric current when a sudden, emotionally exciting stimulus is applied. This can easily be conditioned in the following way. Exhibit to the subject a series of words, one at a time; one word – say the word 'cow' – is repeated at irregular intervals in this series. Whenever the word 'cow' appears, the subject is given an electric shock which provokes the psychogalvanic reflex. After a while, the appearance of the word 'cow' by itself has the effect of causing the psychogalvanic reflex to appear.

Conditioning is related to anxiety for the very simple reason that it has been shown conclusively that the ease with which a conditioned reflex is formed depends very much on the anxiety of the person on whom the experiment is being performed. Conditioned reflexes are formed very much more easily in anxious than non-anxious people. What is more, there is a good deal of what is called 'stimulus generalization' in the anxious person. This is a technical term referring to the tendency of conditioned reflexes to occur even though the conditioned stimulus may be slightly different from the one to which the subject had been originally conditioned. If in the dog the conditioned salivation is to a sound of 216 cycles per second, the dog will also respond with salivation if you suddenly produce a sound of 340 or 580 cycles per second. The more unlike the original sound the new sound is, the less is the conditioned response, until, finally, when the dissimilarity is too great, there is no response at all. There is thus a gradient from stimuli very much like the original one, and causing a strong response, to stimuli not very much like the original one, causing little or no response. This gradient is very much steeper for non-anxious people than for anxious ones. In other words, the anxious person reacts to stimuli quite unlike the original one with almost the same strength as he does to stimuli very much like the original one, while the non-anxious person discriminates very much better between them.

This lack of discrimination of the anxious person also comes out in a different type of conditioning experiment in which the subject is conditioned to expect an electric shock to sound A, and not to expect an electric shock to sound B. In the non-anxious person, this discrimination can be established fairly easily so that after a while, when sound A is produced, there is a decrease in skin response, whereas when sound B is produced there is none. This discrimination also is much more difficult to produce in the anxious person, who will respond to both sounds with a strong decrease in resistance.

By discrimination here, I do not, of course, mean conscious discrimination. If you asked the anxious person whether sounds A and B were different, he would be able to answer correctly just as much as the non-anxious person; his perceptual capacities are not the cause of his difficulties. This is brought out particularly well in some recent work on what has been called 'subception'. In this experiment, the investigator exhibits ten words in random order to his subject, using what is called a tachistoscope, i.e. an instrument for showing cards or slides or pictures for very short periods of time. The time is regulated in such a way that the subjects cannot always recognize the word, nor do they always fail to recognize the word exhibited. Having established the speed at which the subject can respond correctly part of the time, the investigator then conditions the subject's psychogalvanic response to five of these words but not to the other five. He then again exhibits all ten words in random order to the subject, asking him which of the ten has just been shown. The interesting and important finding from this research is that when a word is shown to which the psychogalvanic reflex has been conditioned, the reflex often occurs, although the subject reports that the word he has seen was one of those that had not been conditioned. In other words, although at the level of conscious perception the subject is wrong, and thinks he is dealing with a neutral word, nevertheless his nervous system reacts correctly to the word as a conditioned stimulus. Thus, there is the clear cleavage between conscious report and unconscious emotional reaction which we find again and again in the responses of neurotic and anxious subjects.

After this digression we must come back to our original question. We have seen that we must rule out the psychiatrist's report of changes in the anxiety of his patients for various reasons. As a substitute we must then make use of objective measures, such as those mentioned above. We must establish the reactions to stress and frustration which are apparent in the tenseness and the autonomic reactions of our patients. (The autonomic system is a part of the human nervous system which is particularly concerned with breathing, heart-beat, blood supply, digestion, and other non-voluntary responses of the human organism; it is most closely related to emotional reactions and their expression.) We must investigate the rate at which they form conditioned reflexes, the degree to which stimulus generalization takes place, and the extent to which discrimination is impaired. These are only a few of the large number of objective measures which we can use for the purpose. It is not necessary to give a complete list in order to show what could be done along these lines if we wanted to investigate the hypothesis that the degree of anxiety of our patients was significantly reduced as a result of psychotherapy.

I have purposely discussed only one particular symptom. What is true of anxiety is true of many other traits and symptoms which might be hypothesized to change under therapy. In each case, we start with a rather vague idea of what it is that we are after. This vague idea is then refined and improved, an attempt is made to obtain an operational definition of it, i.e. a definition in terms of some definite experimental operation which can be duplicated by others with the same result, and gradually the term which started out as a very subjective kind of rating begins to take on the properties of exact definition and measurement which characterize scientific usage.

What is the probability that objective measurement of this type would disclose any marked effects of psychotherapy? There is good evidence to suggest that neurotic reactions appear largely on an inherited basis and that a person's liability to break down under stress is a property of his nervous system, which is unlikely to be affected to any considerable extent by psychotherapy. This view is opposed in many ways to much current speculation along Freudian lines, which, as is well known, claims that the major factors in the creation of a neurosis are environmental happenings which take place mainly in the family circle, and particularly in the first five years of life. Much of the support for this Freudian view is based on a fallacy, a fallacy which has quite a respectable history in psychology. It was found very early in the present century that there was a considerable correlation between the intelligence of parents and children. This caused hereditarians to argue that intelligence must be inherited, seeing that obviously the children were similar to their parents with respect to intelligence by way of heredity. Environmentalists, on the other hand, used the same findings to support their claims by saying that the similarity in intelligence in parents and children was obviously due to the fact that intelligent parents provided a stimulating environment to their children, whereas dull parents provided a dull environment to their children. It took a few years before both sides realized that the fact of similarity between parents and children by itself is neutral with respect to the question of heredity or environment.

This lesson does not seem to have been learned, however, by psychoanalysts, who in the field of personality development still claim that the correlation implies a definite causal sequence. Thus, for instance, the Freudians believe that a certain pessimistic outlook is caused by early weaning, whereas late weaning causes optimism in the child. There is, indeed, evidence showing that some such correlation exists and that children who had been weaned early tend to grow up somewhat more pessimistic and conservative than children who were weaned late. It is not necessary, however, to assume that it is the early weaning, i.e. an environmental influence, which causes the later behaviour pattern. It is equally plausible to assume that pessimistic, depressed mothers tend to have pessimistic, depressed children, this being an inherited tendency, and also that pessimistic and depressed mothers tend to wean their children earlier, or indeed are unable to feed them at the breast for any length of time. Thus, the fact of the observed correlation can be accounted for equally easily in terms of heredity and environment, and what is true in this particular case is equally true with respect to many other examples given by the Freudians in support of their hypothesis. What is required is direct evidence rather than this one-sided interpretation of essentially ambiguous results, and such data as are available, particularly from the study of identical and fraternal twins, seem to favour rather strongly the view that heredity plays a very conspicuous part indeed in the causation of neurotic disorders.

This view of neuroticism as hereditarily determined may seem to run counter to our discussion of the recovery rate among neurotics, which appeared reasonably high both with and without psychotherapy. How, it may be asked, can there be any kind of recovery if neuroticism is caused by inherited factors? The answer is that one must carefully distinguish between *neuroticism*, i.e. the inherited emotional instability which predisposes a person to form neurotic symptoms under stress, and ultimately to have a nervous breakdown; and *neurosis*, the result of the imposition of emotional stress on a nervous system predisposed to react through the neurotic mechanisms. Neurosis may appear in a person showing little emotional instability, through overwhelmingly strong environmental stress; it may fail to appear in a person strongly predisposed, because of lack of environmental stress. There is an obvious comparison of neuroticism and neurosis on the one hand and intelligence and education on the other. A very intelligent person, though predisposed to react favourably to education, may yet be ignorant because of lack of educational facilities in the neighbourhood; a rather dull person, though lacking in innate ability, may yet acquire a modicum of knowledge through special coaching and training. We are not likely to change the innate, predisposing factor through psychotherapy or any other technique which does not interfere surgically with the central nervous system; we may hope, however, to relieve the environmental stress causing the exacerbation of the predisposing factors, just as we may hope to improve the educational facilities, lack of which is preventing so many people from reaching a standard of education for which their innate abilities would qualify them.

11

PSYCHOANALYSIS, HABIT, AND CONDITIONING

FOR many years now, there has been very little opposition to the claims of psychoanalysts that theirs was the only theory which accounted for the presence and form of neurotic symptoms, and that equally theirs was the only admissible form of therapy. While psychiatrists in general have taken those claims with a grain of salt, and while there have been considerable advances in the physical methods of treatment, yet the majority of neurotic disorders have nearly always been treated by some form of psychotherapy.

In recent years, there has been growing up a good deal of dissatisfaction with this position. The failure of psychotherapists to give proof of the efficacy of their procedures, noted in the preceding chapter, has been only one of many contributory causes. Another one has been the growth of a firmly based psychological theory of learning, which offers an alternative explanation to the Freudian one of many of the phenomena of neuroses. Until quite recently this alternative hypothesis had not given rise to actual practical measures, and consequently no direct comparison was possible. In recent years, however, there have been considerable advances along this line and for the sake of an example we may consider the new approach in its application to a problem that has bothered humanity for many hundreds and, indeed, thousands of years. That is the problem of enuresis.

Pliny already reports on the great concern which the ancients felt about this incontinence of urine, and tells us that the most common folk-remedy for this condition was to feed the afflicted child with boiled mice. Other remedies included the wearing of a clean smock at baptism and the consumption of wood lice and the urine of spayed swine.

These somewhat odd methods find their complement in more recent medical history, which is replete with recommendations of innumerable drugs and hormones, special diets, injections, operations, electrical and other stimulation, and such varied recommendations as sleeping on the back and not sleeping on the back. Most of these methods seem to work, up to a point, in the hands of those who believe in them, but on the whole success has been relatively poor.

Freud, as one might have expected, succeeded in introducing a sexual angle into the study of enuresis, maintaining that 'whenever *enuresis nocturna* does not represent an epileptic attack, it corresponds to a pollution'. Others have argued that enuresis is an hysterical manifestation through which deep-seated anxieties are 'converted into a physical symptom'. These and similar psychiatric views have led to the problem being regarded as essentially one of psychological influences and determinants, and consequently treatment nowadays is largely through some form of psychotherapy. Success, on the whole, is not achieved in a very large proportion of the cases, except in so far as many children after the passage of a year or two tend to have spontaneous remission of the symptoms in any case. One psychiatrist who held the view that enuresis was entirely dependent on personality dynamics obtained cures in only 50 per cent of the cases treated by him.

Quite different would be the view taken by those who look upon control of the bladder as a problem in learning theory, and enuresis as a failure in learning. Using the principle of conditioning, Mowrer argued somewhat along these lines : extension of the bladder in the neurotic child does not lead to awakening but to a reflex sphincter relaxation, and therefore to the onset of urination. What is needed is some mechanism that would cause the child to awake when the bladder was distended but before the reflex sphincter relaxation took place. He accordingly suggested a rather neat instrument, which takes advantage of the electrolytic properties of urine. He developed a special type of pad, consisting of two thicknesses of heavy absorbent fabric, which served to separate two equally large pieces of bronze screening. This combination is quilted together and is light in weight, durable, and not uncomfortable for the child to sleep on. While the pad is dry, there is no electric contact between the two pieces of screening. As soon as the urine strikes the pad, however, it quickly penetrates the fabric and makes a contact. This contact makes an electric circuit, which causes a bell to ring, which in turn wakes up the child, during the process of urination. The child then goes to the bathroom to complete the process.

According to the principles of conditioning, the frequent correlation of bladder distension and being awakened because of the bell ringing should produce final awakening to the bladder distension itself (the conditioned stimulus), even though the bell (the unconditioned stimulus) is now withdrawn, and it would be expected, therefore, that after a number of repetitions the child would now wake up before urination takes place. This method, which had actually been used by others before Mowrer, ever since the turn of the century, is said to give extremely good results. Mowrer reports 100 per cent success and others who have used the method concur in its unusual effectiveness. Personality changes, in so far as they have been observed, have tended to be in a favourable direction, and in no case has there been any evidence of 'symptom substitution'. This is important because it is sometimes said that any attempt to deal directly with the problem of enuresis would necessarily result in the child's developing some other kind of symptom.

Mowrer rightly points out that the difference in attitude which gives rise to the conditioning and the psychotherapeutic methods of treatment, respectively, are perennial points of dispute between clinician and educator. To the specialist engaged mainly in therapeutic work, the bad effects of education are most obvious and he is likely, therefore, to have a poor view of training in education. The educator, on the other hand, as the authorized agent for perpetuating accepted values and traditional ways of culture, is likely to value more highly the importance of his calling. This difference in attitude easily leads to charges by the clinician that the educator is brutal and sadistic, and to the countercharge by the educator that the clinician is idealistic and unrealistic. This is a much wider problem than can possibly be dealt with here; there does seem to be a distinct tendency in contemporary culture for the educator to be replaced by the clinician, not because of any conscious and deliberate policy or because there are any facts showing the superiority of the one approach over the other, but rather for non-rational and emotional reasons.

There is a good deal of room here for investigation, and, indeed, the problem is a very crucial one to the psychologist because it involves the whole question of just what it is that constitutes a neurosis. Mowrer, for instance, points out that much current psychotherapy is predicated on the assumption that neurosis is simply a result of mislearning and over-learning, and much time is accordingly spent in trying to get the patient to 'reality test', i.e. to perform X, which he has long thought of as dangerous but which realistically is not, and to discriminate between 'then' and 'now', i.e. 'to see that conditions have changed, that attitudes, beliefs, and practices which, though perhaps justified at an earlier stage in the patient's life history, are no longer necessary or useful'.

Opposed to this general view is Mowrer's stress on the inadequacy of the learning of the neurotic. As he points out, the growing human being has to master that enormous accumulation of vicarious learning which we call culture. Some items of culture provide no difficulty as they serve to solve immediate problems, but culture also contains elements which at least in the early stages of life are unwelcome to the human animal. These are the moral injunctions which are necessary for the continued functioning of the group, but which to the infant appear foreign and function-less, mere barriers in his path to satisfaction and pleasure. From this point of view, culture stands for restraint, re-nunciation, and sacrifice. It forces the human mind to live in the future rather than in the present. The difficulties in the way of achieving this learning are very great and the neurotic, in Mowrer's view, is a person who has failed to carry out this learning, who has failed to achieve the integration which is dependent on acquiring this cultural heritage.

The difference between these two views is very marked, and it is clearly imperative to choose between them as they give rise to quite different principles of treatment for the neurotic. The Freudian view favours the clinical, Mowrer's view favours the educational approach. There is all too little experimental evidence available to decide between these two approaches and it is here perhaps even more than in the practical field that these experiments on enuresis are important. The success of the educational, and the relative failure of the therapeutic, approach here cannot necessarily be generalized to other fields, but they indicate at least that there is some factual support for hypotheses alternative to the Freudian and psychoanalytic ones and that more effort should be put into the construction of therapies not based on the particular hypothesis Freud enunciated in the closing years of the nineteenth century.

I have dealt at some length with enuresis, but it should not be thought that conditioning is applicable only to this particular disorder. Another example of conditioned reflex treatment can be found in the field of alcoholism. In some form or other, the idea of outbalancing the craving for alcohol by means of a revulsion established artificially goes back a long way; Pliny may again be quoted as discussing quite a number of methods apparently used in his time. Modern methods are based on the use of drugs, such as emetine hydrochloride, the injection of which produces nausea and vomiting. The conditioning procedure is as follows. The patient is taken to a room, arranged in such a way that all distracting stimuli are eliminated. Treatments are given in the morning because patients react better when fasted and rested. After preliminary medication the emetine is then injected, and immediately prior to the expected vomiting attack the patient is exposed to the sight, smell, and taste of those alcoholic beverages which he preferred in his drinking days. These sessions last about half an hour and are repeated daily for five or six days. They are followed by half a dozen preventive one-day treatments (reinforcements) given at intervals ranging from four to twelve weeks. Thus, the whole procedure takes about a year; sometimes further reinforcements are given during the second year.

Theoretically, this application of conditioning procedures seems perfectly sound. The conditioned stimulus, the alcohol, becomes associated with the unconditioned stimulus, the emetine injection, and after a number of repetitions the unconditioned response, vomiting, tends to recur after the application of the conditioned stimulus, i.e. at the sight, smell, and taste of alcohol. Results of this procedure are rather encouraging and, on the whole, superior to those which have been reached by psychotherapy. Here then is another field in which firmly established habits can be broken up by the conditioning method of retraining and relearning.

Conditioning, however, is only one of many possible methods of habit-breaking in the armamentarium of the psychologist. A second one, which is very satisfactory when it can be applied, is that of substitution. If it is desired to get rid of habit A, it is often possible to substitute a habit B, which is innocuous but which makes use of the same motor pathways as habit A, and thereby inhibits it. A very simple example of this is the use of chewing-gum in order to get rid of the smoking habit. It is impossible to smoke at the same time as you are chewing gum, and consequently, if you develop a gum-chewing habit you will automatically reduce the number of cigarettes you smoke. This was realized quite clearly by the cigarette manufacturers when chewing-gum was first placed on the market, and their alarmed reactions paid tribute to this method of habit destruction.

There are, however, many unsatisfactory features about the substitution method. In the first place, the substitute habit may be worse than the original one; many people would regard gum-chewing as being even less desirable than cigarette smoking. In the second place, some people manage to combine two activities which, in theory at least, are antagonistic, and no one who has ever seen a Texas cowboy chewing gum, smoking, talking, eating, and drinking whisky all at the same time, will feel terribly confident about the antagonistic action of these various oral activities. In the third place, it is usually very difficult to find any habit which will act as a substitute and which the prospective habit destroyer is willing to take up. For all these reasons, the substitution method is of rather limited usefulness.

Quite the opposite is true of a third variety of habit-destroying mechanism, namely, that of suggestion. We cannot be said to understand at all well the way in which suggestion works, but there is ample factual evidence to leave us in no doubt about its potential power. One typical experiment, for instance, was concerned with the efficacy of suggestion as compared with orthodox medical treatment in getting rid of warts. Two groups of children were used, the control group, which received ordinary treatment for their warts, and the experimental group, which was submitted to suggestion treatment. This consisted essentially in drawing a picture of the child's hand, with the wart on it, on a large sheet of paper, and then, with a certain amount of hocus pocus, drawing circles around the wart and reducing its size on the picture day by day until the wart had completely disappeared in the picture. This procedure, which makes use of suggestibility no less than the famous method used by Tom Sawyer in *Huckleberry Finn*, was shown to be far more effective than the orthodox medical treatment; more warts disappeared in response to suggestion in the experimental groups than did among the members of the control group.

Nor is it necessary for suggestion to be conscious in order to be effective. There is one rather interesting experiment which has troubled thoughtful people a good deal. Nail biting is known to be a habit particularly resistant to extinction. In this experiment a number of nail-biting children were brought together and arbitrarily divided into an experimental group and a control group. Nothing was done with the children in the control group, who slept togther in a large room adjacent to another large room in which the experimental group children were sleeping. Both groups were observed over a period of a month to study the effects of the therapeutic agent on the experimental group. This therapeutic agent was simply a large electric gramophone which was put on rather softly after the children had gone to sleep and which repeated endlessly 'I will not bite my finger nails. Finger nail biting is a dirty habit. I will never bite my finger nails again', and so on. The record was not put on until the children were asleep and it was taken off before they woke up in the morning. None of them reported at the end of the experiment that they had heard the record at all. Nevertheless, there was a very marked effect of the suggestion; far more children in the experimental group left off nail biting than did in the control group. Thus does reality catch up with the wild extravagant fantasies of Huxley's *Brave New World*!

The most frequent use of suggestibility, however, has been in connexion with hypnosis, particularly in relation to a phenomenon known as post-hypnotic suggestibility. This is a very curious phenomenon which has been known for well over a hundred years. A suggestion is given to a person in the hypnotic trance, telling him that after waking up he will carry out a certain act. The suggestion may be to the effect that he will go out of the room, pick up an umbrella, bring it back and open it up in front of an audience at a given time, say when the clock chimes five, or when the experimenter blows his nose. The subject will in almost every case carry out the suggestion. If asked later why he did this particular thing, he will rationalize his conduct by some kind of semi-reasonable explanation. Thus, he may say, for instance, that as the group was talking about superstitions, he just got the umbrella and put it up in the room to show that he was not superstitious. To anyone acquainted with the real motive, namely, the post-hypnotic suggestion, these pseudo-motives are very interesting because they are so similar to the pseudo-motives often given by people to justify actions the real reasons for which are unconscious to themselves, or, if conscious, dishonourable.

These post-hypnotic suggestions are very strong indeed. On one occasion a person who had a considerable degree of knowledge of hypnotic procedures was hypnotized with his consent, and he was told that at the end of the hypnotic session he would be awakened, and ten minutes later the hypnotist would blow his nose. At this signal he was to get up from his chair, go across the room, and sit down in another chair. When the time came and the hypnotist blew his nose, the subject became vaguely uneasy and finally said, 'Look here, I feel a definite compulsion to go over to that chair. I bet you have given me a post-hypnotic suggestion. Well, I'm darned if I will go all the same.' After this, he took part in the discussion for a few more minutes and then finally, and quite suddenly, got up, crossed the room and sat down in the other chair. Thus, even when a person is trying consciously to fight the post-hypnotic suggestion and is fully conscious of it, he may nevertheless give in in the end.

Many attempts have been made to use this type of suggestion for the breaking of habits. Hypnotizing a person and telling him that in the future the sight of alcohol will make him recoil with feelings of nausea and horror does work for a while, but after two or three days the force of the suggestion declines and finally disappears completely. It could be maintained by rehypnotizing the patient every few days, but for various reasons this procedure is not practicable and not recommended.

While the effects of a post-hypnotic suggestion wear off with many repetitions, there is evidence that post-hypnotic suggestions may remain active for an astonishingly long time. Authentic cases have been reported where a person was told to write a post-card, using a certain form of words, to the hypnotist at 12 o'clock noon of that same day in a year's time, and the hypnotized subject, although quite unconscious of this suggestion, carried it out in every detail. There thus appears to be a good deal of promise in this method; the reason why, at the moment, it does not appear to be particularly useful is connected with the unfortunate associations which the term hypnosis arouses in so many people. Stage exhibitions and quackery of one kind or another have brought hypnosis into disrepute, and few people are willing to risk their reputation by doing the necessary experimental work which alone can take phenomena like post-hypnotic suggestion out of the category of odd and interesting happenings and, by explaining their mechanism, make them subservient to human welfare.

Apart from conditioning, substitution, and suggestion, there is one further method for the breaking of habits which is firmly based on psychological principles, although at first sight it may appear to be somewhat paradoxical. The nature of habit is obviously that of automatic, unconscious repetition. This was fully understood by the poet who wrote of the centipede's plight when his conscious attention was drawn to the movement of his innumerable feet. While he was going along by habit and without paying attention he was doing all right; the moment he tried to repeat the movement pattern consciously, he became hopelessly lost and could not move an inch. In a milder form this is true of human locomotion, too. If the reader will try and run down the stairs, not in the usual automatic way of not paying attention to the actual movement, but consciously directing his attention to each step, deciding each time exactly where he will put his feet, he will very soon find himself at the bottom of the stairs with a broken leg and a firm conviction of the importance of unconscious habit. The same principle, of course, explains the efficacy of the golfer's gamesmanship who draws his opponent's attention to details of his swing and follow-through. While these are carried on automatically they work perfectly well; the moment conscious attention is paid to them, however, they cease to become habits and become new and difficult achievements. In other words, you may break a habit by taking it out of the field of

unconscious and repetitive behaviour and by paying close
attention to all the details of it.

How does this principle work in actual practice? Dunlap
made considerable use of it in disrupting habit patterns
which were resistant to other types of therapy. A child who
persistently bit his nails, for instance, would be told to go
for half an hour every day, sit in front of the psychologist
and consistently, painstakingly, and consciously bite his
nails throughout that period. A persistent smoker who could
not give up the habit was told to come day after day to sit
with the psychologist for an hour and smoke cigarette after
cigarette without respite, consciously paying attention to
every inhalation and to all the sensations in his throat and
mouth. Nail biting and cigarette smoking soon disappeared
from the habitual activities of the subjects, and the cure
appeared to be relatively permanent. Dunlap applied his
principles in other fields too, and showed that paradoxical
as the prescription of carrying on with the habit which you
are trying to break may sound, it nevertheless was impress-
ively successful in a large number of cases. Again, as in the
case of suggestion, there has been little follow-up of this
principle, largely because of the all-pervading faith in
psychotherapy, which characterizes modern psychology and
psychiatry. In spite of repeated failures with alcoholic
neurotics, nail biters, drug addicts, and so forth, psychotherapists still claim that their procedures are the only ones
applicable to the correction of this type of habit. Fortunately there are signs that a more critical view is coming to
the fore and that experiments with other methods will be
carried out to show just how much can be done with them.
There is a sound theoretical basis for the procedures described here – conditioning, substitution, suggestion, and
repetition – and any increase in our knowledge of the basic
processes underlying these methods will undoubtedly be
reflected in the efficacy of the treatment based thereon.

Possible combination of two or three methods will probably not only be more efficacious than any one of them, but
may multiply its usefulness. The most useful part for psycho-

therapy to play may be not as a *substitute* for these more fundamental methods but rather as an *adjunct*. Some of the writers who have used habit-breaking methods of the type described here have added a statement to the effect that in their view, psychotherapy should accompany the treatment. That seems a reasonable point of view; there are stresses and strains arising in the breaking of any firmly anchored habit which may require the help of an outsider, as they would otherwise be beyond the patient's ability to bear without impairing his nervous stability. But this point again is subject to experimental scrutiny; all we can safely say is that the habits of emotional maladjustment which either accompany or, in the opinion of some, form the nucleus of neurotic disorders, may with advantage be attacked by new methods whose usefulness in this connexion has already been shown, and whose theoretical justification promises well for their success.

12

WHAT IS WRONG WITH
PSYCHOANALYSIS?

IT is impossible to deny that Freudian theories have had a tremendous influence on psychiatry, on literature, and perhaps also on that whole complex of laws, folkways, and *mores* which we often refer to as 'sexual morality'. Moralists are inclined to doubt whether this influence has been essentially for the good, but after the initial outcry which was perhaps inevitable most people have settled down to an easy and even enthusiastic acceptance of psychoanalysis. This acceptance is not altogether in line with psychoanalytic teaching, which would lead one to anticipate resistance and hostility. Such resistance and hostility as there are can be found almost exclusively among psychologists and anthropologists, i.e. among those who have made a professional and detailed study of the theories and claims of psychoanalysts; among lay people the terms 'psychology' and 'psychoanalysis' have come to be almost synonymous, and in the literary world Freudian terms and concepts have been accepted so completely that modern novels are frequently indistinguisable from psychiatric case records.

This would appear to be an almost unique phenomenon in science. In no other science are we likely to find certain theories and hypotheses popularly accepted but rejected by many experts in that science. There are a few cases where this has been known to happen; the Lysenko affair has shown that in genetics also *vox populi* may be *vox dei*, to the extent of having genuine scientists excommunicated and threatened for not accepting views the evidence for which was practically non-existent, but which found favour with lay judges. Possibly another parallel may be found in the history of the heliocentric theory of the universe in which laymen supported those who believed the earth to be the centre of the world, against the consensus of opinion of those best qualified to judge.

In thus equating psychoanalysis with popular opinion we may seem to be moving in a topsy-turvy world. Is not Freud the great innovator, comparable with Galileo or Darwin? Is it not true that like these great scientific geniuses he also was at first stoned by the common multitude, only to be recognized and honoured after many years of persecution? Perhaps this apparent paradox is not quite as paradoxical as it may seem.

There are two kinds of psychology, just as there are two ways in which we may approach any other set of phenomena. Eddington has contrasted these two approaches in his famous example of the two tables – the sensible table, which we can see and touch, which has weight and thickness, and is part of our everyday environment, and the scientific table, made up of electrons and protons, consisting essentially of nothingness interrupted by extremely fast-moving electric charges. We may accept the scientific table on the authority of the physicist's say-so, and because we have found in the past that predictions based on the physicist's view of the world tend to be correct; nevertheless, most of us find it impossible to look at the world consistently in this fashion, and prefer to deal rather with sensible entities which in some mysterious way we think we understand. It is obvious to us that the earth is flat, that the sun moves around the earth, and that you cannot make a silk purse out of a sow's ear. We may give up these views reluctantly and under protest when the factual support for the contrary views becomes too strong, but we usually do so with very bad grace, and a secret hankering after the good old ways.

The same opposition occurs with even greater force in psychology. German philosophers have brought out this point quite clearly in contrasting *verstehende* psychology with *erklärende* psychology, i.e. a common-sense psychology which tries to *understand* human beings, and a psychology which tries to *explain* their conduct on a scientific basis. It is often said that psychology has a long past, but a short history;

it is the common-sense type of psychology which has been the stand-by of writers, philosophers, and all others who had to deal with human beings, and which accounts for the long past, but it is the explanatory, scientific type of psychology which arose towards the end of the last century which is referred to as having had the short history. These two kinds of psychology are so frequently mixed up that a few words may be useful in clarifying the issue.

In our dealings with people we can hardly be said to proceed on a haphazard basis of pure chance. Experience teaches us to expect certain reactions from certain types of people; close acquaintance may enable us to predict with considerable accuracy the reactions of our friends, or of members of our family. We may know quite well that Mary is a bit old-maidenish, so that it is better not to tell risqué stories in front of her, while Joan is a bit of a fly-by-night who can always be relied upon to liven up a party. Dick is reliable and so honest that one would not be well advised to discuss in front of him ways and means of obtaining income tax relief which departed ever so little from the paths of rectitude, while Fred is forever cutting corners, and is quite likely one day to overdo it and find himself in jail. Dolores is 'one for the boys' and 'an easy lay'; Mac is a tightwad and High Church; Jim has no money sense at all and tends to take a scientific view of most things; Dolly is a 'one-man woman' and house-proud. We all make these generaliza-tions with respect to the people we know well, and we are quite prepared to act on them. We may even pride ourselves on our 'understanding of human nature', and on the accuracy of our diagnosis. We often believe that such judge-ments can with accuracy be formed almost at first sight, and many people go as far as to think that external physical signs, such as a weak chin, or red hair, or a Jewish nose, are infallible signs of a person's character. We may not know consciously how we arrive at our judgements, but we will defend to the death our claim to their correctness.

Similar judgements are made every day on the physical plane also. We judge things to be heavy or light, we consider the air to be humid or dry, we expect material objects to fall when they are unsupported. We should be surprised to find that water did not wet us, or the sun did not heat us. We have a whole set of expectations built up through experience, and fortunately for us these expectations are frequently right.

Some physical concepts may appear similar to those of everyday life, e.g. those of time and space. It is, however, important to realize that they are far from identical. Newton has pointed out in the *Scholium* which precedes his *Principia*, that sensed time and sensed space, i.e. our everyday notions of these concepts, are not to be confused with 'true or mathematical' time and space; anyone who confuses the two 'is guilty of vulgar ignorance'. Physical science does not attempt to *understand* everyday phenomena in common-sense terms, although ultimately it started out from this type of observation; physical science tries to *explain* natural phenomena in terms of laws of wide generality which subsume the individual phenomenon in question.

Exactly the same is true of psychology. The 'understanding' psychologist is trying to gain an intuitive insight into the working of another person's mind on the basis of his common-sense knowledge of human nature. He may have derived his knowledge from self-observation and introspection, or from the observation of other people in a great variety of situations, or even from reading Shakespearian plays and modern novels; there is no denying that he is often amazingly astute and accurate in his intuitions. This type of insight, based on wide experience and probably natural aptitude and interest in human beings, is a very valuable quality in many walks of life, and almost indispensable in the psychiatrist, the personnel manager, the social leader, and the politician. However, valuable and useful as it may be, psychological insight and understanding by themselves have nothing whatsoever to do with psychology as a science, just as little as facility in dealing with physical 'things' is an essential asset for the physical scientist. From observation I venture to assert that many of the greatest psychologists are if anything below average in this quality of 'insight' into human motives and purposes, and similarly physicists of the highest standing are frequently incapable of adjusting the carburettor in their cars, or even of fixing a burned-out fuse. The expectation frequently voiced, namely, that psychologists should have learned a lot about 'human nature', using the term in this sense, is quite unjustified. The psychologist knows no more about 'human nature' than the next man, and if he is wise he will not let his claims outrun his discretion.

If the psychologist as a scientist is not trying to understand other people, then what precisely is he trying to do? He is trying to explain their conduct in terms of a system of general scientific laws. In doing so he may use terms which he has taken over from everyday speech, terms like intelligence, emotion, trait, type, ability, and so forth, just as the physicist took over terms like space, time, weight, mass, and many others from the language of his day. But it would be an error to equate the muddled, inexact, ill-defined terms of common usage with the exact, precisely defined, clear-cut concepts of the scientist. There are similarities, and a certain amount of overlap, but there certainly is nothing approaching complete correspondence.

This fact often leads to misunderstanding. The psychologist makes a statement regarding, say, the inheritance of intelligence, using that word in a relatively precise way to stand for a set of measurable phenomena. The layman understands the statement to refer to his own idea of intelligence, which may be and usually is rather different from that of the psychologist, and offers objections which are not at all relevant to the intent of the original statement. The psychologist finds it difficult to counter these criticisms because all the terms he uses have special connotations which would require explanation, frequently involving highly complex mathematics, and all of which can only be understood in terms of the whole system of thought of which they form a part. These bars to understanding are particularly mischievous because their presence is often quite

H

unsuspected, and the argument may go on for hours and hours without reconciling the positions of the protagonists in the slightest. Scientific statements are highly complex statements deriving their meaning essentially from a whole set of facts, hypotheses, and theories; they cannot meaningfully be debated in the absence of full knowledge of all these facts, theories, and hypotheses.

How are these considerations relevant to psychoanalysis? Perhaps I can best make clear the connexion by stating quite briefly and dogmatically that psychoanalysis in my view is trying to *understand*, rather than to *explain*; that consequently it is essentially non-scientific and to be judged in terms of belief and faith, rather than in terms of proof and verification; and that lastly its great popularity among non-scientists derives precisely from its non-scientific nature, which makes it intelligible and immediately applicable to problems of 'understanding' other people. This judgement I believe to be a statement of fact, rather than a value judgement. Religion and art are two other non-scientific disciplines which in spite of their lack of concern with scientific truth have contributed greatly to human happiness; to say that they are less valuable than science implies a scale of standards and values which itself is subjective and non-scientific. To judge whether a given discipline is or is not scientific is possible without value implications; it necessitates nothing but a commonly agreed definition and standard of scientific procedure. Such a definition and such standards exist, and may be found in the writings of logicians and philosophers of scientific methodology; those who are acquainted with these writings will agree that in spite of occasional disagreements on minor issues there is an overwhelming amount of agreement on the main points.

Many psychoanalysts would probably agree with this analysis, and maintain that their work differed in many important respects from orthodox scientific procedures. Jung is but one of a large number of analysts who consciously reject scientific methodology in favour of subjectivity, intuition, and unconscious 'understanding'. There can be no argument here; those who look for religion, faith, beauty, or other non-scientific values need fear no scientific criticism. Neither, on the other hand, should they make any claims to having established scientific truths; they cannot reject the methods of science and yet claim the results. This desire to have the best of both worlds is very frequent among analysts, but it would be difficult to proffer any logical argument in its defence. Non-scientific analysts may, of course, quite frequently be right in their surmises, hunches, and intuitive insights, just as many people who have never heard of psychology or of psychoanalysis are often astonishingly astute in their understanding of human motives. To be correct in particular instances is not necessarily a sign of the scientific worth or correctness of one's views, theories, or hypotheses. (The obverse of this statement is more nearly true; to be wrong in particular instances discredits a scientific theory to such an extent that it needs to be replaced completely by another, or at least heavily revised.)

While thus many analysts disclaim any intention of being scientific in their work, no such thing could be said of the great majority who in their writings claim that what they say is not merely useful, interesting, exciting, and ingenious, but also true in the scientific sense of that term. Freud himself certainly held such a view, and most of his followers would probably agree with his contention. This makes it possible to apply our agreed criterion, and to see to what extent psychoanalysis lives up to its pretensions.

It is here already that many analysts enter their first objection. They say that traditional ideas as to what constitutes scientific method and scientific truth are unduly narrow, and that the proof they are willing to offer is none the less scientific for lying outside the confines of orthodoxy. In other words, starting out with the claim that 'psychoanalytic conclusions are scientific truths', a claim which is interesting only because we have come to appreciate that 'scientific' truths tend to be correct because they have been arrived at by a particular method, the analysts immediately proceed to alter the meaning of 'scientific' in such a way as to make it include the psychoanalytic findings in question. Such habits of subtle redefinition are, of course, quite familiar in politics; prestige words like 'democracy' are frequently applied to dictatorships by a process of definition which turns their customary meaning inside out. The high-priest of all who indulge in this pastime, of course, is Humpty Dumpty, whose discussion of the meaning of 'glory' has become a classic in the art of sowing semantic confusion.

'I don't know what you mean by "glory",' Alice said. Humpty Dumpty smiled comtemptuously. 'Of course you don't – till I tell you. I meant "there's a nice knock-down argument for you!".' 'But "glory" doesn't mean "a nice knock-down argument",' Alice objected. 'When *I* use a word' Humpty Dumpty said in rather a scornful tone, 'it means just what I choose it to mean – neither more nor less.' 'The question is', said Alice, 'whether you *can* make words mean so many different things.' 'The question is', said Humpty Dumpty, 'which is to be Master – that's all.'

A well-known exponent of this practice, Mrs Baker Eddy, redefined 'science' in terms of religion, thus arriving at Christian Science. Communists redefine 'science' in terms of Marxian 'dialectical materialism', thus arriving at the 'people's democracies' with their 'dictatorship of the proletariat'. The palmist of Brighton pier redefines 'science' in terms of her particular mercenary art, thus arriving at 'scientific fortune-telling'. The claim that psychoanalysis is scientific has no ascertainable meaning whatever unless we define the term 'science' in the way agreed on by the great majority of those who have considered the history and practice of science. This is the important question; whether psychoanalysis is scientific in some other meaning of the term, created merely in order to enable the answer 'yes' to be given, is neither here nor there.

What, then, is the evidence on which psychoanalysis is based? Essentially it is clinical rather than experimental. I have already discussed the differing attitudes of the clinician and the experimentalist in the introduction, and shall not here repeat what I have said there. Suffice it to remember that clinical work is often very productive of theories and hypotheses, but weak on proof and verification; that in fact the clinical method by itself cannot produce such proof because investigations are carried out for the avowed purpose of aiding the patient, not of putting searching questions to nature. Even when a special experiment is carefully planned to test the adequacy of a given hypothesis there often arise almost insuperable difficulties in ruling out irrelevant factors, and in isolating the desired effect; in clinical work such isolation is all but impossible. The often-heard claim that 'psychoanalytic hypotheses are tested on the couch' (i.e. the couch on which the patient lies during the analytic session) shows a clear misunderstanding of what is meant in science by 'testing' hypotheses. We can no more test Freudian hypotheses 'on the couch' than we can adjudicate between the rival hypotheses of Newton and Einstein by going to sleep under an apple tree.

What type of evidence other than the clinical do Freud and his followers adduce in support to their claims? There are two main varieties. The first relates to the integrated nature of the whole body of hypotheses, theories, practices, and treatments which makes up modern psychoanalysis. An integrated system of constructs in science has unique advantages; it also has considerable dangers inherent in it. The advantages lie in the mutual support which the various parts of the system give to each other; the dangers lie in the tendency for interpretations to be biassed in terms of the analyst's preconceived notions. This danger is particularly marked in psychoanalysis because interpretation of observations forms such a large portion of the whole structure.

It is increased by another feature of psychoanalysis which is unique in science, and is reminiscent rather of the practices of the ancient order of Loyola. Every psycho-analyst must pass through a training analysis in which all his actions, dreams, and fantasies are interpreted in Freudian terms, and in which he forms strong emotional bonds with his teacher, bonds which predispose him to accept such interpretations as correct, and which will make it impossible for him to make objective, unbiassed judgements about the true relevance of analytic concepts. That this danger is not imaginary is attested by the admission of well-known psychoanalysts. Glover, for example, in arguing against the views of another Freudian which he regarded as pernicious and dangerous, accounted for the adherence of certain analysts to these views in terms of their 'emotional certainty of the truth of the analyst's views' acquired in their training analyses under the heretic. But what is sauce for the goose is sauce for the gander, and if the views of the adherents of Melanie Klein are due to their 'emotional bias' acquired during the training analysis, surely the same explanation can be given of the views held by Glover and his adherents? In fact, *ad hominem* arguments of this kind form the stock-in-trade of Freudian argumentation; it is because they are recognized not to have scientific validity that they have not usually been turned back on to psychoanalysts themselves.

It is not often realized to what extent this 'emotional biassing' through training analysis forms a complete barrier between analyst and critic. Thus Freud states that 'the teachings of psychoanalysis are based upon an incalculable number of observations and experiences, and no one who has not repeated those observations upon himself or upon others is in a position to arrive at an independent judgement of it.' Thus Freud demands effectively that one must believe in his system before one can criticize it, a demand which is hardly in line with orthodox scientific procedures! Similar claims are made by the Jungians, where Jacobi states that 'theoretic conceptions and explanations are adequate only up to a certain point for the comprehension of Jung's system of thought, for in order to understand it completely one must have experienced its vital working on one's self.' When it is realized that there are some fifteen or more hostile 'analytic' systems making similar claims, it will be clear that no one can be competent to judge between them because no one would have enough time and money to undergo fifteen separate and incompatible personal training analyses!

Claims made for Freudian hypotheses in terms of their forming part of a 'system' must therefore be rejected as irrelevant. There are quite a number of such 'systems', all disagreeing on fundamental issues, and all relying on proof of the clinical ('couch') variety. But if they are all based on evidence obtained 'on the couch', how can we hope to judge between their divergent claims? If the clinical experience of the claimants is the only type of proof attempted, and if these clinical experiences are in flagrant contradiction, then we must either rely on faith, declare the whole matter incapable of a solution, or ask for more acceptable proof. When Freudians claim that their patients produce in their dreams symbols clearly similar to those described by Freud, while Jungians claim with equal fervour that their patients produce in their dreams symbols similar to those posited by Jung, we must look for more experimental evidence before deciding between these claims – unless, indeed, we try to account for both findings in terms of quite a different type of hypothesis, making suggestibility to the known expectations of the analyst responsible for the results of Freudians and Jungians alike!

Such more experimental, factual type of evidence is the second variety offered by analysts, and we must look at it with particular care. Let me quote a particular argument in illustration; an argument taken from Freud's writings and selected because I have found that to many audiences it makes a very strong appeal. Freud argues for the hypothesis that all dreams are in reality wish-fulfilments, and quotes in support reports about the common experiences of explorers and others that when they are starving in their camps they tend to dream about food. Thus the need for food generates the wish for food, and the dream, ever ready to fulfil these wishes, obliges with vistas of two-pound steaks and strawberry shortcake. Here, then, we have outside support for our hypothesis, and the scientific proprieties appear to be fulfilled.

Let me restate this argument in more formal terms. On the basis of detailed observation of the dreams of many patients, we arrive at the hypothesis that 'dreams are wish-fulfilments'. From this hypothesis we deduce that starving men should dream of food. If this can be shown to be so, our hypothesis is supported; if this can be shown not to be so, our hypothesis is decisively disproved. Now Freud does not provide us with experimental evidence of any kind; he relies on anecdotal evidence of the most unreliable variety, second-hand, selective, and incomplete. Little value can be attributed to it. Fortunately we have more recent reports of adequately controlled, well-carried-out experiments into human starvation, experiments in which the participants lost almost a quarter of their body weight. Detailed records were made of their dreams, and comparisons with properly-fed individuals failed to show any tendency, however small, for the starving subjects to report more food-dreams than the control group. Thus experimental procedures show Freud's anecdotal evidence up as inconclusive and irrelevant; they also disprove his fundamental hypothesis regarding the nature and purpose of the dream.

Similar findings have again and again attended the detailed investigation along experimental lines of Freudian generalizations. Orlansky, Sears, and many others have summarized the experimental literature dealing with Freudian concepts, and the outcome, by and large, has been that for every hypothesis supported there are at least two where the evidence is doubtful, or clearly contrary to expectation. This is by no means a bad average as scientific hypotheses go, but it does seem to dispose of the Freudian system as such. Much may be salvaged, and taken over into newer systems of personality description; indeed, psychology will for many years to come be deeply indebted to the intrepid genius who infused new life into a rather philosophical and academic discipline. But however highly we may value these hypotheses and insights, psychoanalysis as a self-contained system claiming to afford a scientific view of human nature is dead, even though the embalmed corpse may still be exhibited to the faithful.

How does psychoanalysis counter the factual arguments

brought against it? In the first place, by claiming that its therapeutic procedures work, thus lending important support to the theories and hypotheses on which it is based. I have examined the evidence regarding the effectiveness of psychotherapy in another chapter of this book, and we may notice only the conclusion, to the effect that the available evidence, which is technically faulty and of very doubtful value, being based almost entirely on the opinion of each psychotherapist regarding the success of his own therapy, gives no support whatever to the contention that psychotherapy alleviates the mental suffering of neurotics. Some two patients out of three do tend to improve during therapy, but similarly two patients out of three improve without being given any psychotherapy at all. Thus this argument can hardly be used in order to bolster up the contentions of the Freudians.

The second defence of the psychoanalysts relates to a feature of their system which will be familiar to those who have made a study of semi-religious systems, ranging from biblical prophecy to dialectical materialism. The original statements are couched in such vague, general and complex ways that deductions cannot be made with any degree of definiteness; interpretation thus becomes necessary, and a class of self-styled 'experts' arises, claiming to expound the pure truth of the original, and relating it to current problems and current thought. As Ellis, himself an analyst, points out, 'analytic theory has so far been formulated in such a loose and unverifiable manner as to encourage some analysts to verge dangerously close to mysticism, than which nothing is less scientific.' He goes on to direct attention to the fact that analysis has tended to attract more than its due share of individuals who seem to be mystical-minded, a fact he attributes to four main causes: '(a) analysis has *not* held strictly to scientific principles, but has allowed considerable non-scientific leeway to its devotees; (b) it has attracted to its ranks many neurotics who have great need of mystical, non-logical defences, and who must continually fall back on religio-mystical philosophies to bolster their inabilities to face the grim realities of contemporary life; (c) it has tolerated vague, generalized formulations which are ever but a step removed from mysticism, and which may easily be mystically interpreted; (d) it has frequently been cultish and obscurantist: which is precisely what mystics inevitably tend to be, too.' Be that as it may, the fact is indisputable that Freudian theories are not simple, straightforward statements of hypotheses from which testable deductions can be made; they are highly involved, loose *obiter dicta* which require interpretation before being intelligible, which are frequently contradictory, and which do not easily lend themselves to processes of scientific proof and disproof. This makes them almost completely resistant to disproof; if deductions from psychoanalytic hypotheses are not verified it can always be maintained that the deduction rests on an erroneous understanding of the hypothesis, and that an alternative 'interpretation' of the hypothesis would indeed predict the experimentally-found facts. Thus Freudian hypotheses are indeed quite invulnerable, being too indefinite for factual deductions to be made with any certainty; by the same token they are also unscientific and useless.

It is the third defence of the psychoanalysts, however, which constitutes a master-stroke of tactical brilliance. They make use of concepts such as 'reaction formation', which allow a person who theoretically should show behaviour pattern A to react away from this pattern to such an extent that he shows instead the opposite pattern, Z. Thus the person who because of various hypothetical childhood events is supposed to be timorous may through reaction formation be outwardly aggressive and tough; thus the hypothesis is verified regardless of whether the patient is found to be either timorous or aggressive. Jung makes use of a similar mechanism by stating that persons who are outwardly introverted are unconsciously extraverted, while those who are outwardly extraverted are unconsciously introverted – thus making it possible to 'explain' any type of conduct simply by referring it either to the conscious or to the unconscious portion of the patient's personality. It is this feature of analytic thought, more than any other, which serves the analyst as a defence mechanism, because all reactions whatever can thus be explained after a fashion, even if none can be predicted. However, it is not *ex post facto* explanation which constitutes science, but prediction which can be verified. Here the concept of reaction formation is of course quite useless, because it does not help us in deciding between a number of possible alternatives. Concepts like reaction formation are essentially *ad hoc* hypotheses which inevitably explain the individual case because they have been put forward especially in order to explain it, but which do not fit into any systematic framework, and which are anathema to scientists because of the ease with which they can be advanced, and the difficulty of proving or disproving them. If we make up an *ad hoc* hypothesis for every new case – which essentially is the method of psychoanalysis – then we shall never go beyond the present position where we can explain everything and predict nothing.

So far we have criticized analytic procedures on general grounds; it may be useful to particularize and state a few of the objections which psychologists have brought forward against various features of contemporary psychoanalysis. In the first place, then, *psychoanalytic conclusions are based on unreliable data*. Its data are introspections (of the analyst) and verbalized statements (of the analysand). Data of this kind are essentially subjective, and therefore present special difficulties to the scientist. These difficulties are not insuperable; verbatim recordings can be made of the analytic session, and Roger and other non-analytic workers have shown how useful and indeed invaluable such recordings can be in tracing the course of therapy, in validating hypotheses advanced by the therapist, and in checking the accuracy of the extremely fallible memory of the therapist. In relying on his memory alone, the therapist easily becomes selective, and what is recorded by him in the case history tends to be what fits in with his preconceived ideas. Thus what is reported by the analyst in articles and books is seldom the whole evidence; it is a highly selected part of the evidence, usually taken from a few highly selected cases. No general conclusions can be drawn from such data, particularly as the analyst seldom attempts the essential cross-check of going through his data to find evidence against his preconceived notions, and in favour of a hypothesis different to the one suggested by Freudian theory.

This would not be so dangerous if the data presented by the analyst were at least direct records, however selected, of what occurred in the analytic session. But usually *psychoanalytic data prejudge the issue* by mixing inextricably raw data and analytic interpretation. The reader who is familiar with Freud's own writings, or with those of any of his followers, will be able to check for himself the ratio of fact and interpretation in the cases there reported. As Wittels admits in his biography of Freud, 'Freud's specific method of investigation ... was not suitable for setting up boundaries and strict definitions. Through insight into himself, he came to understand a psychological phenomenon, and from the beginning his discoveries carried a strong inner conviction of certitude.' As Ellis comments on this passage, 'while an inner conviction of certitude is indubitably a fine trait for a prophet to possess, its liabilities for the scientist should be sufficiently obvious to warrant no further comment.' It is this inner conviction of certitude which presumably makes the analytic writers eager to convince by argument, rather than to prove by fact, and which leads to this inextricable combination of verbal report and interpretation.

Psychoanalysts overgeneralize their conclusions. Freud based his imposing edifice on the verbal statements of a few hundred middle-class Viennese neurotics. Instead of confining his conclusions to the population of which this was a sample – as would have been the proper scientific procedure – he extended them to all human beings, at all times, everywhere. In other words, he thought to have divined universal truth from an extremely unrepresentative sample of human beings. What is true of his neurotic patients (assuming for the moment that his observations were accurate, and his hypotheses correct) is obviously not necessarily true of non-neurotic Trobriand Islanders; indeed, Malinowsky has shown with a wealth of detailed illustrations that Freudian theories are very strongly culture-bound, and have to undergo considerable modification if they are to be applied in any way to other groups. What is true of middle-class people is not necessarily true of working-class people; in another chapter I have discussed the facts supporting this statement at some length, and will therefore not deal with them again here. Nor does the fault lie with Freud alone. Most of his followers have emulated his example, and there are several cases where what has been alleged to have been found true in one case has been generalized to the whole of humanity! Overgeneralization of this kind puts psycho-analysis outside the pale of science; before findings are extended beyond the group on which they were originally established, there must be acceptable proof that such extension is warranted.

Psychoanalysts apply their putative principles to general social phenomena without proof of their applicability. Even if Freud's theories and hypotheses were strictly applicable to human beings as individuals, it would not follow that we could account for social phenomena such as war, industrial unrest, or artistic production by their means. Many analysts, however, have extended these theories to deal with almost all the social problems which beset us, always from a theoretical point of view, i.e. without any reference to fact, and usually without the humility of the scientist presenting a hypothesis. These dubious speculations are presented as facts, and society is urged to take action accordingly. I shall give one example of such hypothesising in another chapter, 'National Stereotypes and National Character'; many others could be given. I have seen it suggested in a serious document intended for official consumption that part of the unrest in the coalfields was due to the unconscious conflicts aroused in the miner by having to use his pick-axe (a phallic male symbol) on 'mother earth' (a mother symbol). To the layman, who finds difficulties in distinguishing between psychology, psychoanalysis, and psychiatry, such far-fetched ideas are likely to bring all three into disrepute, although there is probably no serious psychologist who would subscribe to views of this type. Freud himself has issued a warning against 'indiscriminate psychoanalyzing' of all and sundry; it is unfortunate that his followers have not always followed this sober advice.

Where Freudian hypotheses are used to guide research, this research is often illustrative of preconceptions, rather than a crucial test of the hypothesis. Thus the hypothesis that broken homes produce neurosis may lead to a demonstration that neurotics frequently come from broken homes. This fact, of course, is not crucial unless it can also be shown that people who do not suffer from neurosis tend to come from broken homes in a significantly smaller number of cases. But this second part of the experiment is hardly ever performed by Freudians. Figures published by the American Army showed that a large proportion of neurotics did indeed come from broken homes; they also show, however, that normal and especially well-adapted soldiers also came from broken homes in almost equally large proportion. These figures indicate that the broken home had only a vanishingly small part, if any, to play in the genesis of neurosis.

This neglect of control groups to provide the negative part of the inductive argument is a very characteristic part of Freudian experimentation. Again and again a causal sequence is asserted because certain events are found to occur frequently in the early years of the lives of neurotics; hardly ever is there any attempt to show that these events occur less frequently, or not at all, in the lives of nonneurotics. The analyst may retort that we are all neurotic, after all, unless psychoanalyzed according to the dictates of Freud (of Jung, or Stekel, or Adler, or whoever may be the father-figure of the analyst who is talking), and that therefore these events would be expected to occur universally. But this argument clearly proves too much; we may all be neurotic, but some of us are more neurotic than others, and it is the causes of these individual differences which we wish to know about. If the causes adduced by Freudians are universal, then by that token they cannot help us in accounting for the fact that one person has a nervous breakdown, while another overcomes his difficulties in less neurotic ways.

Psychoanalytic arguments from facts beg the question. Let us turn to the preceding argument that broken homes cause neurosis, and let us assume that it had been established beyond doubt that broken homes were more frequent in the histories of neurotics than in the histories of non-neurotics. To argue from this that the broken homes were in any way responsible for the subsequent neurosis would be a clear example of an ancient logical fallacy, namely, that of the *post hoc, ergo propter hoc* argument. To the statisticians, this fallacy is known as 'arguing from correlations to causes'. All that could be regarded as established would be that broken homes and neurosis are correlated; this correlation tells us nothing whatsoever about the causal sequences involved. The Freudian interpretation is an environmentalistic one; it would be just as reasonable to invoke a hereditary one, somewhat along these lines. Predisposition to neurosis is inherited – neurotic parents, neurotic children. But neurotic parents are likely to have their marriages fail, so that their children will grow up with the background of a broken home. Consequently, we shall find that neurotics will tend to come with disturbing frequency from broken homes – not because the broken home causes the neurosis, but because the parents' neurosis causes both the broken home and (through heredity) the child's neurosis. I do not claim that this second hypothesis, along hereditarian lines, is more likely to be true than the Freudian (although there is considerable evidence for the view that neurotic predisposition and emotional instability are to a considerable extent inherited traits); I am concerned with the calm disregard by psychoanalysts of non-Freudian hypotheses which might explain the alleged facts equally well. Science advances by eliminating counter-hypotheses through carefully controlled experiments; it does not advance by begging the question. When it is realized that the alleged facts themselves are of very doubtful standing, and often merely the projections of the analyst's own wishes and desires, it will be realized why scientists are chary of accepting the analytic account of human nature as anything but brilliant speculation.

Protests against these methods of conducting research and of advancing arguments and proofs are not confined to psychologists; many orthodox psychiatrists are equally severe in their censure. Elliot Slater sums the matter up extremely well when he says: 'There has . . . been an increasing tendency among clinicians to minimize the effects attributable to genetical causes, and to teach a psychiatry in which they receive little or no mention. This tendency has been marked in Britain, but it has assumed formidable strength in the U.S.A. Instead of a harmonious development, in which the psychoses and neuroses, constitution and environment, psychogenesis and physiogenesis receive their due share of attention, interest among practical workers has been devoted more and more exclusively towards psychotherapy, psychoanalysis, social psychiatry, personnel selection, group therapy, and preoccupations with anthropology, sociology, and political theory. In its one-sidedness, this development is not healthy.

'It would not perhaps be putting it too high to say that we are witnessing the manifestation of an anti-scientific tendency which is winning an increasing number of supporters. The customary canons of scientific reasoning are ignored by these schools. Uncomfortable facts are left unconsidered. Hypotheses are multiplied regardless of the principle of economy. Explanations which may be valid for certain members of a class of phenomena are regarded as true for the class as a whole. Interpretations which conform with theory, and which might be true, are regarded as established. Possible alternatives are not considered, and no attempt is made to seek for evidence of critical value which shall decide between them. Criticisms from outside are ignored, and only the initiate may be heard. Utterance is dogmatic and lacks scientific humility and caution. These are the mental mechanisms which we associated with the growth of a religious orthodoxy, and not with the progress of science.'

If this chapter has been critical, it has been so because I am concerned about the future of psychology. However much psychologists may show their desire not to be held responsible for the views advanced by psychoanalysts, society often fails to mark the distinction between scientific statement, based on fact and rigorous logical and statistical reasoning, and the kind of *obiter dicta* discussed in this chapter, based on assumptions and loose and wishful thinking. If the latter are in due course discredited, this discredit will almost certainly attach to the whole of psychology and psychiatry, instead of only to the group responsible.

I would not like to be understood as condemning psychoanalysis hook, line, and sinker. Like most psychologists, I appreciate the breath of fresh air which Freud introduced into the musty dry-as-dust atmosphere of nineteenth-century academic psychology. The brilliance of his mind has opened doors which no one now would wish to close again, and his keen insight has given us a store-house of theories and hypotheses which will keep researchers busy for many years to come. All this one can appreciate without accepting the totality of his views as revelations from a higher authority, and without losing one's critical sense. There is much that is supremely important in Freud's contribution to psychology, but there is also much that is bad. To eliminate the latter, without losing the former, must be the task of a scientifically-orientated psychology. The answer to the question which forms the title of this chapter – What is wrong with psychoanalysis? – is simple: Psychoanalysis is unscientific. It is only by bringing to bear the traditional methods of scientific inference and experimentation that we can hope to reap all the benefit of its founder's genius.

13

NATIONAL STEREOTYPES AND
NATIONAL CHARACTER

A LITTLE while ago there appeared in a number of English newspapers extracts from a Russian periodical called *Odesskiye Novosti*, giving an analytical description of the typical British officer of to-day. Apparently this lucky individual's 'income' runs into thousands, often tens of thousands a year, of which he keeps no account, being incapable of keeping accounts. 'The pay he receives from the Government hardly suffices to keep him in perfume and clothes.' English officers, especially young ones, are mostly rolling in wealth and apparently 'do absolutely no work of any kind; they spend their days and nights in clubs of extraordinary magnificence and opulence'; no wonder that the average officer 'is usually occupied with two girl friends simultaneously, a lady of high society and a girl from ballet or opera'. As a soldier, the British officer in his uniform, which is 'truly magnificent and cut to fit very tight', is 'the most ignorant officer in Europe from a professional point of view'.

It is easy to laugh at such obvious inanities, but these quotations highlight a tendency in human thinking which is not confined to Russia, but is well-nigh universal. This is a tendency for thinking, particularly on social and national issues, to take place not along rational lines but in terms of *stereotypes*. The word *stereotype* derives from the printer's habit of making paper-pulp moulds of the forme which contains the type and cuts for the newspaper page. Molten lead is then poured into this mould and the leaden plate thus obtained is used for striking off the printed copies. Walter Lippmann, the well-known American columnist, has applied the term stereotype to the field of attitudes and ideas because of the rigid character of the mental processes which mould the material of experience into fixed patterns. As Lippmann points out, 'For the most part we do not see and then define, we define first and then see. In the great blooming buzzing confusion of the outer world we pick out what our culture has already defined for us and we tend to perceive that which we have picked out in the form stereotyped for us by our culture.'

Stereotyped ways of looking at things have their obvious dangers. They tend to be maladapted and may lead to disaster if taken too seriously. If the Russians take seriously the picture of the British officer presented to them, they may experience a rude shock when they come to compare the stereotyped picture with reality. Stereotypes also have obvious advantages. They give us an ordered, more or less consistent picture of the world to which our habits, tastes, capacities, comforts, and hopes have adjusted themselves. 'They may not be a complete picture of the world but they are a picture of a possible world to which we are adapted. In that world people and things have their well-known place and do certain expected things. We feel at home there; we fit in; we are members; we know the way around. There we find the charm of the familiar, the normal, the dependable; its grooves and shapes are where we are accustomed to find them.'

Perhaps the most obvious field in which stereotyped attitudes are found is that of national differences. It is not, however, the only one. We all have mental images of certain groups of people which make us endow these groups with certain uniform characteristics. Sometimes these characteristics are picked out for us in cartoons; the *Daily Worker* capitalist with his top hat, morning coat, and bag of gold, grinding the faces of the poor into the dust, finds its counterpart in the *Daily Express* cartoon of the unshaven Bolshevik, bomb in hand, who threatens to blow up Parliament. Old maids, mother-in-laws, politicians, gangsters, Jews, Nazis, workers, yokels, cockneys, taxi-drivers, bus-conductors – there is hardly any large group in society which does not assume some stereotyped characteristics which are attributed to all its members, however unrealistic and inappropriate such attribution may be.

But it is in the field of national differences that stereotypes appear with particular virulence, possibly because in the case of most other groups reality and acquaintance impose a certain check on us, whereas in so far as other nations are concerned we can rationalize our preferences in the complete absence of factual knowledge. Nor is it only the uneducated who hold views of this kind; many a learned professor has written tomes on the national characteristics of various groups, based almost entirely on passing fancies and stereotyped prejudices. The militarism attributed to the Germans to-day is completely absent from the stereotypes about them which were current 100 years ago, when the French were regarded as the militarists *par excellence*, having taken over this characteristic from the Spaniards, who tend nowadays to be regarded more in the light of music-hall characters. History chronicles many other changes – the warlike Swedes of the popular imagination of 200 years ago now stand as an example of patient pacifism to many other nations. It has been well said that one cannot *indict* a whole nation. Neither can one *describe* it, and what is true of a whole nation is also true of the constituent parts of each nation. We have stereotyped views regarding the character of the Irish, the Welsh, the Scots, or the Prussians, Bavarians, and Viennese. These are not likely to be any more accurate than those concerning whole nations.

There are experimental ways of investigating stereotypes. One of the most obvious is to ask a group of people what traits characterize the Germans, the Italians, the Americans, and so forth. Results of such studies on the whole agree fairly well with what might have been expected; there is considerable agreement between different people in any one nation regarding the most characteristic traits of other nations. There is even agreement between different nations; for instance, the Americans and English agree with respect to other groups, and even, though less markedly, themselves. The Germans, for instance, are regarded as scientifically-minded and industrious by English and Americans alike; they are also considered solid, intelligent, mathematical, extremely nationalistic, efficient, and musical by the Americans, and arrogant, aggressive, and over-nationalistic by the English. Italians are regarded as artistic, impulsive, passionate, quick-tempered, musical, religious, talkative, revengeful, lazy, unreliable, and dirty, by both. Negroes fare even worse. They are considered to be superstitious, lazy, happy-go-lucky, ignorant, ostentatious, musical, slovenly, unreliable, dirty, and religious by both Americans and English.

The Irish do rather better. While they too are religious and happy-go-lucky, they are also supposed to be quick-tempered, witty, industrious, nationalistic, quarrelsome, aggressive, and pugnacious. Jews are believed to be shrewd, mercenary, industrious, intelligent, loyal to family, grasping, ambitious, sly, and persistent. They are also credited with being very religious. The Chinese, as one might have expected, are looked upon with more favour by the English, who consider them industrious, courteous, meditative, intelligent, and loyal to their families, than by the Americans, who consider them superstitious, sly, conservative, ignorant, and deceitful. The Japanese stereotype seems to have altered considerably as a result of the war. Where pre-war they were considered intelligent, progressive, industrious, shrewd, and meditative, they are now considered cruel, fanatic, treacherous, though still imitative and industrious. Perhaps a few more years will serve to restore them to their previous status. Turks do rather badly; apparently they are cruel, treacherous, sensual, dirty, deceitful, sly, quarrelsome, revengeful, and superstitious. They make up for all this by being very religious. The French, needless to say, are sophisticated, talkative, artistic, passionate, and witty, whereas the Russians are industrious, tough, suspicious, brave, and progressive.

The English consider themselves sportsmanlike, reserved, tradition-loving, conventional, and intelligent; astonishingly enough, Americans agree, adding, however, that the English are also sophisticated, courteous, honest, industrious, extremely nationalistic, and, I hardly dare put this down, humourless! The Americans consider themselves industrious, intelligent, materialistic, ambitious, progressive, pleasure-loving, alert, efficient, straightforward, practical, and sportsmanlike; the English agree that Americans are materialistic and pleasure-loving, but also consider them generous, talkative, and, most widely used adjective of all, boastful.

The close agreement found in English and American groups is probably due to the fact that these stereotypes derive from books, films, and other cultural media shared by both groups. It is unlikely that a comparison between stereotypes held by Spaniards, Turks, or Russians, would show much agreement with those given here. To judge by German writings, it appears that, to the Germans, the average Englishman is 'a clever and unscrupulous hypocrite; a man who, with superhuman ingenuity and foresight, is able in some miraculous manner to be always on the winning side; a person whose incompetence in business and salesmanship is balanced by an uncanny and unfair mastery of diplomatic wiles; a cold-blooded, prescient, ruthless opportunist; a calculating and conceited egoist.' There is little resemblance between this picture of the Englishman, quoted from an account by Harold Nicolson and another one given by him. 'The French portrait of the Englishman is a picture of an inelegant, stupid, arrogant, and inarticulate person with an extremely red face. The French seem to mind our national complexion more than other things. They attribute it to over-consumption of ill-cooked meat (*O tempora! O mores!*). They are apt, for this reason, to regard us as barbarians and gross. Only at one point does the French picture coincide with the German picture. The French share with the Germans the conviction of our hypocrisy. . . .'

Now most people who hold these stereotypes have probably never seen a member of the group about whose characters they hold such strong views. The almost complete absence of knowledge does not cause them to hold these beliefs any the less fervently, or to allow any kind of doubt to intrude into their minds. It is not so much their wrongness which makes these stereotypes so dangerous; it is not at all unlikely that, on the average, Jews are more loyal to their families, Americans more boastful, Negroes more musical, the Irish more quick-tempered, and the Germans more industrious than other groups. It is the complete absence of any kind of proof, the reliance on vague and unverified opinions floating through the air, and embodied in ephemeral newspaper articles and equally ephemeral films, which makes these views so dangerous.

The stereotypes current about a nation tend to be favourable or unfavourable according to whether that nation is, as a whole, regarded in a favourable or unfavourable light. It is possible to rank nations in order of popularity, and here again, English and American audiences tend to react in a very similar manner, both agreeing to put themselves, as well as the Irish, French, Swedes, and Germans at the top; the South Americans, Italians, Spaniards, Greeks, Armenians, Russians, and Poles in the middle; and the Mexicans, Chinese, Hindus, Japanese, Turks, and Negroes near the bottom. It is not known what the ranking given by nationals outside the Anglo-Saxon circles would be, but it is safe to assume that it would differ considerably from these.

Stereotypes similar to those described also determine our social and political thinking. We often react to party labels rather than to the actual proposals which are put before us. This was demonstrated very clearly in a study in which farmers and workers in the United States were interviewed with respect to their voting intentions, their party preferences, and their approval or disapproval of various lines of action. They were found to disapprove of Socialist and Communist parties and candidates, and yet to approve of the measures proposed by these parties rather more than those proposed by their more conservative opponents. When it is a question of an election, therefore, these people would have voted against the measures which they actually favoured because of their stereotyped view of Socialism!

A similar result was obtained in this country when a reliable and accurate measurement was made of the degree of a person's radicalism or conservatism respectively. There was considerable overlap on this measure between people who voted Conservative, Liberal, and Labour. Some voters for the Conservative Party were found to be considerably less conservative in their attitudes than some who voted for the Labour Party. Thus their faith was determined not so much by their opinions on relevant issues, but by the stereotyped views regarding these parties. Again, it has often been shown that people who overtly denounce Fascism often hold views identical with those held by Fascists. What they disapprove of is the conventional stereotype of the Fascist; they have no objection against the essence of what constitutes Fascism.

Is this tendency to think in terms of stereotypes at all related to other parts of personality, or to any definite set of political and social attitudes? There is fairly strong experimental evidence that in this country, at least, the tendency to hold stereotyped views is more frequently found among Conservatives, with a tendency to hold less stereotyped views among Liberals and Socialists. A tendency to hold stereotyped views is also apparently more frequent in what has been called 'the authoritarian personality'. As this is treated at length in the next chapter, I shall not deal with it here.

We have so far considered differences in national character only from the point of view of the caricature-like stereotypes. Is there no evidence to indicate genuine national differences, and is there no way of accounting for them in terms of reasonable and acceptable causes? There have been a number of attempts at the experimental definition of national differences and there are quite a number of theories in the field, but it cannot truthfully be said that any reasonable progress has been made so far. It seems probable that anthropological evidence regarding differences between different tribes is reasonably satisfactory, and there have been a number of attempts recently to apply these methods to the larger and more complex groups which we call civilized nations. I shall discuss one of these attempts presently, but before doing so, I wish to quote some brief descriptions of two primitive groups to indicate the kind of description which anthropology may give us. These descriptions are relevant to one of the great stereotype debates which forms such an interesting feature of our political life, namely, that between the virtues of competition and co-operation, by showing what happens if either of them is carried to an extreme.

On the one side, we have the Zuñis, a Pueblo group of Indians in New Mexico, who have outlawed competition as a socially active force, and among whom individual initiative is punished by the group as disruptive. They discourage all striving for prestige or power and strike the observer as sober, inoffensive, and modest. They are a very ceremonious people, given to dances and religious observances, which follow an identical pattern laid down by definite rules for any given occasion. They show an almost complete lack of individualism, basing their whole lives on ritualistic observance of semi-religious rules, which determine exactly what is the proper action in each set of circumstances. Emotional involvement is considered part of the disruptive forces of competition and is not allowed, therefore, to intrude into their marriage and separation contracts, which are extremely simple. A wife who wishes to divorce her husband simply waits until he is out of the hut, then packs his belongings together in a little bundle and places it outside the door. The husband, when he comes home, realizes that he has been divorced and slinks away without any great show of emotion. This lack of emotionality also keeps the Zuñis from suicide; where there is no loser in a non-existent competitive struggle, there is no need for taking one's life. When told of the frequent occurrence of suicide among white people, they consider this sufficient evidence for the superiority of their own pattern of culture.

As an example of the opposite extreme, consider a New Guinea tribe, the Dobuans. There competition rules supreme, and they are considered a lawless, treacherous, suspicious, constantly fighting group. They are divided into localities and these into war units, but there is little tribal unity among these. No two individuals are on intimate terms because they are constantly scheming to get each other's possessions, or at least they are considered by everyone to be so scheming. Even the marriage relation becomes the scene for a competitive struggle. Man and wife spend one year in the husband's village, where the wife is treated as a slave, beaten, and made to carry out the most menial tasks with everyone trying to make her life as unhappy as possible. The next year, however, they both move to the wife's village and there the man becomes a slave, maltreated, abused, and beaten. The wife having got her own back in this fashion, the two again move to the man's village, and the whole comedy repeats itself.

Every activity in which the Dobuans engage is competitive and all their lives are based on magic. Where ritual is a stabilizing constant force, magic is disruptive, unexpected, unpredictable. Natural laws do not exist; if your cow dies, it is not because of old age or illness, but because someone else has used magic to beat you in the constant struggle of competition. Your task, therefore, is to find out who is responsible and to use counter-magic to do him an even greater harm. Consequently, magic and charms needed for implementing it are in constant demand, and powerful magic is the most important possession of the Dobuans.

These descriptions are taken from the writings of anthropologists from the 'culture pattern' school, and in a way it can be seen that they partake of the nature of a stereotype. Undoubtedly there exist differences in the behaviour of the Dobuans and the Zuñis, which could be put on a statistical footing, but the striking unity of the picture in each case is probably achieved only by the well-known practice of 'leaving out the warts'. There are individuals and groups among the Dobuans who refuse to take part in the competitive exercise and who are regarded as a little odd by the others. Similarly, there are highly competitive individuals among the Zuñis who have to be warned, excommunicated, or even killed in order to preserve the pattern. But when all is said and done, and when all the necessary qualifications are made, it can hardly be doubted that very real and deep-seated differences do exist between the groups, and that if we regard them as nations, we may consider national differences to be demonstrated.

It would be easy to go on from here and sermonize, as many writers do, regarding the morals to be drawn from these examples of what happens when certain principles like those of co-operation and competition are carried to extremes. I shall instead discuss at some length efforts to carry over this type of thinking and observing into the more complex field of national differences between those nations we have come to think of as civilized, and I shall, in particular, deal with the work of Geoffrey Gorer on the Americans, which has exerted a good deal of influence on many people, who have uncritically accepted his conclusions as facts.

The foreword of his book sets the tone for what is to follow. Gorer declares that his work 'is ultimately based on more than seven years' experiences and encounters, on the love, and friendships, and quarrels, and misunderstandings, and delicate negotiations, and casual incidents which made up my life in the United States'. It can be seen from the outset therefore as being a work based on records of individual experiences rather than an account of generally valid truths, and therefore, as some critics have pointed out, a work of journalism rather than of science. The fact that large numbers of generalizations are made on the basis of these personal adventures does not, of course, make any difference to this verdict; science demands more than generalization, it demands verification, and there is little in

Gorer's account to show that he is even conscious of the necessity of verifying the generalizations he puts forward.

Following psychoanalytic practice, Gorer's hypothesis derives from the relationships obtaining inside the family. In particular, it is based on what he calls the 'rejected father'. Making use of the fact that many Americans are the children of immigrants, he argues that these children would tend to despise and reject their fathers because of their foreign ways, their difficulties of assimilation, and their general non-American, European ways. The children, of course, go to American schools, learn American ways, and become in every way identified with American culture. 'The more successful the immigrant father was in turning his children into Americans . . . the more his foreignness became a source of shame and opprobrium and the less important did he become as a model and guide and exemplar.'

One would imagine that the mother, being equally foreign with the father, would suffer the same rejection, but apparently this does not fit in with Gorer's hypothesis. 'Whatever her language and ways, the mother retained emotional importance as a source of love and food and succour.' This, be it noted, is just an assertion; Gorer offers no kind of evidence such as might be obtained from interviewing a well-selected sample of a few hundred first-generation Americans; it is based entirely on the needs of his hypothesis. Gorer derives far-reaching conclusions from this idea of the rejection of the father. He declares that Americans are particularly opposed to authority, and that in some ways this is due to their rejection of the father, who is a kind of original authority figure. He compares the birth of the American republic with Freud's famous primal scene, in which the downtrodden sons combined to kill the tyrannical father; the sons, overwhelmed by their crime and afraid that one of their number will attempt to take the murdered father's place, then make a compact to establish their legal equality, based on the common renunciation of the father's authority and privileges. On these lines, he argues, arose the equalitarianism and the dislike of authority which he believes to characterize Americans.

From the rejection of the father and the non-rejection of the mother, Gorer derives the hypothesis that the mother became the dominant parent in the American family, almost, as he says, by default, rather than by any demands on her part for excessive privilege or influence. Much follows, in his view, from the fact that the American mother thus took upon herself the dominant rôle in the rearing of her children. As he puts it, 'the idiosyncratic feature of the American conscience is that it is predominantly feminine. Because the mother plays the major rôle in disciplining the child and in rewarding and punishing it, the child associates duty and right conduct with feminine influence.' This apparently makes the rôle of the daughter easy and straight-forward, but is rather different for the son, who 'carries around, as it were, encapsulated inside him, an ethical, admonitory, censorious mother'. But these rules, emanating as they do from the women, are felt as impositions, as con-cessions to feminine demands rather than as good in them-selves. This identification of moral conduct with femininity leads to the obvious result that in those fields of life con-cerned with things rather than with persons, i.e. in business above all, where the female element is almost completely lacking, moral rules do not apply.

Enough has perhaps been said to give the reader a general view of the kind of argument which Gorer is putting up, and I will not try to summarize the rest of his book. I will instead discuss the scientific validity of the methods of argumenta-tion which he employs, by taking a few examples of a rather more specific kind and dealing with those in rather greater detail. Gorer explains that Americans tend to bring up their babies on a rigid feeding schedule, paying little attention to the needs of the baby, which cannot be properly dealt with in any such rigid way. Because of this rigidity of the feeding schedule, most American babies learn to experience hunger, and the fear of hunger. Apparently, however, this is not the end. The fear of hunger remains, though in a disguised and

irrational form. 'Symptoms of it can be seen in the frequently expressed fears that America will be reduced to
want, perhaps to actual starvation, if it lets its food or
resources or money outside the country; by the quite
excessive anxiety induced by an unbalanced national
budget; by the fear of depletion in any of its aspects.'

These consequences are serious enough. However, there
are others which also have their importance in determining
the outlook and behaviour of our grown-up Americans.
Gorer's argument runs something like this. Having established to his satisfaction the various consequences of the
feeding schedule, he points out that relevant to this point
also is 'the very great erotic fetishist value given to women's
breasts in contemporary America. They have almost completely replaced the earlier value given to legs. As a stimulating sight, well-separated and well-developed breasts under
a tight-fitting over-garment are thought to surpass any
amount of nudity.' He mentions the fact that various film-
stars have made their reputation through tight sweaters and
that one film, 'The Outlaw', made a national reputation
because of the emphasis given to the heroine's bosom. 'The
cleft which separates the breasts is almost the greatest object
of erotic curiosity, and a number of English films in which
actresses wore Restoration costume have been considered
too indecent to be shown to the American public without
fichus.' Gorer adds that the addiction of most American
men to milk as a drink also has symbolic significance.

This argument of Gorer's should not be taken as a parody
or a burlesque, as one might feel inclined to do at first reading. It is offered quite seriously, and although this may
appear as a task of supererogation, it may be looked at from
the critical point of view for a few minutes. Firstly, what are
its implications, and secondly, what is the evidence offered?
The facts appear to be that a well-shaped feminine bosom
is attractive to the average male American, and that
American censorship works in mysterious ways. I should not
myself doubt the accuracy of these observations. The real
point which arises is that they are both derived by Gorer

from the alleged fact that American babies are brought up on a rigid feeding schedule. Now, this implies a causal relationship which, if it means anything, must mean that inhabitants of other countries, brought up without the blessings of a rigid feeding schedule, show no interest in those aspects of the feminine figure so graphically described by Gorer, and that their censorship departments have no objection to extreme degrees of what I believe is technically known as 'cleavage'. No one who is familiar with censorship battles in this country, or on the Continent, will agree on the second point; attempts by film-stars to reveal have always been counterbalanced by attempts on the parts of moralists to hide, and while the battle has swung one way and another in various countries, at various times, it would be rather difficult to correlate success and failure in it with the prevalence of certain feeding schedules.

As regards the first point, it is rather more difficult to speak authoritatively because, interesting as the subject would no doubt be, and enthusiastic as many Ph.D. students would be to tackle it, there are no reliable figures on relative male preferences for legs or breasts, either in this country, on the Continent, or in America. In their absence it must be left to the personal experience of the reader to judge whether Gorer's argument is a reasonable one.

The really interesting point, of course, is this. Gorer posits the correlation between two events which most people would regard as being quite unconnected, namely, the nature of a child's feeding schedule and the nature of those feminine characteristics which attract him sexually when he is grown up. Now, as a hypothesis this seems somewhat unlikely. However, anyone who took it seriously could quite easily conduct an experiment to find out whether, in actual fact, this correlation existed. Taking, say, 100 males brought up on a rigid feeding schedule and a control group of 100 males identical in age, social background, and intelligence, brought up on a free feeding schedule, there should be no difficulty in an interview procedure to establish the nature of their anatomical preferences. But this is not Gorer's way.

The hypothesis is stated as a fact; no verification is given, and the most far-reaching consequences are based on hearsay and selected, largely irrelevant, facts.

However, Gorer does on occasion quote facts, but when he does so these facts are frequently subject to criticism. He states, for instance, as a fact the belief of Americans 'in the basic equality of American citizens'. As evidence he quotes public opinion polls in which representative cross-sections of Americans were asked to assign themselves to a social class; in every case about four-fifths have described themselves as middle class. As he says, 'Although objectively such self-description is almost meaningless, subjectively it is extremely revealing. . . . This belief in a basic equality, modified by differences in income due to industry and skill, is held unquestioningly by about seven-eighths of the population of the United States, even though inspection will show that by the criteria of commensality, intermarriage, and associations they can be objectively divided into three social classes.'

We may perhaps take a closer look at the evidence. The poll to which Gorer refers is one carried out by the *Fortune* magazine in February 1940. A representative cross-section of the community were asked to put themselves into one of the three classes mentioned to them, i.e. upper class, middle class, and lower class. On the whole, 8 per cent claimed to be upper class, 79 per cent to be middle class, and 8 per cent to be lower class, the remainder falling into the 'Don't Know' category. Among the prosperous, 75 per cent claimed to be middle class, whereas among the poor 70 per cent did. These figures indeed appear to support Gorer.

There is, unfortunately, one fatal flaw in these data which would not escape anyone familiar with the forms of speech of Americans, or English people for that matter. The term 'lower class' is not one which the great majority of people apply to themselves. In that three-class structure of which Gorer speaks, the terms 'upper' and 'middle' class are widely accepted, but the third calls itself 'working class', not 'lower class', and consequently no reasonable and

I

reliable conclusion can be drawn from the *Fortune* survey, which seems to have been excessively faulty in its construction. This has been shown quite clearly in the work of Centers, who found that when people were given the opportunity of calling themselves 'upper class', 'middle class', 'working class' or 'lower class', only 1 per cent chose the term 'lower class' as designating their particular position; 51 per cent called themselves 'working class'. As Centers points out 'the answers will convincingly dispel any doubt that Americans are class conscious and quite as quickly quell any glib assertions like *Fortune*'s "*America is middle class*".'

It would seem to follow from these data that Gorer's original assertion of belief in equality of Americans, on which so much of his book is based, is false; the evidence which he uses to support it has been shown conclusively to be based on technical errors so frequently encountered in the work of the *Fortune* polls, and that exactly the opposite conclusion must be drawn to that publicized by *Fortune*. What becomes now of the band of brothers drawing up a mutual contract of equality and resistance to authority? Instead, we see a class-structure in which the participants are quite conscious of their particular position and of their relations to others in this structure.

Here is but one example of many that could be given, where the facts are in direct contradiction to Gorer's hypothesis. But he makes no attempt to give any discussion of the factual evidence; he merely uses it to illustrate his hypothesis whenever it is found to be compatible with his theory, or when it can be made to appear so. The theory is the primary interest. Facts are only important in so far as they may be used to bolster up parts of the theory. If the facts are in contradiction, they are ignored. If there are no facts in existence, so much the better; hypothesizing and theorizing will then go on in a much freer atmosphere. The reader will see now why earlier on I quoted the view that much of Gorer's work must be considered as journalism rather than science.

He and others of the same school have substituted new

stereotypes for old instead of giving us facts regarding national differences, arguing from these facts to hypothetical underlying causes, and then verifying these deductions in the usual scientific manner. They have argued rather from the preconceived assumptions of psychoanalysis to hypothetical causes, which are then presented as facts without any attempt at empirical verification. If that be so, why, it may be asked, discuss this contribution at such length? The main reason is that while, from the scientific point of view, this type of work is negligible, nevertheless it plays an important and detrimental part in the development of psychology. This it does in several ways.

In the first place, the reader who is not a specialist in this subject is likely to accept these arguments and pronouncements as being scientific contributions of substance. He may therefore take seriously the alleged facts and be ready to base his conduct on them. There is some evidence that writers of this school have persuaded politicians, and other responsible public leaders, of the accuracy of their analysis of the psychology of the Russians or the Japanese, and as these analyses have no more factual basis than has Gorer's work on the Americans, it follows that action based on them is likely to be ill-conceived, faulty, and misguided. Stereotypes tend to make bad signposts for action.

Reasons for the wide acceptance of pseudo-psychological writings of this type are not far to seek. Not having to worry about stubborn facts, the writer is able to give a consistent picture, and drawing upon the stereotypes and agreeing with the prejudices of his reader in his neglect of established facts, he can discard the many qualifications which burden the pages of the more cautious scientist. Addressing himself to the general public he uses journalistic techniques of persuasion and suggestion rather than scientific techniques of impartial presentation and cautious deduction. No wonder that many people feel that here at last they are given a solution to a riddle which has puzzled them throughout the years.

The second point is possibly even more serious. Critical

readers, particularly those who have had a training in more rigorous sciences, will read this type of book with manifestations of incredulity, and consider themselves confirmed in their belief that psychology is not, and cannot be, a science, ignoring the fact that books like this are in no way representative of social science, but, on the contrary, ignore and flout its canons. Social science may easily become identified with this type of work, and consequently rejected *in toto*.

A third consequence has been that bad money is driving out good. Gresham's law applies to social science as well as to economics, and the facile ease of the theorizer has discouraged public support for the more difficult, more laborious, and much more time-consuming work of the scientist. It is certainly possible to make a genuinely empirical study of national differences; indeed, it may be said that such a study would be of the utmost importance in the future development of the United Nations and the effective implementation of the resolutions passed by many internationally-minded bodies. Yet no such empirical studies are likely to be undertaken or financed while those in power remain convinced either that the correct answer can be obtained by arm-chair theorizing, or else that social science is incapable of giving any answer at all. It is by encouraging these two opposing tendencies, both equally inimical to the development of scientific psychology, that the work of Gorer and his colleagues deserves to be classed as one of the abuses of psychology. Instead of replacing stereotyped thinking about national differences by factual discussion, it adds new stereotypes to the old. Until the day that such stereotypes are replaced by facts, it may be salutary to state most emphatically that at the present moment there is no evidence of an acceptable kind for any large-scale generalizations regarding differences between nations.

14

THE PSYCHOLOGY OF ANTI-SEMITISM

THERE are few topics in social psychology on which more has been written than on anti-Semitism. Most of the writers have used an historical or a sociological approach; others have written critical, ethical, and hortatory articles and books. In this chapter, we shall only be concerned with a strictly psychological approach. I have no desire to deny the importance of other approaches, but, to paraphrase a well-known declaration of U.N.E.S.C.O., 'Prejudices arise in the minds of men', and consequently experiments on the psychology of prejudice may possibly throw some light on this vast subject, in addition to anything we may learn from history and sociology.

To start with, then, there is good evidence that both in Britain and other countries there exists a social attitude towards Jews which may be called anti-Semitism, and which is fairly widespread. In the United States, as well as in Great Britain, the number of people who have no hostile, deprecatory, or at least unfavourable attitudes toward the Jews as a whole constitutes no more than a quarter of the total population. This anti-Semitic attitude is held with varying strength. In a typical middle-class English group, some 12 per cent were found to maintain that 'The Jews corrupt everything with which they come into contact'; 31 per cent believed that 'Jews in their dealings with others are an absolute menace, money-grabbing, and unscrupulous'; and 4 per cent believed that the 'Jews are the most despicable form of mankind which crawls on this earth'. On the other hand, a number of people consider the Jews as a rather superior type of people; thus, 6 per cent believed that the Jews had survived persecution because of the many admirable qualities they show.

In spite of this wide variation in attitude, there is considerable agreement in the population with respect to those traits which are supposed to characterize the Jew. In this country, Jews are widely considered to show the following traits by the proportion of the population indicated in brackets: – shrewd (59 per cent); mercenary (38 per cent); industrious (35 per cent); intelligent (32 per cent); loyal to family (30 per cent); grasping (28 per cent); persistent (27 per cent); religious (22 per cent); ambitious (21 per cent); talkative (14 per cent); gregarious (12 per cent); over-nationalistic (12 per cent); and artistic (11 per cent). Some of these adjectives, it will be seen, are favourable, others are unfavourable. That the stereotype of the Jew does not consist simply of a collection of unfavourable traits is shown by the fact that the following traits were practically never mentioned as characterizing the Jews: – aggressive, argumentative, arrogant, boastful, cowardly, cruel, fanatic, frivolous, humourless, ignorant, impulsive, imitative, loud, lazy, naïve, passionate, quarrelsome, quick-tempered, revengeful, stupid, superstitious, slovenly, suggestible, treacherous, or unreliable – all of them traits attributed to certain national and racial groups, as shown in the chapter on 'National Stereotypes and National Character'.

Is the stereotype of the Jew justified? Is there any tendency for Jews to show these various traits more frequently or more strongly than Gentiles of the same intelligence, social class, and education? Unfortunately, there is very little evidence about the psychological peculiarities, if any, of the Jew. When Jews are tested on intelligence tests and compared with similar samples of Gentiles, they are often found to be very slightly superior; this superiority, however, may not be one of innate intelligence so much as of traditional drive towards higher education, which inevitably must exert some slight influence on scores on the type of verbal intelligence test used.

The only other trait on which Jews have been shown to be differentiated significantly from Gentiles is that of aggressiveness, the usual finding being that Jews are rated as more aggressive than are Gentiles by people who know them well. It would be wrong, however, to interpret this finding as arguing in any way for an innate racial trait. Several studies have shown that those Jews who have encountered persecution, hostility, and derision because of their race are far more aggressive than Jews who have not had such unfavourable experiences. In other words, the aggressive Jew may be a reaction to anti-Semitism rather than its cause.

It is a solemn thought that these few facts, together with some irrelevant information regarding the greater percentage of left-handedness in Jews, a rather peculiar distribution of blood-groupings among them, and other similar snippets of information, are the only scientific information we have on this important question of what Jews are really like in contra-distinction to non-Jews. Here is a field of research that should certainly be investigated, and one which might yield results of very great interest and importance. In the absence of any such research, however, which will tell us whether there is anything in the Jew as an individual or in Jews as a group which causes anti-Semitic reactions, let us turn to the personality of the anti-Semite himself.

Here our first question must surely be the following: Is anti-Semitism a specific reaction unrelated to other types of attitudes, or is it merely one of a whole complex of opinions regarding a great variety of issues? Here, fortunately, the answer is quite definite, straightforward, and without any qualification whatever.

Large-scale experiments, both in the United States and in this country, have shown conclusively that anti-Semitic reactions are not specific but are closely related to a variety of other social attitudes. For proof of this statement, let us see first of all how anti-Semitism itself can be measured; afterwards, we can go on to show how it is related to various other social issues.

The first step in the construction of a measuring instrument consists in collecting a large number of attitude statements about the group in question from personal interviews, statements in papers and books, and various other sources, care being taken that these statements are written down in precisely the way in which typical members of the public make them originally. After eliminating duplicated items, one is left with a few hundred statements which are then submitted to a large group of judges, which should consist, if possible, of the same sort of people as those to whom the scale will ultimately be administered. Each judge is given the whole set of statements, printed on separate slips of paper, and is then asked to arrange them in 11 piles ranging from one extreme indicating strongly anti-Semitic attitudes, through neutral, to the other extreme of strongly pro-Semitic attitudes. After each judge has completed this task, all items on which the judges show disagreement as to the degree of favourableness or unfavourableness are eliminated, because, clearly, if the reader of the statement may interpret it as being either pro- or anti-Semitic, then his reaction to the statement cannot be properly evaluated.

The investigator is left with a large number of items on whose degree of favourableness or unfavourableness the judges agree closely. A selection is then made of, say, 24 statements ranging all the way along a scale from very anti-Semitic to very pro-Semitic, and covering the intervening ground comprehensively. The resulting list of statements is then printed in random order, together with five possible replies (strongly agree, agree, uncertain, disagree, strongly disagree), and presented to each member of the population to be tested. The score on the test is a product of the degree of pro- or anti-Semitic attitude, and the strength with which that attitude is held. To clarify the discussion, a typical scale of this type, which has been used extensively in this country, is given below.

OPINIONS ON THE JEWS

In this questionnaire you will find 24 different opinions on the Jews. We want to know in each case whether you agree or disagree with the view expressed. Underneath the statement of each opinion you will find five alternative reactions:

strongly agree   agree   uncertain   disagree   strongly disagree

Underline whichever alternative gives the most correct picture of your own view. PLEASE DO NOT LEAVE OUT ANY STATEMENTS even when you find it difficult to make up your mind. Your views will remain quite anonymous! You are asked not to sign your name.

Thank you for your co-operation.

(1) Dislike of the Jews comes mainly from misunderstanding.
strongly agree   agree   uncertain   disagree   strongly disagree

(2) Jews monopolize everything to the detriment of the English.
strongly agree   agree   uncertain   disagree   strongly disagree

(3) The Jews are an isolated group in society because of their religion.
strongly agree   agree   uncertain   disagree   strongly disagree

(4) Jews will stoop to any kind of deceit in order to gain their own ends.
strongly agree   agree   uncertain   disagree   strongly disagree

(5) Jews are as valuable, honest, and public-spirited citizens as any other group.
strongly agree   agree   uncertain   disagree   strongly disagree

(6) There are both 'good' and 'bad' Jews, as there are both kinds of Englishmen, and there is not much to choose between them on the whole.
strongly agree   agree   uncertain   disagree   strongly disagree

(7) The Jews as a whole cannot be held responsible for the misdeeds of a minority who run foul of the laws and customs of this country.
strongly agree   agree   uncertain   disagree   strongly disagree

(8) Jews corrupt everything with which they come into contact.
strongly agree   agree   uncertain   disagree   strongly disagree

(9) There is no reason to believe that innately the Jews are less honest and good than anyone else.
strongly agree   agree   uncertain   disagree   strongly disagree

(10) The dislike of many people for the Jews is based on prejudice, but is nevertheless not without a certain justification.
strongly agree   agree   uncertain   disagree   strongly disagree

(11) The Jews are mentally and morally superior to most other people.
strongly agree   agree   uncertain   disagree   strongly disagree

(12) The Jews have too much power and influence in this country.

strongly agree   agree   uncertain   disagree   strongly disagree

(13) The Jews have a stranglehold on this country.

strongly agree   agree   uncertain   disagree   strongly disagree

(14) The Jews have survived persecution because of the many admirable qualities they show.

strongly agree   agree   uncertain   disagree   strongly disagree

(15) Jews in their dealings with others are an absolute menace, money-grabbing and unscrupulous.

strongly agree   agree   uncertain   disagree   strongly disagree

(16) Jews are just as loyal to the country in which they live as any other citizens.

strongly agree   agree   uncertain   disagree   strongly disagree

(17) Jews lack physical courage.

strongly agree   agree   uncertain   disagree   strongly disagree

(18) The Jews are a menace to any nation and to any country in which they happen to live.

strongly agree   agree   uncertain   disagree   strongly disagree

(19) The Jews are a decent set of people on the whole.

strongly agree   agree   uncertain   disagree   strongly disagree

(20) The Jews should give up their separate customs and become average citizens of this country.

strongly agree   agree   uncertain   disagree   strongly disagree

(21) There are too many Jews in the highly-paid professions.

strongly agree   agree   uncertain   disagree   strongly disagree

(22) Jews can't be expected to behave any better towards the rest of the world than the rest of the world behaves towards them.

strongly agree   agree   uncertain   disagree   strongly disagree

(23) The Jews are the most despicable form of mankind which crawls on this earth.

strongly agree   agree   uncertain   disagree   strongly disagree

(24) The Jewish menace has been much exaggerated.

strongly agree   agree   uncertain   disagree   strongly disagree

Results obtained from the responses of a large group of people enable us to answer one preliminary question, i.e. is anti-Semitism a general attitude, or is it made up rather of quite specific opinions? Thus, it may be possible that one person may think that the Jews are mercenary but not that they are too powerful; another may believe that the Jews have a stranglehold on this country but also that they are as loyal to the country in which they live as are any other citizens. It is logically possible to believe that there are too many Jews in the highly-paid professions, but also that the Jews are a decent set of people on the whole; that the Jews have too much power and influence in this country but also that they have survived persecution because of the many admirable qualities they show. In other words, it is logically possible for people to hold some favourable and some unfavourable views regarding the Jews, and if this were so, then on the whole it would be unreasonable to speak of anti-Semitism as a kind of general attitude; we would rather be dealing with a number of specific opinions.

In actual fact, a person who holds one unfavourable view regarding the Jews will tend very strongly to hold other unfavourable views, even though the two views may be logically incompatible. Thus, for instance, one and the same person may believe that Jews are too seclusive, keeping themselves to themselves and not mixing with Gentiles, and also that they are too intrusive, trying to be over-assimilative. In one study, two attitude scales were constructed, one dealing with seclusiveness, taking the stand that Jews are too foreign and unassimilated, and accusing them of being clannish, of keeping apart, and not being sufficiently concerned with other groups and their ways; the other scale taking the stand that Jews were intrusive and accusing them of over-assimilation and over-participation. When Jews seem to be conforming in social behaviour, according to this second view, they are actually just 'imitating' and hiding their Jewishness; their attempts to join organizations are based on prestige-seeking and the desire to pry; their admission into the Government or into Gentile neighbourhoods only leads to attempts by them at control and domination; their seeming philanthropy is based on selfish motives; and, finally, because they lack a culture of their own, they must copy or 'sponge' on the culture of the country in which they live. Logically, the points of view expressed in these two scales are exactly opposite; nevertheless, the large majority of those endorsing the views expressed in the one scale also expressed the views endorsed in the other! Thus, evidence for the existence of a generalized trait of anti-Semitism is extremely strong. In addition, we can see already that this trait is based on emotional rather than on logical grounds because it leads to logical contradictions.

So far we have dealt only with prejudice directed against the Jews. This prejudice might possibly be only an example of a more general tendency towards ethnocentrism, i.e. the belief that one's own nation and social group are superior to all other nations and social groups. This hypothesis appears to be fully justified because it has been shown over and over again that people who hold anti-Semitic views also tend to hold views denigrating Negroes, coloured people in general, nations and races other than those of the anti-Semite himself, and even social classes other than those to which he himself belongs; a belief in the inferiority of women is also frequently found in anti-Semites. There is thus a general tendency to glorify the 'in-group', i.e. the group to which the anti-Semite belongs, and to hold strong prejudiced views regarding any and all 'out-groups'.

This finding is important because it shows that we cannot deal with anti-Semitism in isolation. Anti-Jewish prejudice in a way is merely accidental; where there are no Jews, other groups will take their place. The Jews merely stand for the 'out-group', and prejudices regarding them are created regardless of their own behaviour by certain quite general processes in the psychology of the anti-Semite. If we wish to deal with anti-Semitism, therefore, we must broaden our quest and look at ethnocentrism as a whole.

Even that, however, is not enough. Ethnocentrism itself is not found in isolation. It tends to go together with a great variety of more general beliefs, opinions, and attitudes. The most important complex of attitudes correlated with ethnocentrism and anti-Semitism is perhaps that which is commonly known as conservatism. In one study carried out in Britain, the following questions were asked of groups of Conservatives, Liberals, and Socialists, equated for age, sex, and education: 'Do you think that Jews are as valuable, honest, and public-minded citizens as any other group?' and 'Do you think that the Jews have too much power and influence in this country?' 40 per cent of the Conservatives believed that Jews were as valuable, honest, and public-spirited citizens as any other group as compared with 58 per cent of the Liberals, and 67 per cent of the Socialists. In other words, Conservatives were definitely more anti-Semitic than Liberals, and Liberals more anti-Semitic than Socialists. Similarly, with the other question, 68 per cent of the Conservatives believed that the Jews had too much power and influence in this country, a belief held by only 52 per cent of the Liberals and 39 per cent of the Socialists. These figures, agreeing as they do with a great number of other researches, done both in America and here, show quite clearly the close relationship between Conservative political opinions and anti-Semitism.

In the same investigation, a whole host of other questions was asked, many of which discriminated at a high level of significance between anti-Semites and people not holding anti-Semitic beliefs. Anti-Semites believe that coloured people are innately inferior to white people; that war is inherent in human nature; that persons with serious hereditary defects and disease should be compulsorily sterilized; that our treatment of criminals is not harsh enough, and that we should punish rather than try to cure them; that conscientious objectors are traitors to their country, and should be treated accordingly; that no sex education should be given at school; that marriage between white and coloured people should be strongly discouraged; that all human beings are not born with the same potentialities; that patriotism in the modern world is not a force that works against peace; that crimes of violence should be punished by flogging; that religious education in schools should be compulsory; that the principle 'spare the rod and spoil the child' has much truth in it and should govern our methods in bringing up children; that women are not the equals of men in intelligence, organizing ability, etc.; that the death penalty is not barbaric and should not be abolished; that the Japanese are by nature a cruel people; and that there would be another war in 25 years. The conclusion was drawn from a survey of these various items that anti-Semites, in addition to being ethnocentric and conservative, also tended to be patriotic, religious, anti-feminist, and sadistic-aggressive, as shown by their endorsement of flogging, the death penalty, and so forth.

Independent studies in the United States have since given strong support to these views and added various other items as indicators of anti-Semitic tendencies. Nine main groups of items were found to correlate highly with anti-Semitism – ethnocentrism in these studies. The first group of items is referred to a '*conventionalism*', or the rigid adherence to conventional middle-class values. Examples of this attitude are 'One should avoid doing things in public which appear wrong to others, even though one knows that these things are really all right'. The second group of items is referred to collectively as '*authoritarian submission*', or submissive, uncritical attitude towards the idealized moral authorities of the 'in-group'. Examples of this attitude are 'What this country needs is fewer laws and agencies, and more courageous, tireless devoted leaders whom the people can put their faith in.' The third group of items is labelled '*authoritarian aggression*', or a tendency to be on the look-out for, and to condemn, reject, and punish, people who violate conventional values. As an example, we may quote the item 'Homosexuality is a particularly rotten form of delinquency and ought to be severely punished'.

The fourth group of items deals with opposition to the subjective, the imaginative, and the tender-minded and is called '*anti-intraception*'. Intraception is a somewhat technical term meaning 'the dominance of feelings, fantasies, speculations, aspirations – an imaginative, subjective, human outlook' as opposed to extraception, 'a term that describes the tendency to be determined by concrete, clearly observable physical conditions (tangible objective facts).' As an example we may quote the item 'There is too much emphasis in colleges on intellectual and theoretical topics, not enough emphasis on practical matters and on the homely virtues of living.'

The next group of items is headed '*superstition and stereotopy*', i.e. a belief in the mystical determinants of the individual's fate and a disposition to think in rigid categories. As an example the following item may serve: 'Although many people may scoff, it may yet be shown that astrology can explain a lot of things.'

Next comes the belief in '*power and toughness*', i.e. a preoccupation with the dominance-submission, strong-weak, leader-follower dimension; identification with power figures; and exaggerated assertion of strength and toughness. This attitude is expressed by items such as 'Too many people to-day are living in an unnatural, soft way; we should return to the fundamentals, to a more red-blooded, active way of life.' Another group of items is summarized by the terms '*destructiveness and cynicism*', or a generalized hostility and vilification of the human species. Instances of these attitudes are 'No matter how they act on the surface, men are interested in women for only one reason', and 'When you come right down to it, it's human nature never to do anything without an eye to one's own profit'.

The last two sets of items are called '*projectivity*', identified as the disposition to believe that wild and dangerous things are going on in the world; and the projection outwards of unconscious emotional impulses and sexual strivings, i.e. an exaggerated concern with sexual goings-on. Examples of these two tendencies are 'To a greater extent than most people realize our lives are governed by plots hatched in secret by politicians', and 'The sexual orgies of the old Greeks and Romans are nursery-school stuff compared to some of the goings-on in this country to-day, even in circles where people might least expect it'.

If these various types of opinions are in fact held more frequently by people with anti-Semitic views than by people who are not ethnocentrically inclined, then it should be possible to predict a person's score on an anti-Semitism or ethnocentrism questionnaire from his answers to items of the type just described, which are logically quite independent. This can be done with considerable accuracy, and successful efforts to do so have been reported not only in the United States and in Great Britain, but also from studies carried out in Germany, Sweden, and other Continental countries. It seems, therefore, that anti-Semitic and ethnocentric attitudes are themselves only part of a wider cluster which may, with some justification, be called Fascist-mindedness or Authoritarianism. The relationship between items in this cluster and Fascism has been established by showing that acknowledged Fascists show a strong tendency to endorse all these various items; the term 'Authoritarianism' has been coined especially to draw attention to certain features of this complex of attitudes which are believed to be theoretically important. Whichever term we choose, there is no doubt that here is something of fundamental importance in social psychology.

One hypothesis which may help us in accounting for the origin of this clustering of attitudes may be formulated by relating social attitudes to personality. That such an hypothesis is not entirely unreasonable was shown several years ago by S. Crown, who demonstrated a distinct tendency for people who held anti-Semitic views to be more emotionally unstable and neurotic than people who did not hold such views. This connexion between prejudice and emotional instability was discovered in a large-scale questionnaire study; it has since been confirmed in interview experiments in which a smaller number of people was studied intensively through psychoanalytic interviews over a period of time.

Emotional instability alone, however, would hardly account for the authoritarian personality and the general complex of ethnocentric, Fascist-minded attitudes; it would appear necessary to have much more specific hypotheses, and attempt to verify these through direct studies of people with high and low scores on tests of 'authoritarianism' respectively. This has been done by a group of research workers in America whose findings have thrown a flood of light on the personality organization of the 'authoritarian personality'. A brief summary of the results obtained will now be given.

The procedure adopted by these psychologists was a very simple one. They took groups of people who made particularly high scores on a questionnaire containing items like those described above, and contrasted them with other groups of people making particularly low scores. Comparisons were carried out by means of interviews, questionnaires, and psychological tests, and, on the whole, these different approaches gave remarkably congruent results. The simplest way of discussing the final outcome will probably be by taking a series of headings which summarize the main points.

In the first place, then, we find that the high scorers and the low scorers are differentiated by what may be called an opposition between *repression* and *awareness*. The outstanding finding of the research was that the extremely unprejudiced individual tended to manifest a greater readiness to become aware of unacceptable tendencies and impulses in himself; the prejudiced individual, on the other hand, showed the opposite tendency of not facing these impulses openly, and thus failing to integrate them satisfactorily into his total personality. Thus, the prejudiced person represses consciousness of undesirable thoughts and qualities, while the non-prejudiced person remains aware of them and accepts them as part of himself. Among these tendencies, which are repressed by the prejudiced person, are mainly fear, weakness, passivity, sex impulses, and aggressive feelings against authoritative figures, especially the parents.

This tendency to repress these feelings leads to a second group of qualities which differentiates the high scorer from the low scorer, namely, the tendency to *externalize* as opposed to the tendency to *internalize*. The prejudiced person makes use of a mechanism which was first described by Freud, but has since been established on firm experimental grounds, namely that of projection. There is a tendency in people to attribute personal qualities they themselves possess, but do not admit possessing, to other people. Thus a person who is stingy but will not admit this to himself will tend to attribute stinginess to others to quite an unreasonable extent. Thus, similarly, those qualities which the prejudiced person represses in himself tend to be projected and attributed to other people; it is not the prejudiced person himself but others who are seen as hostile and threatening, or else his own weakness leads to exaggerated condemnation of everything that is weak.

Another aspect of externalization consists in a tendency toward avoidance of introspection and of insight in general, thus rendering the content of consciousness rather narrow. Another consequence is that since the energies of the person are largely devoted either to keeping instinctive tendencies out of consciousness, or to striving for external success and status, there is less room for interpersonal relationships or for taking pride in work as an end in itself. 'The comparatively impoverished potentialities for interpersonal relationships may exhibit themselves either in a relatively restricted, conventional but dependable approach to people, as found primarily in the more conservative subgroup of the high scorers, or in a ruthless, manipulative approach, as found in the more delinquent subgroup.' There also seems to be relatively little enjoyment of sensuality or of passive pleasures such as affection, companionship, or art and music on the part of the typical high scorer. Instead of these internalized pleasures, there is an inclination toward mobility and activity, and a striving for material benefits.

The non-prejudiced individual, on the other hand, being conscious of his own less acceptable tendencies, does not externalize them by projection, but integrates them into his personality. He tends to be oriented toward real achievement, toward intellectual or aesthetic goals, and toward the realization of socially productive values. 'His greater capacity for intensive interpersonal relationships goes hand in hand with greater self-sufficiency. He struggles for the establishment of inner harmony and self-actualization, whereas the high scorer is concentrated on an effort to adjust to the outside world and to gain power and success within it. One of the results of greater internalization is the generally more creative and imaginative approach of the low scorer both in the cognitive and in the emotional sphere, as compared with a more constricted, conventional, and stereotypical approach in the high scorer.'

This lack of an internal focus of the prejudiced person leads to the next focal point of distinction, *conventionalism* versus *genuineness*. 'One of the outstanding characteristics to be found in both the conservatively inclined, as well as in the delinquent subvariety of the high scorer, is the adoption of conventional values and rules. High scorers generally seem to need external support – whether this be offered by authorities or by public opinion – in order to find some assurance concerning what is right and what is wrong.' This conformity to outside values in the extremely prejudiced person can be seen most clearly in his attitude toward his parents, which is one of stereotyped admiration, with little ability to express criticism or resentment. Many indications are usually found in the interview that there is often considerable underlying hostility toward the parents, which is frequently repressed and which prevents the development of a truly affectionate relationship. At the opposite end, the greater genuineness of the non-prejudiced person is evident in his equalitarian conception of the parent-child relationship, which makes it possible for him to express criticism and resentment openly, and at the same time to have a more positive and affectionate relation with the parents.

The conception of sex rôles shows a similar division. The male high scorer's view is highly conventionalized; he thinks of himself as active, determined, energetic, independent, rough, and successful in the competitive struggle. The rôle of the woman is one of passivity and subservience. There is relatively little genuinely emotional involvement in his non-marital sex relations, and of his wife the prejudiced person tends to require the conventional prerequisites of a good housewife. 'On the whole, sex is for him in the service of status, be this masculine status as achieved by pointing toward conquests, or be it social status as achieved by marrying the right kind of woman. At the opposite end, the non-prejudiced men tend to look primarily for companionship, friendship, and sensuality in their relations to the other sex. Similarly, the unprejudiced woman looks primarily for mutual interest and affection in her choice of a mate, where the high-scoring woman, on the other hand, clings to a self-image of conventional femininity defined by subservience to and adulation of men, while at the same time showing evidence of an exploitive and hostile attitude toward them.'

These differences in emotional reaction link up with the next differentiation, which may conveniently be labelled '*power-* versus *love-orientation*'. Related to conventionalism is a tendency toward admiration of and search for power, which is much more pronounced in the typical high scorer. 'The comparative lack of ability for affectionate and individualized interpersonal relations, together with the conception of a threatening and dangerous environment, must be seen as underlying the prejudiced individual's striving for the attainment of power, either directly or by having the powerful on his side. . . . In this context we often find a frame of mind best characterized as 'over-realism', a tendency to utilize everything and everybody as means to an end.' This ruthless opportunism is often considered as an essential attribute of masculinity by the prejudiced man.

On the other hand, the search for affection and love in one's personal relationships is an important determinant of the behaviour of the typical low scorer. Emotional attachments are formed, however, not only in contact with other people, but also in relation to his work. 'Though far from being indifferent to recognition, low scorers place comparatively little emphasis on their activities as means to an end; rather, these activities tend to become a source of pleasure and satisfaction in their own right, or else the emphasis lies on their social implications. . . . Finally, interest and liking for art, music, literature, and philosophy are more often found in the lower scorer. It may be considered that such interests contribute substantially to the greater resourcefulness, and to the comparative diversion from power and status, that is characteristic of the low scorer.'

The last group of traits which differentiates the prejudiced from the non-prejudiced may be summed up under the heading of '*rigidity* versus *flexibility*'. This is accounted for in terms of the necessity of maintaining rigid defences in order to keep unacceptable tendencies and impulses out of consciousness. If these defences are loosened, there is a danger of a breaking-through of the repressed tendencies which have not lost their dynamic strength, and whose abrupt or unsuccessful repression prevents rather than helps in their control and mastery. 'An ego thus weakened is more in danger of becoming completely overwhelmed by the repressed forces. Greater rigidity of defences is necessary to cope with such increased threat. In this vicious circle, impulses are not prevented from breaking out in uncontrolled ways.' A great deal of energy is spent on keeping these basically unmodified instinctual impulses repressed. This process, with its attendant projections and externalization, and its lack of internal strength and individualism, provides a rather labile and precarious balance, and in order to prevent it from leading to breakdown a firm, rigid, simple, and stereotyped cognitive structure is required, with no place for ambiguity. 'The tendency to impose preconceived and often stereotypical categories upon experience may thus be envisaged as a more general trait in subjects scoring extremely high on Ethnocentrism . . . it is in the low scorer that we find the more flexible emotional and cognitive adjustment; this is also reflected in his greater reluctance to "reify" concepts, in his more pronounced appreciation of the complexity of social and personal relations, as well as in his more profound sympathy with the psychological and social sciences studying these relations.'

In this attempt to characterize the personality of the ethnocentric, prejudiced, authoritarian personality, I have followed the psychoanalytic terminology used by the original writers, although this terminology is often difficult to understand and tends to mix up fact and theory inextricably. The attempt to understand, however, seems worthwhile in this case because the results are rather striking in their cogency, and in their power to create a personality picture which agrees in most essentials with a great variety of other more objective research findings reported by many authors. There are certain points, however, which should be remembered before evaluating the results.

In the first place, the results quoted only indicate tendencies. Not all highly prejudiced individuals show the personality patterns described, and not all people free from prejudice show the opposite personality pattern. Thus, while personality may account for a certain portion of prejudice, it certainly does not account for all of it. In the second place, we are dealing here with *extremely* prejudiced and *extremely* unprejudiced people; what is true of them is not necessarily true of the *slightly* prejudiced or the *relatively* unprejudiced. Many people repeat parrot-like anti-Semitic and ethnocentric slogans, simply because they have never thought about the subject at all, or because they are too stupid to know what they are saying, or because this kind of talk is current in the particular environment in which they live. Where this is so they have no emotional involvement with the views they are repeating, and in that case, no explanation in terms of personality structure would be called for. Probably the great majority of anti-Semites, defined in terms of their verbal statements, would fall into this category. On the other hand, it should be remembered that it is the fanatical few who are the danger much more than the sheep who willingly follow where they are led, and it is in these leaders that we may expect the personality structure described above to be particularly pronounced.

In the third place, most researches have dealt with the Authoritarian Personality as defined by anti-Semitism and Fascism; evidence is available to show that Communists share with Fascists that 'tough-mindedness' which is such a marked feature of the personality description of the ethno-centric. With them, the superiority of the working class is as axiomatic as is the superiority of the middle class with the Fascist; with them the inferiority of their own country as compared with the U.S.S.R. is as certain as is the superi-ority of his own country is with the Fascist. Their scape-goat is not the Jew, but the Capitalist. It is because of this fact that in dealing with the psychology of anti-Semitism, I have had more occasion to comment on the *conservative* 'authori-tarian personality'; it would be quite wrong to imagine that nothing comparable could be found on the left of the political spectrum.

As a last point, some critics have pointed out that work of this type deals essentially with verbal statements rather than with actions, and that what a person says and what a person does are two different things. This belief that 'action speaks louder than words', and that therefore the clue to a person's attitudes can be found by observation of behaviour rather than in terms of verbal statements, is so widely shared that a short note seems required.

It is certainly possible for a person to disguise his true attitude by giving voice to opinions which he does not really hold. The dangers of drawing wrong conclusions from be-haviour, however, are hardly less real. The fact that a person goes to church is hardly reliable evidence that he holds strongly religious opinions; his action may be prompted rather by a desire to impress others, to conform, or to make useful contacts. A person may paste a leaflet asking people to vote 'Conservative' on his window, not because he holds conservative views but because he fears repercussions if he gives an indication of his socialist opinions. A person having no anti-Semitic opinions of any kind may yet be found to take part in a pogrom for fear of being denounced himself. Verbal statements may not always be an accurate indicator of a person's attitudes, but actions also may give an entirely false impression. One should always search for objective evidence to show that actions or verbal statements are in fact a true reflection of attitudes.

This can be done in various ways. One of the most impressive is that of duplication. If the same consistent results can be found time and again with different social and national groups, then it is extremely unlikely that wilfully false statements can be responsible for this unanimity. Thus, it is a fact that many different investigators have reported results essentially similar to those summarized in this chapter, lending strong credence to the general correctness of the resulting picture.

Equally important is the fact that it is possible to make deductions from these hypotheses which can be verified. Let us take a specific example. We have seen that the prejudiced person is supposed to be more rigid than the non-prejudiced person. It should be possible to put this view to a strict experimental test by constructing a measure of rigidity and applying it to people scoring high and low respectively on the ethnocentric-authoritarian scale. One such test was constructed in the following manner. There is a well-known type of intelligence test in which the subject is told that he is to measure out so many gallons of water from a large container. In order to do that, he is given three smaller vessels, none of which is of exactly the right size, so that in order to measure out the required amount, he has to pour water from one of the containers into the others in a series of moves which will finally give him the required amount.

The 'rigidity' test consists of a series of such problems. The first eight can be solved by making the same sequence of moves; this sets up a pattern which the rigid person will tend to follow in the next two problems, which can also be solved in the same way as the others but for which a much easier solution exists. The non-rigid person, of course, would be expected to find that easier solution because in him the pattern set by the first eight problems is not so rigidly established. The eleventh problem cannot be solved at all along the lines of the original eight, and the next two problems can again be solved both by the original method and by a much simpler one. A score of rigidity is derived in terms of the number of times that the subject deviates from the original pattern on the last five problems. The hypothesis calls for a high score of rigidity to be made by those who give ethnocentric and authoritarian answers on the questionnaire, and a well-controlled experiment has shown that this is actually what happens. We thus have independent evidence of the correctness of the original hypothesis.

Taking it all in all, these many and varied strands of evidence constitute a rather strong web which will undoubtedly require modification in many important details but which will certainly be found useful in supporting practical measures to combat anti-Semitism. Such measures, of course, lie outside the sphere of psychology, and their discussion will not therefore form part of this chapter.

15

GALLUP POLLS AND PUBLIC OPINION

FOR democracies and dictatorships alike, the old adage *vox populi, vox Dei* holds with almost equal strength. The dictator who, like Mussolini, decides on a course of action which is opposed by the great majority of his subjects invites disaster, just as much as a statesman in a democratic country whose policies go against the interests, real or imaginary, of the people who are called upon to support him at the next election. Ever since ancient times, therefore, politicians, military leaders, and statesmen have shown great interest in methods of finding out the opinions of those on whom they are ultimately dependent.

It must not be imagined, of course, that these attempts were made necessarily because of a wish to modify policy in accordance with public opinion. Much more frequently the attempt was made in order to find out whether further propaganda was required in order to make popular opinion agree with that of the leader. When a leader feels that popular opinion would not support a given action, such as the banning of the Communist Party by Hitler, he may order certain actions to be taken, such as the burning of the Reichstag, which will modify public opinion sufficiently to make it possible for him to carry out his original purpose.

Whatever the purpose, therefore, of seeking to know the opinions and attitudes of the public, the desire itself is quite universal and very strong. In a way, the whole machinery of democratic government through election, referendum, and so forth, is based on the hypothesis that it is possible to obtain a genuine estimate of 'public opinion', and until recently no better methods were available, unless we chose to place reliance on intuition and subjective estimates by so-called experts. Clearly, the vote cast at an election is very non-specific, because it is given to a party representing not one view on one subject, but a large number of views on a large number of subjects, between which the voter cannot discriminate in his vote. Thus he may agree with the Conservatives on tariff reform, with the Liberals on 'equal pay for equal work', and with the Labour party on nationalization. His final vote will not give any indication of these finer divisions, and whatever party he votes for, it is certain that he will be voting against points of view he may hold very strongly himself.

The need to obtain more accurate measures on individual issues and to get a better picture of the views held by the man-in-the-street than could be obtained by observation of the size and temper of the crowds that come to hear political speeches, the views that constituents communicate to candidates and party workers in conversations, letters written to political journals, and so forth, led to the development of 'polling techniques' as they are called nowadays. These appear to have originated in the *straw votes* conducted in the early part of the century by American newspapers which questioned people in the street about their voting intentions. Another development which helped in the formulation of present polling methods was the use of the 'mail canvas' correspondence, which was started about a century ago by some agricultural journals, and was then taken over by the United States Department of Agriculture, first for the collection of information about crops, and subsequently for the collection of opinions on various subjects. The best-known example of this type of work is the series of polls conducted by the *Literary Digest*, which contacted millions of U.S. citizens during the 1920s and the beginning of the 1930s through its postcard ballots. These polls were concerned not only with voting intentions, but also with opinions on subjects like prohibition and New Deal policy.

These early attempts at prediction of elections and ascertaining of public opinions and attitudes on various subjects were sometimes extremely accurate in their forecasts; thus the *Literary Digest* in 1932 predicted the number of votes cast for Roosevelt with an error of less than 1 per cent. Successes such as this, however, tended to be relatively rare, and in a large number of cases forecasts were found to be extremely inaccurate. It was dissatisfaction with this inaccuracy which led to the developments now often identified with the name of Gallup, and the modern system of public opinion polling.

In some ways the problems which face the person who wishes to ascertain public opinion on any given subject are relatively simple. All he has to do, to put it briefly, is to go and question people directly about their attitudes. This is what the layman would do almost instinctively, and, with certain refinements, that is exactly what the pollster does to-day. There are three problems, however, which arise in this connexion and these require careful consideration. The three main problems are: firstly, whom to ask, or the problem of *sampling*; secondly, what to ask, or the problem of *interviewing*; and thirdly, what conclusions to draw from the results, or the problem of *interpretation*.

Let us take the problem of sampling first. What we want to know is the opinion held by a given group of people, say all the adult inhabitants of the British Isles, which is usually too large to make possible the questioning of all the members of that group. Fortunately, it is possible to get a very accurate estimate of the views held by the total group by questioning only a relatively small sample of that group. If we question a small sample, however, we must make quite sure that this sample is *representative* of the whole population; in other words, we must make sure that men and women, old and young, northerners and southerners, working-class and middle-class people, urban and rural dwellers, all appear in the same proportion in the sample as they do in the total population. Obviously, if men and women differ in their attitude towards a given subject, then by including only men in our sample we would get a completely wrong idea of the attitude held by the whole group in which we are interested. We may select our sample to be either a random one, i.e. one in which every member of the total group has an equal chance of being chosen, or a stratified sample, in which we make sure that people are chosen in predetermined proportions. But in either case, the overriding necessity, before any conclusions can be drawn, is that the sample on the whole must be truly representative.

A good example of what can happen when it is not is given by the fate of the *Literary Digest* poll in 1936. Mailing out its usual postcard ballots, the *Digest* received two million answers, yet it made the very large error of 19 per cent in predicting the Roosevelt vote, an error so large that the poll was abandoned. When it is remembered that in 1932, only four years previously, the *Digest* poll was correct within 1 per cent, it may be asked what happened in those four years to account for this difference. The answer is a relatively simple one. The *Literary Digest* postal ballot was directed largely at middle-class people, people who read magazines of that type, who owned telephones and cars, and whose political views on the whole could be described as conservative. Thus, they formed an extremely biassed sample of the total population rather than a representative one. This did not matter in 1932, because at that time the differences between the two main political parties in the United States, the Democrats and the Republicans, were not related to Conservatism and Liberalism respectively. Both parties were equally conservative in their attitudes, and consequently the percentage of voters in the middle-class section of the population polled by the *Digest* split in about the same proportion as the rest of the population, so that a forecast based on their views was reasonably accurate. Roosevelt and the New Deal transformed the scene by making the Democratic party more liberal and thus attracting working-class support, while the Republican party, by contrast, became more identified with conservative opinion, thereby attracting more middle-class support. By 1936, therefore, the division between the parties had become in part a division between social classes, and by polling only one social class, namely, the middle class, the *Literary Digest* obtained an estimate of support for Landon, the Republican candidate, which was out of all proportion to the support this candidate really commanded in the whole population.

In the same year that the *Literary Digest* failed so

abysmally, in spite of its poll of two million people, to predict Roosevelt's return, Gallup, with a very much smaller sample of only 3000 people, came very much nearer to the actual poll and predicted the return of Roosevelt. This showed that it is not the *size* of the sample but rather its *constitution* that is important, because Gallup's sample was constructed according to the rules of representative sampling. Gallup's practical proof of the superiority of representative sampling over the uncontrolled methods prevailing earlier is an interesting demonstration to those who distrust statistical arguments, but it should be noted that the need for effective sampling was pointed out on purely theoretical and statistical grounds long before the failure of the *Digest* poll showed these criticisms to be justified. Indeed, the theory of sampling has been worked out by mathematicians in very great detail, and it is possible to estimate the likely error in prediction, when the size of the sample is known, by simple formulas.

How is sampling actually accomplished? There are two main methods, called 'quota sampling' and 'area sampling'. In quota sampling, which is the method used by most of the public polling agencies, interviewers are assigned a definite number of people of specified characteristics whom they are to interview, i.e. they may be told to contact three over-50 males, five under-30 women, and so forth. This method, although it is very widely used and has the advantages of simplicity and cheapness, also has very definite disadvantages. It requires the interviewer to estimate such variables as age, social class, and so forth, variables which are not always accurately and correctly gauged. He may, of course, ask the person whom he is interviewing as to his age, and social class, but answers regarding the first are not always accurate, particularly when women are being interviewed, and answers regarding the latter tend to be inaccurate in men, who seem to upgrade themselves with fair regularity! Possibilities of fraud and cheating on the part of the interviewer, i.e. of making up the replies by himself without actually interviewing anybody, or by wrongly fitting the interviewees into the categories he has been assigned, can probably be eliminated by proper training and adequate payment, as well as by selection of interviewers, which takes into account certain personality characteristics. But when all is said and done, quota sampling consistently shows greater errors in prediction than can be accounted for in terms of the statistics of sampling theory. This would not matter so much if the errors were random, but, unfortunately, errors seem to show a distinctive bias. This bias, in all countries where polling organizations are working, appears to be in the direction of overestimating the vote for Conservative middle-class candidates, and of underestimating the vote for Socialist and working-class candidates. In the United States it shows itself by a persistent underestimate of the Democratic vote and an over-estimate of the Republican vote – a tendency dramatically emphasized in the 1948 election, when Truman became President, in spite of the confident forecasts by pollsters to the contrary.

The average error of the election forecasts made by polls is now in the neighbourhood of 3 per cent, a figure which depends in part on the exact electoral system of a country, but which seems to be remarkably steady on the whole within all the countries which have carried out polling. An average error of 3 per cent may give the appearance of relative accuracy, but it is easy to overrate the effectiveness of polling. The success of methods of prediction is frequently tested by comparing these methods with the results of some simple predicting device. One such rule-of-thumb device is that of merely predicting that the vote in each state or constituency will divide exactly as it did in the preceding election. If polls are to be of any use, it seems reasonable to expect that their forecasts should be an improvement on this method. In America, the accuracy of this rule-of-thumb prediction during the period where comparisons are possible (1936–1948) has been found to be almost as good as that attained by polling. This may be due to the fact that this was not a period of rapid political change; in England comparison is more favourable to polling. Whichever way we look at it, however, there is little doubt that sampling can be made and should be made much more accurate than it is at present, even though this might be a rather costly thing to arrange.

A method for ensuring more accurate sampling is the so-called 'area' method. In this, the total area to be sampled is divided into districts and these again into dwelling units. By a process of random selection, certain dwelling units are chosen and certain people within each dwelling unit specified, so that the interviewer has no choice as to whom he should interview. This method ensures random sampling and is therefore technically superior to quota sampling. Its disadvantage is that it is extremely costly. The interviewers have to go from one part of town to another for consecutive interviews, and if the interviewee is not at home, they have to call back again and again until he is at home and can be interviewed. No substitution is allowed, for the very simple reason that people who are at home most of the time differ in many respects from individuals who tend to be out a good deal. Thus, in a survey in which an attempt was made to assess the number of people who were contributing to the war-time food drive by digging 'Victory' gardens, it was found that the percentage of 'diggers' among those who were at home when the interviewer first called was higher than among those who were out and could only be reached on later occasions; in fact, the more visits that were necessary, the lower was the percentage of people engaged in digging!

Government agencies, both in the United States and in this country, tend to make use of area sampling because they often make policy decisions on the basis of the information received, so that high accuracy is essential. Gallup and other polls have hitherto avoided area sampling on the whole because they do not consider the increased accuracy to justify the increase in cost.

Having found our sample, the problem arises of what questions to ask and how to prevent biassing effects from vitiating the results. The first problem that has to be faced is that of expressing one's question in such a way that the interviewee, however low his intelligence, and however poor his education, will understand the question. This may sound easy, but in actual fact it is a very complex and difficult problem. One example may serve to illustrate how even experienced public opinion experts may fail in this respect. An American Government agency polled Negroes from the Southern States on their attitudes toward the question of taxation of profits and found, to their consternation, that the interviewees were solidly opposed to this measure. As usually the poorer groups favoured taxation of profits, an expert was sent down from Washington to investigate the matter. He reported back after a brief survey, saying that the Negroes failed to see any justification in the Bible for the taxation of prophets! This true story may illustrate the difficulties facing the expert in framing his questions. The answer appears to lie in a technique called 'pretesting', i.e. in administering the set of questions believed to be adequate and intelligible to a small sample of the population for the specific purpose of finding out how well the questions are understood. If the pretesting is unsatisfactory revisions are made until the pretests show an adequate intelligibility.

Intelligibility, however, is not all. A question to be meaningful must also relate to existing opinions and attitudes on the part of the subject, as otherwise answers may be meaningless. Shortly after the war, one polling agency asked the question 'Do you think King George of Greece should be allowed to return to his country?', and the fact that over 60 per cent of the people questioned answered 'Yes' was interpreted in many quarters as an expression of opinion favouring the conservative side in the struggle for power that was going on in Greece at the time. An independent study carried out at the same time asked a rather different question, namely, 'Have you ever heard of King George of Greece?', with the result that only a very small proportion of the population were found to have any acquaintance whatsoever with this particular monarch. Thus, a large

K

proportion of 'Yes' answers was a reflection rather of the natural tendency to say 'If this chap is the King of Greece, why the dickens shouldn't he go back to Greece' rather than an indication of preference for one side or the other in Greek politics. Pollsters must be very cautious in their attempts to measure existing attitudes not to create pseudo-attitudes which give quite the wrong picture of public opinion.

Even when questions are clearly worded and relate to very real issues there are special points which have to be borne in mind. One of these is the effect of context. Before America entered the war, two samples of Americans were polled with respect to the advisability of allowing United States citizens to join the English or German armies. In the one sample the questions were put first about the English army and secondly about the German army; 45 per cent answered 'Yes' with respect to the English and 31 per cent answered 'Yes' with respect to the German army. In the other group the question regarding the German army was put first and that regarding the English army second. Here 40 per cent answered 'Yes' with respect to the English army and 22 per cent 'Yes' with respect to the German army. Thus, quite different figures were obtained, depending on the order in which questions were put.

It is easy to see what happened here. Americans on the whole were more favourable to the English side and tended to say 'Yes' to the question 'Should United States citizens be allowed to join the English army?' When faced with a similar question regarding the German army, the fact of American neutrality made them give a similar answer there, although this tendency was weakened by their dislike of the German war machine. On the other hand, if the question 'Should the United States permit citizens to join the German army?' was put first, the most natural answer to most Americans was 'No', and when the same question was put about the English army the fact of United States neutrality made many correspondents reply in the same way as they had to the question about the German army.

Another important consideration which affects the answers of interviewees to a very considerable extent in the question of explicit or implicit statement of alternatives. To the question 'Should we start thinking about peace now?', which was put by a polling agency in the middle of the war, 81 per cent of the interviewees said 'Yes', but when the alternative was made explicit and the question was put 'Should we win the war first and then start thinking about peace?', only 41 per cent were in favour of thinking about peace now. Thus, very marked apparent changes in attitude can be produced by the explicit statement of alternative answers.

A third problem arises when questions have to be asked regarding issues on which certain attitudes are generally regarded with disfavour as conflicting with the national policy or with current stereotypes. When questions of this type are asked, interviewees may not reveal their true opinions but may instead give what they consider to be the socially approved answer. Clear evidence of this was given in the following experiment. The question was asked by two groups of people: – 'Do you think that the Jews have too much power and influence in this country?' One group was asked this question in the ordinary way by interviewers who wrote down the answer; the other group was given a slip of paper on which to write their answer, which they were then told to fold and put into the slot of a large box marked 'Secret' in gigantic red letters, which the interviewer was carrying around with him. Of those interviewed in the ordinary way, 56 per cent admitted to anti-Semitic views on this question; of those taking part in the 'secret' ballot 66 per cent answered 'Yes'. The difference of 10 per cent is very much larger than could have been expected on the basis of chance, and indicates a distinct tendency among some people to give socially approved answers to this question when interviewed in the ordinary way.

This tendency of interviewees to give answers which they consider to be in line with the interviewer's own opinions, or with widely held social views, may also account for certain findings regarding interviewer bias. In one experiment carried out in the United States before America came into the war, a question was asked regarding help for England. Before going out to interview, however, the interviewers themselves were asked about their opinion on this question, and the results of their interviews were then compared with their own views. Those interviewers who were in favour of helping England found that among the interviewees 60 per cent were in favour of helping, while 40 per cent were in favour of keeping out. Interviewers who themselves wanted to keep out rather than help England found that 44 per cent of the interviewees wanted to help England and 56 per cent wanted to keep out. There clearly is some degree of bias creeping into the results, although interviewers are, of course, trained not to give any indication of their own views.

While desirable, this is difficult and may often be impossible. The interviewer's accent, education, and social class may already predetermine to some extent the replies of the people he is interviewing. Thus, on one occasion, an American group was polled on its attitude toward trade unionism. Among working-class people interviewed by a middle-class interviewer, 41 per cent only were in favour of trade unionism; working-class interviewers reported 56 per cent favourable towards trade unionism. Clearly, the interviewees expected middle-class interviewers to be against, and working-class interviewers to be in favour of trade unionism, and framed their replies accordingly.

There clearly are great difficulties in avoiding bias; several methods are open to the polling agency in their attempts to avoid such bias. One such method is the so-called 'split ballot' technique, in which two samples are interviewed using differently-worded questions for each sample. If the results agree, this may be taken as evidence that the wording of the question has not introduced undue bias. Where differences do appear, a repetition of the whole investigation with newly-worded questions becomes necessary. As regards interviewer bias, it is possible to ascertain the views of interviewers in the first place, and make corrections for the differences found among respondents questioned by interviewers holding different views. While these possibilities exist, they are not always being used by polling agencies, who often feel that studies of this kind are expensive and experimental, and not absolutely necessary. In their absence, expert guidance can often avoid the more obvious errors, but from the scientific point of view, the reliance which can be placed on results reported by these agencies is much lessened by this failure to investigate all possible causes of error on each occasion.

We have dealt so far with the two questions of whom to interview and how to ask our questions. We must now tackle the fundamental question of how to interpret the resulting data. Certain types of data, of course, do not require much interpretation. A pre-election forecast, indicating that candidate A will poll 60 per cent of the votes and candidate B 40 per cent, has little scientific importance and is of purely journalistic interest. It merely tells us to-day, with a certain degree of inaccuracy, what we would know in any case tomorrow with complete accuracy. Even the claim that these forecasts prove the general accuracy of polls cannot be accepted as extending to other types of questions; it is possible that polling may be accurate with respect to a person's voting intention but quite inaccurate with respect to his views on the legalization of brothels, or the reality of God.

It is when we come to general social problems, such as the incidence of anti-Semitism in the population, that problems of interpretation become acute. As an example, let us take replies to the question mentioned above, 'Do you think that Jews have too much power and influence in this country?'. Apparently, some 66 per cent of the population think so. Can we conclude from this that 66 per cent of the population are anti-Semitic? The answer obviously is 'No'. If we had asked a different question, say 'Do you agree that the Jews monopolize everything to the detriment of the English?', we would have obtained quite a different percentage. Depending on the exact question we ask, we can make the incidence of anti-Semitism appear to vary from some 3 per cent to something like 80 per cent. There clearly is something radically wrong in this method of assessing general social attitude.

The difficulty seems to arise in connexion with the habit of polling agencies to report their results in terms of per cent 'Yes', 'No', and 'Don't Know' answers to individual questions. A comparison may make the difference clear. Supposing we wanted to get a measure of the average height of the population. We might do this by issuing a number of investigators with sticks of equal height, asking them to measure a representative sample of the population and to report what proportion of the sample were taller than the stick, as tall as the stick, or smaller than the stick. This would give us a set of answers similar to those obtained by the polling agencies, i.e. it might be found that 70 per cent were taller than the stick, 5 per cent were equal in height, and 25 per cent were shorter. This fact would tell us nothing about the average height of the population unless we knew the exact height of the stick. But the phrase 'the height of the stick' involves a whole system of measurement in terms of which height can be specified, and if such a system of measurement exists already, it would be just as simple and much more accurate actually to measure the true height of each person in the sample and report the findings in terms of average number of inches.

Unless we know the exact degree of anti-Semitism of a given question, knowledge of the percentage of people who agree with this statement in the population tells us very little about the prevalence of anti-Semitism. What we need is not a single question with a statement of the percentage of 'Yes', 'No', and 'Don't Know' answers, but rather a scale of measurement such as that reprinted in the chapter on the 'Psychology of Anti-Semitism', where a statement of the average degree of anti-Semitism revealed by that scale would correspond to the use of a yardstick in our example. No doubt, statements in terms of scale values will be less easily interpreted by the newspaper-reading public, but they would have some scientific value which is absent in the percentage reports given by the polling agencies at the moment.

These considerations do not, on the whole, affect the practical usefulness of the polls; they do, however, seriously diminish their importance from the point of view of social science. The contributions which the polls have made in the scientific field are very small. Certain generalizations have been made on the basis of polling data which appear to be important, such as, for instance, the observation that the opinion of working-class groups tends to prevail with respect to internal policy within a democratic country, whereas the views of middle-class groups tend to prevail with respect to foreign policy. But such generalizations are rare, and most of the findings are statements of single, particular facts, to the effect that on a particular occasion a particular proportion of a certain sample of the population said 'Yes' to a particular question.

Now facts are the raw material of science, but science requires far more than facts. Outside the framework of a theory or an hypothesis which they can help to verify or disprove, facts are of no particular relevance or importance. It is an error, therefore, to assume that public opinion polls are scientifically valuable because they report facts which are fairly reliable. If these facts were integrated into a general system or theory, they might be of the utmost scientific importance. As it is, they may occasionally be quoted in support of some theory or other, but there are few experts in the fields of social psychology or sociology who have found these results useful or valuable.

It is from the practical point of view, then, that we must evaluate public opinion polls and the various organizations such as the Social Survey, the B.B.C. 'Listener Research', and the many American Government agencies which try to ascertain attitudes and opinions on a great variety of issues by means of polling and sampling techniques. A few examples may serve to indicate the type of work done by these organizations. These examples are taken almost at random from the very large number which can be found in the literature. Some relate to relatively small matters, others to issues of greater importance. The first example I wish to give is taken from the work of the Social Survey, an agency of the British Government which was set up during the war and has been doing very important work ever since. Its work is done entirely in response to demands by various Government Departments, wishing to base their policy on factual information. In 1948 the question arose as to the number of war medals which ought to be struck. There are approximately 7 million people who, if they wished to claim, had a right between them to about 20 million medals. The question arose as to the proportion of these 7 million who would claim their medals, and the Social Survey was asked to undertake an enquiry. They estimated that about 35 per cent of the people entitled to make claims would do so; the number who actually did claim medals was found to be 34 per cent. Basing itself on this estimate the Government ordered a much smaller number of medals to be struck than would have been necessary otherwise, and the saving to the Government amounted to between £100,000 and £150,000, i.e. a sum which by itself, for this one single job, paid for the whole running cost of the Social Survey for one year.

The second example relates to a telephone directory survey, also undertaken by the same agency. Subscribers in the greater London area had always had both London and Outer-London directories, and the Government of the day, wishing to economize on paper and money, wondered if those telephone directories were really necessary. It accordingly asked the Social Survey to investigate the actual use made of London directories with a view to deciding whether they could be withheld from subscribers without great inconvenience, and without greatly increasing the number of calls at the Directory Enquiry Service. The result of the enquiry was that the telephone directories could be withdrawn without any great inconvenience to subscribers and without additional demands on the telephone enquiry system, and accordingly the Outer-London directories were withdrawn. Results since have shown the wisdom of this decision, and again several thousand tons of paper and between £150,000 and £200,000 in money have been saved. Examples of this kind could be multiplied indefinitely, each showing the possibility of predicting human action in the mass, and of framing political and social action accordingly. Social policy based on guessing is more expensive and less efficient than social action based on knowledge, and polling agencies like the Social Survey produce that knowledge at a minimal cost. It is difficult to avoid the conclusion that if we are serious in our attempts at planning, then the sphere of action of those agencies concerned with accumulating knowledge on which such planning must be based will be and must be considerably enlarged. If commercial institutions are spending more and more money on 'market research', i.e. on attempts to find out facts relevant to the sale of their products, then surely the Government whose actions affect the whole country should be even more richly supplied with facts on which to base such actions.

Of quite a different order of importance is another example of the usefulness of opinion measurement, this time carried out by a special agency of the United States Army. At the end of the war, there was an urgent demand among American troops for immediate demobilization and the return home. The High Command worked out a system which appeared so obviously unjust and objectionable to the men concerned that for a while there was a threat of open mutiny among American troops overseas. To deal with this situation, psychologists and other social scientists were instructed to work out a 'points' system of discharge based on the expressed views of the men concerned. Within a very brief period of time, during which large numbers of soldiers were interviewed, a points system was worked out which represented, as it were, a consensus of opinion among those affected by the scheme. This system was found fair and equitable and worked without any major hitch, thus avoiding what might have been a considerable disaster, not only in American internal relations and politics but also in the general political situation of the world at the time.

We may now summarize the main conclusions from this survey. The measurement of attitudes and opinions on a wide variety of subjects is possible and can be carried out with relative precision by the use of suitable methods of sampling and interviewing. Results which have been obtained through the use of these methods in the past have shown the enormous practical importance which such measurement may have in the context of democratic planning; indeed, it would not be an exaggeration to say that in their power to look ahead these methods are to the body politic what the eyes are to the human being. There is little doubt that the near future will see a rapid growth in the use made of these and similar techniques, thus substituting knowledge for surmise, and statistics for guesswork.

Preoccupation with practical issues, however, has led those in charge of these techniques to neglect the scientific uses of these methods in terms of hypothesis construction and verification. This is an unfortunate development because development tends to be most rapid where pure and applied science work together, each enhancing the progress of the other. In the field of attitude measurement, traffic has been almost entirely one way; academic scientists have worked out the methods, the statistical formulas, and the techniques followed by practical workers; they have had very little in return. It is this absence of two-way traffic which has made social science more academic and less related to reality than it might otherwise have been, and it has prevented many fruitful advances in the practical field which would have followed closer collaboration. For this lack of integration, those in charge of the practical side of polling must bear their share, but undoubtedly a much greater share of the blame falls on to those people and bodies who are responsible for the current almost total neglect in this country of social science as a whole. There is no Chair of Social Psychology in the United Kingdom, to give but one example of the depressing state of affairs, and no department whose main function it is to institute and integrate advances in this vitally important field. We have to rely almost exclusively on experiments carried out in the United States, where there has been much closer integration of practical and academic work, and where public support of social science is very much stronger. Much lip service is being paid to the idea that the pace of development of physical science has outrun our power to control its products, and that we should try to achieve comparable advances in our control over ourselves and our human environment. There is little evidence in the policy of the Government or the Universities to show that these views are held at all sincerely. If they were, we would soon experience a blossoming forth of Social Science Departments, a growth of interest in the research carried out by such departments, and an improvement in the quality of such research. Without such public support, social science cannot live but only stagnate, and those who blame the psychologist or the sociologist for not having at his fingertips the remedies for all our evils might reflect that the social scientist cannot work in a vacuum or without the requisite support which alone can enable him to exist and make advances in his chosen field.

16

PSYCHOLOGY AND POLITICS

IT will have become abundantly clear to the reader that psychological findings often have an important bearing on political questions and controversies. This connexion between politics and psychology may be quite direct, as for instance in the use of Gallup polls as election guides (with the losing candidate usually accusing the pollsters of bias, and the winning candidate praising their strict adherence to scientific impartiality). However, far more important than these small-scale party wrangles is the impact of psychology on more fundamental areas of political thinking and political action.

Political parties, in so far as they are not merely predatory groups gathered together to share the spoils of office, tend to have certain fundamental tenets and beliefs which underlie their policies. These tenets and beliefs are linked with a certain picture of human nature, of the principles of human motivation, of the extent to which human nature is modifiable, and of the methods by means of which human beings can be guided and controlled. Often these views are held implicitly rather than explicitly; they appear too obvious to the person holding them to deserve discussion, and he may regard them as axioms dissent from which would put the objector beyond the pale of reason.

When these axioms are examined impartially in the light of scientific facts, politicians tend to react severely and often traumatically. Perhaps the clearest examples of such conflict between science and political credo can be found in dictatorship countries. In Nazi Germany, all evidence throwing doubt on the superiority, or even the very existence, of 'Aryan' peoples was ruthlessly suppressed. Textbooks had to be rewritten in conformity with political dictates, and independent scientists who refused to prostitute their calling in this way were deprived of their livelihood. Some of these events are tragic; others are comic. A well-known psychologist who in pre-Hitler days had described his 'degenerate' type as being blond-haired in its physical aspect hurriedly discovered that the degenerate type was in reality dark-haired. If science has its heroes, it also has its clowns; both are likely to expose their character in the conflict between science and politics.

In the U.S.S.R. also the ruling dogma has come into conflict with scientific facts. The belief that all human beings are created equal, and are infinitely modifiable, easily leads to a denial of the importance of hereditary causes and limitations. When firmly-established facts oppose political dogma, the reaction of the politician almost invariably is to deny the fact, rather than to change the dogma; in a dictatorship, the politician's denial extends beyond the facts to the very rights of existence and independent research of the scientist himself. In 1936, the work of the 'testologists', or 'pedologists', i.e. of Russian psychologists using mental tests in the field of individual differences, was brought to an end by a resolution of the Central Committee of the Communist Party of the Soviet Union. Among other things, this resolution declared that 'the CC CPSU considers that both the theory and practice of so-called pedology represent pseudo-scientific and anti-Marxist positions. These positions are based, first of all, on the main "law" of contemporary pedology – the "law" of the dependence of children's development on biological and social factors, on the influence of heredity and some sort of unchanging environment. This deeply reactionary "law" is in complete contradiction to Marxism and to its practice of Socialist construction. . . . Such a theory could have appeared only as a result of the uncritical transference into Soviet pedagogy of the views and principles of anti-scientific bourgeois pedology which has as its aim the preservation of a ruling class and which therefore undertakes to prove that special talents and special rights justify the existence of exploiting classes and "higher races", while on the other hand it has the task of proving that the working class or "lower races" are doomed to physical and emotional failure.'

At the end of a lengthy argument along these lines, the following resolutions *inter alia* were put forward : that (1) The connexion of pedologists with the schools be ended, and that all pedological textbooks be removed. (2) The teaching of pedology as a special science in the Institutes of Pedagogy and the Technicums be abolished. (3) The books published to date on the theory of contemporary pedology be criticized in the press. (4) Those practising pedologists who are willing, be transferred into the field of pedagogy as teachers. This conflict, which in essence was not unconnected with the notorious Lysenko affair, thus ended with the virtual destruction of Russian psychology; what remains is essentially a weak step-child of physiology, without principles or methods of its own.

It is interesting to note that the resolution itself admits that the real reasons for the opposition to 'pedology' did not lie in any scientific proof that the methods used had not been objective, or that the results reached had not been adequately supported. The crime of the 'pedologists' was simply that their conclusions were 'in complete contradiction to Marxism and to its practice of Socialist construction.' There is no attempt other than this appeal to political dogma to disprove the contentions of the early Russian psychologists – just as 300 years ago there was no attempt other than appeal to religious dogma to disprove Copernicus's and Galileo's heliocentric theory.

It would be erroneous to conclude from this example that psychology, having come into conflict with the extreme left, must therefore be considered to give succour and comfort to the political right. Nothing could be further from the truth. In the U.S.A., where social psychology is probably more highly developed than in any other country, psychologists are generally regarded as dangerous 'Reds' and 'Bolsheviks'; the very term 'social science' is enough to cause Conservative businessmen to shiver in their shoes and demand congressional action against the Communist influence in the Universities. Psychology, it appears, is very much the Cinderella of the sciences; proscribed by the extreme right and left, it is barely tolerated in democratic countries where one might have expected a somewhat more hospitable welcome. What is the reason for this universal dislike?

Politicians of all creeds tend to regard psychology with suspicion, not because it is in league with any particular brand of politics, but because it attempts to substitute factual evidence and scientific reasoning for stereotyped thinking and undeviating adhesion to dogma. The politician is used to seeing dogma opposed by counter-dogma; to find a case argued on its factual merits deprives him of his favourite weapon. No wonder that he will deride and oppose an approach which, in the long run, may appear to threaten to put him out of business.

An example may make the difference between the political and psychological approaches clearer. Let us consider the debate that raged several years ago over the problem of the appropriate school-leaving age. Many of the arguments brought forward, of course, had no connexion at all with psychology; it is obvious that by virtue of his training the psychologist has no special competence to deal with the economic issues involved. Nevertheless, it seemed generally agreed that psychological questions did have an important part to play; thus the ability of many children to benefit from an additional year's schooling was one of the central problems under discussion. The important point to note is that both sides tried to settle the issue by *fiat*, some saying flatly that the children would, others that they would not benefit. But this is a question of fact which can be answered on the basis of existing knowledge, or in any case which could be answered on the basis of a properly planned experimental enquiry. Why debate an issue in terms of *opinions* when it can be debated in terms of *facts*?

Occasionally the politician, instead of completely ignoring the point, will put forward his objection to this view. Usually this objection takes the following form. 'You claim that social science has available facts and methods which might throw light on the problems and questions which face us. But this contention appears unfounded. We have asked social scientists to advise us on certain problems, such as those of absenteeism in the coal mines. Either they have failed to give an answer at all, making feeble excuses about not having done any research in this field, or else their answers have been quite absurd and irrelevant to any practical action that might be taken. We would like nothing better than to be given answers to our problems; unfortunately this vaunted social science does not appear in a position to provide these answers. By all means carry on with your studies; in the meanwhile we have a job to do which will not wait for the results of your experiments.'

This answer is superficially plausible, but it does not stand up to close scrutiny. Let us begin our reply by noting what happens in other sciences in a similar situation. Let us take as our first example the production of an atomic bomb. Physicists declare that it may be possible (although they cannot be sure of this) that an atom bomb could be produced after several years of research and extremely expensive plant-building. Politicians agree on the desirability of the project, and the physicists go ahead to study the numerous problems arising out of their assignment. In due course the bomb is produced, at staggering expense, and research is continued over ten or more years to improve the first very inadequate design. The following differences will be noted between the events here recorded, and those in our absenteeism example: (1) The psychologist is asked for an immediate answer, while the physicist is allowed to experiment for several years before being asked to justify his work. (2) The physicist has almost unlimited funds at his disposal, both for preliminary work and for the final contract, while the psychologist has to work with hardly any financial support at all. (3) The physicist is brought into close touch with the material he is studying; the psychologist is usually carefully prevented from coming into contact with coal miners, or whatever the group he may be studying.

It will be clear that the comparison between the physicist's work and that of the psychologist makes failure almost certain for the latter. It is as if a physical scientist were told: 'I want you to tell me whether I can find certain metals in the Antarctic. I forbid you to go there, or to talk to people who have been there; I shall give you no funds whatsoever for carrying out your research; and I want an answer immediately.' No physicist would expect to succeed under those conditions, and probably no physicist would even try.

Granted, then, that the usual requests which the politician may make to the psychologist are absurd because of the conditions under which the latter has to work, what sort of a request would be considered reasonable? Let us take again the absenteeism example, and let us suppose that society were really serious in its desire to solve this problem. It would begin by setting up a Research Institute – possibly under the aegis of the Social Science Research Council whose formation has been discussed so frequently, and to so little effect – staffed by some of the leading social scientists in the country, and in close touch with appropriate University Departments. Finance, for once, would be adequate to make possible large-scale investigations along proper lines of sampling design, and the statistical evaluation of the data. Investigators would be given, not only permission but actual encouragement to contact miners, trade union leaders, officials, and all those connected with the industry. There would be no pressure to whitewash any particular group; stress would be only on factual reports, scientific impartiality, and reasonable recommendations growing out of the facts. There would be room for experimentation; if the hypothesis were advanced that decentralization and closer control of miners themselves over management, e.g. through workshop committees, would lead to a lessening of absenteeism, then experiments of this type would be carried out in at least one or two pits. There is, of course, no guarantee that an answer to the problem would be found, but in the light of such experience as we have had with similar questions the probabilities of success appear reasonably good.

It might be necessary to do more than just set up a specific research organization. Scientists have to be trained, and in this country very few social scientists are being trained at the moment. It might be necessary to offer scholarships to promising students willing to take up psychology or sociology; it might even be necessary to institute a Chair in Social Psychology, or in Experimental Sociology. There are all sorts of difficulties which might be cited to prove how impossible plans of this kind are. There does remain the obstinate fact, however, that there are occasions where social science has been tried, on a large scale, and where it has not been found wanting. Perhaps pusillanimity is the surest way to failure, on the national scale no less than in the individual life.

While lack of financial support and other facilities is a very serious impediment to the development of social science, perhaps even more serious and fundamental is the ambivalent way in which many intelligent people look upon it. On the one hand, they regard it with a certain amount of derision and ridicule, on the basis, firstly, that civil servants, trade union officials, politicians, businessmen, and other 'practical' people know perfectly well what they are doing, and do not need advice or help from 'academic' and *ipso facto* hopelessly unpractical types; secondly, that the very notion of submitting human conduct to scientific scrutiny and attempting to formulate laws for its apparent hopeless irregularity contradicts common-sense notions of free will and other shibboleths and is therefore absurd and ridiculous.

When brought up sharply against the facts, as for instance by the demonstration that the 'practical' businessman's interviewing practices are worse than useless, or that the 'experienced' politicians' and journalists' predictions regarding the outcome of an election are hopelessly wrong, as for instance in the case of the 1945 election when the Gallup poll predicted a majority for Labour while all the 'experts' forecast a Conservative victory, opinion easily veers in the opposite direction, and the psychologist is credited with magical powers of insight and understanding which he himself would never claim. Such a mixture of derision, fear, and adulation is often found in psychopathology; the threat which any new science constitutes to old-established ways of thinking and of doing things has, as history shows again and again, promoted this type of ambivalent reaction with unfailing regularity.

Examples of 'derision' may come to mind more easily than examples of 'adulation', but it is only necessary to recall the widely-held belief, which has no support in factual experiment, that 'psychological treatment' would solve all our problems of penology, with the successfully-treated criminal presumably resuming life as a useful and honest citizen, or the equally prominent belief, which is equally unsubstantiated, that wars could be abolished by submitting everyone to psychoanalytic treatment at an early age. This belief in the 'magic' power of psychology is probably no less of a hindrance to its recognition than is outright rejection; in neither case is the psychologist recognized as a scientist who is applying the tried methods of science to a new and difficult subject, and in neither case is he encouraged to carry on his investigations into human problems in the only place where they can be successfully prosecuted – in the mine, the workshop, the camp, the prison ward, the union lodge, or the factory.

Slowly, very slowly, the climate of opinion is changing, however. Private industry, particularly in the U.S.A., has begun to see the unlimited possibilities of control and prediction which social science has to offer, and in this country the Armed Forces, the Civil Service, and the Government itself (through the Social Survey) have introduced psychological methods of selection, of attitude measurement, and of prediction. There is little doubt that the influence of psychological methods in the various spheres mentioned will increase rapidly; in the U.S.A. the number of psychologists employed by industry, by Government agencies, and in various other 'practical' and 'applied' jobs has increased at a truly astonishing rate, and the beginnings of a similar development can be traced here also. Ignorance, fear, and other emotional barriers to an easy acceptance of the scientific approach often prevent the maximum utilization of psychological discoveries, but greater familiarity with the methods of social science may in due course remove these obstacles. Very few students nowadays go through college in the U.S.A. without having some courses in psychology, and when the vast numbers of students in American colleges are recalled, as well as the fact that from them will be recruited the leaders of industry, government, and the professions, it may be confidently prophesied that the next generation will not regard psychology as an alien intruder, but rather as a familiar friend and helpmate. It would be a pity if Britain, having pioneered in the development of psychology as a science through such men as Galton, Spearman, and McDougall, should forfeit her chance to join in the reaping of the rewards.

It would be wrong to imagine that psychology only impinges on politics in its immediately practical aspects. From some points of view other areas of contact may be more important and fundamental. As pointed out at the beginning of this chapter, political philosophies are in part at least based on firmly-held views of human nature, and if psychology can throw some light on the truth or falsity of these beliefs then presumably psychology is relevant to the political philosophies derived from them. We have already noted the conflict which arose in the U.S.S.R. between a political belief predicated on the hypothesis of human equality in ability and other important traits, and the scientific facts of inequality and hereditary influence. Can similar conflicts be traced between scientific fact and assumptions underlying theories of political democracy?

For many years I have included the following question among those given to students of the University of London Extension Courses in Social Psychology: 'What would be the form of government most suitable for human beings if (*a*) all men were created equal in ability; (*b*) if there were great innate differences in ability?' Well over 90 per cent of the replies indicated a belief that democracy would be the ideal form of government if all men were equal in ability, while some form of autocracy or dictatorship would be more appropriate if there were great innate differences in ability. Granted that the latter alternative has received far more support from scientific studies than the former, must we conclude that our democratic faith is based on an illusion? Or shall we accept the fact that dictatorship in Russia is apparently compatible with a belief in human equality so strong as to lead to the banishment of all contrary evidence as proof that 95 per cent of University Extension Course students can be wrong?

The fact that both the U.S.S.R. and the U.S.A. subscribe to the hypothesis of the equality of man, in spite of the wide divergence in their political systems, should make us pause before giving too hasty an answer. If the Russians insist on the limitless improvability of man, and on the essential equivalence of one individual to another, then we must remember also the American belief that 'one man is as good as another, if not a darn sight better'. Perhaps there are a few errors in the argument from the facts of inequality to the desirability for dictatorship which may cause us to come to a somewhat different decision.

In the first place, those who argue that inequality naturally leads to dictatorship usually assume that the most intelligent would and should be the leaders or dictators. This is most unlikely, both by historical precedent and by psychological experiment. History has few examples of highly-gifted men of real intellectual ability who have donned the mantle of dictator; the best have been rated at I.Q. values of 130 or thereabouts, i.e. very much below the real intellectual giants. Experiment has shown that leadership usually falls to those who are somewhat brighter than their fellows, but not too bright; the child or adult with an I.Q. of 160 or more has interests, modes of thought, and ways of argument quite outside the understanding of his fellows. Except in exclusively intellectual pursuits, the extremely intelligent is as unlikely to be chosen as leader as is the extremely dull. Dictatorship, therefore, would not easily lend itself to the equation of leadership with ability; quite on the contrary, it would almost certainly ensure that the intelligent would be overruled by those whose modest talents and ruthless personalities placed them in positions of power. History affords many examples of this, some of them of very recent date indeed.

If dictatorship does not lead to the placing of the most highly gifted into leadership positions, neither can it be said that present-day democracy succeeds very well in doing so. The tragi-comic events which followed John Stuart Mill's entry into the political arena may serve as one anecdotal example. Few who read faithfully the speeches of British Members of Parliament, or of American Senators, will deny the lack of even elementary factual knowledge, the absence of logical consistency, and the barrenness of intellectual understanding so often betrayed there. For the achievement of high office in democratic countries, outstanding intelligence is probably as much of a handicap as it is in dictatorship countries; the qualities demanded for success are more of an emotional, 'crowd-appeal' kind than of an intellectual nature. Even so, however, the interplay of democratic processes and the rivalry of party machines do give intelligence a better chance to make itself heard in the long run than does the rigidity of a dictatorship. Probably the ancient Greek system of choosing public officials by lot would give the highly intelligent person a better chance still, because lots are not intrinsically biassed against intelligence.

Could we do better than any of the methods outlined so far? Few psychologists have ventured to speculate in this field, but many would probably agree with Paul Horst in his belief that 'the highest goal that measurement and evaluation psychologists can strive for is the development of those instruments and techniques required by a society which aspires to capitalize to the fullest upon the fact that most men are created unequal.' He also makes certain recommendations which may at first sound strange, but whose desirability may nevertheless with advantage be made the subject of debate.

One obvious possibility considered by him but finally rejected is the extension of the Civil Service system (selection by ability as psychologically tested, promotion by competence as shown on the job) to include more and more elective offices. 'Indeed', he writes, 'why should not our United States Congressmen and Senators be required to demonstrate their selective proficiencies in science, economics, sociology, political science, and other fields of knowledge relevant to intelligent legislation? As a matter of fact, it might not be too much to ask that a candidate for the presidency of the United States have some knowledge of the forces that influence the state of health of our national structure and that he be called upon to demonstrate at least a bare minimum of such proficiency. We could then directly approach the problem of an improved governmental structure by insisting that relevant individual differences be measured and only the most competent be selected for office.'

This method, of course, would mean that all public offices would be filled by examination and test, and that elections would become a thing of the past. Practical difficulties and sentimental and emotional pressures alike would presumably make such a scheme unworkable, and consequently Horst considers a second possibility. 'Another alternative would be somewhat arbitrarily to define, as we do now, the jobs to be filled by examinations and those to be filled by election, but to capitalize on individual differences among the voters to be sure that only the most competent to vote would be permitted to do so. In the first case, the candidates would take the examinations, and, in the second, the voters would take them, allowing the candidates to establish their candidacy very much at as present.'

Whatever we may think of this proposal at first blush, there is no doubt that literacy qualifications have not been found incompatible with democratic government, and this extension from literacy to knowledge and ability might be less revolutionary than it appears. Over several years now I have been investigating social attitudes by means of a questionnaire which includes among others the question: 'Do you think that only people with a definite minimum of intelligence and education should be allowed to vote?' In urban middle-class samples Conservatives show an actual majority in favour of this proposal (55 per cent); Liberals are almost evenly divided (47 per cent in favour); Socialists are opposed to it, though not as strongly as one might have expected (39 per cent in favour). Working-class samples are less favourable, but nevertheless show sizeable minorities who agree with the proposal. Responses of American samples and of Swedish and German groups are similar, indicating that in all these countries there is some dissatisfaction with the type of politician thrown up by the present electoral system.

Horst finally comes down in favour of a combination of the two methods discussed. 'Of course, if we really took individual differences seriously, and wanted to make the most of them to ensure topnotch public service personnel, we could combine the two systems. In this case, the candidates would have to pass qualifying examinations before being allowed to run for office, and the electorate would have to pass appropriate examinations before being allowed to vote for candidates.'

These ideas, of course, are not meant to be taken too seriously; the objections to them are so obvious that it would be a task of supererogation to list them. Nevertheless, they should not be dismissed too easily as phantasmagoria of modern 'science fiction'. Is our political system really so perfect that improvements are impossible? Are we sure that those best qualified always succeed in reaching positions of influence and political power? Unless we can give an unqualified 'Yes' as an answer to these questions, suggestions for possible improvements should be debated and discussed in terms of their merits.

I have given but one example of the way in which research

findings of modern psychology may have an impact on politics. The attentive reader will be able to find many other discoveries mentioned in the pages of this book which are relevant to our political thinking. He will not, I think, find that the shadowy and far from precise picture of human nature that is beginning to emerge from psychological research is more in line with the presuppositions of one political party than with those of the others. It seems more likely that parties of the right and left have both taken hold of certain psychological truths which they have then stressed to the exclusion of other, equally important truths. A synthesis is obviously desirable, but this synthesis must not be a simple averaging of contrasting beliefs, but rather an organic growth such as can only take place on the basis of independent, unbiassed, scientific research into the laws governing human behaviour. To all those who doubt the usefulness of psychology in this context, because of its alleged impracticability or because of its very real immaturity, I may perhaps quote the answer which Faraday gave on the famous occasion when he first exhibited a small model of the dynamo he had just invented. A lady approached him and said: 'This is a very nice little thing, Mr Faraday, but of what use is it?' 'Madam', replied the great man, 'of what use is a baby?'

RECOMMENDED
FOR FURTHER READING

1. Terman, L. M., and Oden, M. H. *The Gifted Child Grows Up.* London: Oxford Univ. Press, 1948. (for Chapter 3)

2. Viteles, M. S. *Industrial Psychology.* New York: Norton, 1932. (for Chapter 5)

3. O.S.S. Assessment Staff. *Assessment of Men.* New York: Rinehart & Co., 1948. (for Chapter 7)

4. Ghiselli, E. E., and Brown, C. W. *Personnel and Industrial Psychology.* New York: McGraw-Hill Book Co., 1948. (for Chapter 8)

5. Kinsey, A. C., Pomeroy, W. B., and Martin, C. E. *Sexual Behavior In The Human Male.* London: Saunders, 1948. (for Chapter 9)

6. Eysenck, H. J. *The Scientific Study of Personality.* London: Routledge & Kegan Paul, 1952. (for Chapter 10)

7. Mowrer, O. H. *Learning Theory and Personality Dynamics.* New York: Ronald Press Co., 1950. (for Chapter 11)

8. Bird, C. *Social Psychology.* London: Appleton-Century Co., 1940. (for Chapter 13)

9. Adorno, T. W., Frenkel-Brunswik, E., Levinson, D. J., and Sanford, R. N. *The Authoritarian Personality.* New York: Harper & Bros., 1950. (for Chapter 14)

10. Cantril, H. *Gauging Public Opinion.* Princeton: Princeton Univ. Press, 1947. (for Chapter 15)

INDEX

Marriage, 79, 191
Marxism, 174
Masturbation, 182
McDougall, W., 308
Measurement, 23, 206
Memory, 32, 63
Mental age, 25
M.I.5, 140
Midianites, 139
Mill, J. S., 310
Monogamy, 187
Mowrer, O. H., 210
Mundugumor, 180
Mussolini, B., 282
Myers, C., 168

Nail biting, 215
Neurosis, 193, 208, 212
Neuroticism, Inheritance of, 206
N.I.I.P., 118
Nudity, 188
Numerical ability, 32, 47

Occupational selection, 109
O.C.T.U., 66, 151
Odesskiye Novosti, 243
Office of Strategic Services, 140
Orgasm, 182
Orlansky, J., 232
O'Rourke, L. J., 115
Orphans, 86

Parry, J. B., 115
Pedologists, 301

Perceptual Ability, 32, 55
Persistence, 36
Personality, 27, 73, 200
Personality Tests, 201
Perversion, 189
Petting, 186
Phrenology, 28
Pliny, 209, 213
Poirot, Hercule, 140
Porteus Maze, 25
Power, 34
Predictability, 14
Prefrontal Leucotomy, 200
Pre-marital relations, 186
Probability, 11
Psychiatry, 13, 205
Psychoanalysis, 13, 178, 195, 207, 221
Psychogalvanic reflex, 203
Psychology, 7, 9, 221

Quota sampling, 286

Rats, bright and dull, 91
Reaction formation, 234
Reaction time, 114
Reading speed, 166
Reasoning ability, 32, 58
Regression, 87
Reliability, 105
Repression, 273
Republicans, 285
Rigidity, 277
Roosevelt, F. D., 283
Rothney, J. W., 67